I0814975

Praise for *Post-Traumatic Parenting*

"This book is an emotional road map for any parent trying to break generational cycles. Dr. Robyn Koslowitz is bringing light to such an important topic. By telling her story, she tells the story of so many others. In this space, we can truly heal. We are all just walking each other home (Rumi) This book is an example of just that."

Kimberly Shannon Murphy, award-winning stuntwoman and author of *Glimmer: A Story of Survival, Hope, and Healing*

"To the millions of parents who feel alone carrying childhood trauma into their parenting—Dr. Robyn Koslowitz's *Post-Traumatic Parenting* is the gift and guide they need. In this completely original book, full of heart and scientifically proven methods, parents will find a home with hope and direction. Reading this book won't just give parents ideas about healing; they will feel themselves healing through the compassionate anecdotes and strategies that fill every page. Dr. Koslowitz's wise words provide an antidote to the isolation and even shame that parents working through trauma feel, and lay out clearly 'in the heat of the moment' steps to create connection between yourself and your child, compassionately lighting up the way to help you be the parent you want to be."

Tamar Chansky, PhD, author of *Freeing Yourself from Anxiety* and *Freeing Your Child from Anxiety*

"Robyn Koslowitz's book finally brings attention to the effects of trauma on parenting and its impact on children. Perfect for parents who worry that their trauma could adversely affect their children, who have trouble saying 'no,' or who feel they have to be perfect at parenting in order to spare their children. Koslowitz aims to put an end to the effects of intergenerational trauma."

Janina Fisher, PhD, author of *Healing the Fragmented Selves of Trauma Survivors* and *Transforming the Living Legacy of Trauma*

"This is the book that I have been waiting for! It offers exactly the kind of wisdom and guidance that post-traumatic parents need as they strive to be their best selves in caring for their children. Koslowitz has written a book that is accessible, eye-opening, and inspiring. She shares her own story in the service of helping others heal, offering validation, explanation, and direction for those who are struggling to change lifelong, trauma-related patterns."

Deborah L. Korn, PsyD, clinical psychologist and trauma specialist; coauthor of *Every Memory Deserves Respect: EMDR the Proven Trauma Therapy with the Power to Heal*

"If you have ever experienced trauma, this book is a must-read. Post-traumatic parenting is a vital resource that empowers parents to transform their challenges into strength and connection."

Nicole Amoyal Pensak, PhD, PMH-C, clinical psychologist and author of *Rattled: How to Calm New Mom Anxiety with the Power of the Postpartum Brain*

"This is a powerful and insightful book about parenting with trauma. Dr. Koslowitz immediately establishes a connection with the reader by sharing her own personal experience with trauma and its impact on her parenting journey. She normalizes the experience of feeling "broken" or "damaged" by trauma, creating a sense of community and validation for readers who may be struggling with similar challenges. Her discussion of post-traumatic parenting types brings parenting research forward. This is one of the most important and readable works on parenting published in recent years."

Erin O'Connor, EdD, program leader of early childhood education at NYU Steinhardt; chief of education at Cooper Parenting; and cohost of the *Parenting Understood* podcast

"*Post-Traumatic Parenting* is amazing. I've been impressed in ways that were quite surprising—especially in having it evoke emotions and experiences related to being a parent and the (now adult) child of parents who were themselves traumatized. There were times, while reading, that I felt overwhelmed by tears, as I felt myself becoming increasingly compassionate toward my children, my parents, and—most difficult of all—myself. I found myself feeling more open to considering how a history of experiencing trauma affects our parenting, and what this means for me and my patients in our understanding of ourselves in the context of a larger culture."

Mark B. Borg, PhD, author of *Don't Be a Dick*

"Parenting under the best of circumstances is demanding! The challenges become particularly pronounced when parents have experienced trauma in their own youth. In her book, Dr. Koslowitz comprehensively explains how parents can heal from their own trauma so that they can be more emotionally responsive and available to their children. In user-friendly language, she explains how post-traumatic parenting can manifest itself in different ways, and then offers practical healing strategies. Post-traumatic parenting has not received enough attention in the mental health field. Fortunately, Dr. Koslowitz's book fills that gap."

Sandee McClowry, PhD, RN, FAAN, developer of New INSIGHTS into Children's Temperament and professor emerita, New York University

"In *Post-Traumatic Parenting*, Dr. Robyn Koslowitz offers a profoundly compassionate and practical road map for parents who have faced their own traumas, yet dream of building a future with their children marked by resilience, trust, and love. Dr. Koslowitz speaks directly to parents who find themselves struggling with the weight of past wounds, offering guidance that is both deeply empathetic and firmly rooted in psychological expertise. Her approach goes beyond conventional parenting advice, addressing the unique and often overlooked needs of parents carrying post-traumatic stress.

"Drawing on both her personal experiences and her expertise as a child psychologist, Dr. Koslowitz provides insights that empower parents to not only recognize the effects of their trauma, but to transform these challenges into strengths. This book is a true game-changer, filled with actionable strategies and tools designed to support parents in building joy, healthy attachment, and vibrant, lasting connections with their children.

"If you've ever felt burdened by your past and questioned your ability to parent differently, *Post-Traumatic Parenting* is the encouraging, insightful, and healing companion you need to finally break the cycle and become the parent you've always wanted to be. This book is a must-read for any parent ready to embark on a journey of transformation and hope. For today's parents, it's a book that we have all been waiting for."

Shimon Russell, LCSW

"This book is an emotional road map for any parent trying to break generational cycles. Dr. Robyn Koslowitz is bringing light to such an important topic. By telling her story, she tells the story of so many others. In this space, we can truly heal. We are all just walking each other home (Rumi) This book is an example of just that."

Kimberly Shannon Murphy, award-winning stuntwoman and author of *Glimmer: A Story of Survival, Hope and Healing*

"What we've experienced growing up colors how we parent our own children. And for people who have experienced trauma, the echoes can be especially loud. Dr. Robyn Koslowitz explains with deep compassion the links between our past and our present experiences, and she offers concrete and immediately usable guidance to help parents show up for their kids in a way that fits their deepest values. This book provides both an explanation for why trauma may be the hidden factor in your parenting struggles, and more importantly, what to do about it. I strongly recommend this caring and practical book for any parent who wants to move beyond their traumatic past toward greater understanding and more empowered and empowering relationships with their children."

Eileen Kennedy-Moore, PhD, creator the the *Kids Ask Dr. Friendtastic* podcast

POST-TRAUMATIC PARENTING

POST-
TRAUMATIC
PARENTING

BREAK THE CYCLE AND BECOME THE PARENT YOU ALWAYS WANTED TO BE

ROBYN KOSLOWITZ, PhD

BROADLEAF BOOKS
Minneapolis

POST-TRAUMATIC PARENTING
Break the Cycle and Become the Parent You Always Wanted to Be

30 29 28 27 26 25 3 4 5 6 7 8 10

Cover design: Broadleaf Books
Graphics for the book developed by Emily May/May Marketing and Media

Print ISBN: 979-8-8898-3117-4
eBook ISBN: 979-8-8898-3118-1

To my parents

We always said I'd be a published author. Now, that dream has come true. Thank you for dreaming big for me.

To my father

The power of your presence can be seen by the devastation caused by your absence. Thank you for teaching me how to think, how to believe in myself, and how to always follow my inner compass.

To my mother

Thank you for teaching me how to live, how to love, and how to listen. As Strickland Gillian wrote, "Richer than I you can never be. I had a mother who read to me." Thank you for the stories, for telling me yours, and listening to mine.

CONTENTS

INTRODUCTION

- Do you feel bad for your children, because they are unlucky to have you for a parent?
- Did you grow up believing you were lazy, unmotivated, or stupid and wonder now how can you be qualified to parent?
- Do you watch other parents having close, connected, joyful relationships with their kids and despair about why you can't have that?
- Do you feel depleted by the chaos in your home?
- Do you blame yourself for times you feel angry or frustrated with your kids?
- Do you feel ashamed of the way you interact with your kids?
- Do you think someone—anyone—else would be a better parent for your children than you?
- Do you set family goals and values like cycle breaking and find yourself unable to live up to them?
- Do you find yourself thinking, *I'll never parent like my parents*, and then find yourself yelling, threatening, rejecting, criticizing, or punishing—exactly like your parents did?
- Do you look at other parents who seem to be managing so well and silently ask, What's wrong with me?

If you answered yes to any of these questions, you're not alone.

I've been there.

You are not any of the labels that were thrust upon you. You're not lazy, stupid, worthless, or useless. In fact, your trauma has set you up to be exceptional—to be incredible. Once you see how trauma is the invisible factor that creates these fears, it's going to be so much easier to address it and become the parent you've always wanted to be.

I've helped hundreds of parents do it.

I did it myself.

My trauma story can be told in four parts.

Part I

The Trauma of Absence

The trauma of absence is all the stuff that didn't happen for me, because I grew up in a house with an ailing, fragile parent. I'm the youngest of four children, and my three older brothers were all out of the family house by the time I was five years old. In many ways, I was raised as an only child.

My father had a very severe heart condition, which I was aware of for as long as I can remember. He had his first scary heart episode when I was five. I remember the scene vividly because for years I believed that it was my fault. Up until then, my father had been a strong, physically capable man. He used to love to pick me up and swing me to the top of the refrigerator in our apartment's kitchen. One day, he swung me to the top and then he clutched his chest. That was the beginning: race to the hospital, diagnosis, and years of watchful waiting.

For the rest of his life, my parents were stressed all the time. And although they were good, well-intentioned parents, I always felt a pressure to make them proud and to never get my father angry. I knew that if he got angry, he would clutch his chest, and that was terrifying for everybody. I also learned that when you live with someone with a chronic illness, the rest of the family is preoccupied with keeping that person alive and dealing with their own anxieties. It's not that my mom was emotionally unaware; she was a fantastic mother. She worked hard to supplement the family income and she was very tuned in to my needs, but she was anxious and protective of me even before my father's illness, and she didn't have the bandwidth for extra stressors in her life. So, I missed out on a lot of normal exploratory experiences that other kids got to try (and sometimes fail at, since failing is a part of learning) because I knew that I couldn't stress her out.

Consequently, many crucial childhood experiences just didn't happen for me, even though I thought my life was normal and I was mostly happy. I didn't have playdates, for example. I never went to the playground and wasn't taught a lot of sports or play skills that other kids my age had. Instead, I taught myself how to read when I was four. So when the other kids my age were playing outside, I would double down on what I did know how to do. I was very busy with my dolls and my books and my fantasies. I was that kid who brought a book to school for recess—I had some friends, but books were my comfort zone. You know what happens to the kid who brings a book to school for recess? In elementary school, it's tolerated, more or less. By middle school, it puts a target on your back.

Can you relate to this? Over the years, I've heard so many stories of the trauma of absence. Young women who were late to school because they didn't have responsible parents who could get their younger siblings up, dressed, fed, and out the door. Adults who recall the shame of wearing dirty or outdated clothing, because their adults weren't able to care for them. Children who were mocked for an immigrant parent's accent, for being poor, or for having a disability. *Trauma isn't only what happened to you. It's also what didn't happen for you.*

Every few months, an ambulance would race to our house. My father would be loaded in, and my mother and I would ride along to the hospital. He was constantly going to the hospital because he thought he was having a heart attack or because his nitroglycerin pills didn't work. My dad's bouts were a chaotic surprise, so there was never time to get me a sitter. Since my mother didn't want to leave me home alone, and because I was a shy, introverted kid, I didn't want to wait out the crisis at a neighbor's place. So, I'd sit with her in antiseptic, overcrowded New York City hospitals, doing my homework or devouring novel after novel. I remember being admonished by my fifth-grade teacher for my penmanship. "Sweetheart, you write so beautifully. But the essay was written with such sloppy handwriting! It's like getting a beautiful gift wrapped in garbage. Don't disrespect yourself this way." It never occurred to me to tell my teacher that I wrote the essay on my lap, in an ambulance. I just hung my head in shame and promised to do better.

Were you like me, held to account for the consequences of your trauma by teachers who meant well but ended up traumatizing you further? Does this past experience make interacting with your own children's teachers more difficult?

Part II

The Acute Trauma Incident

Months and years passed by, all the same. Then when I was sixteen, everything changed. By that point, my father was actually feeling better.

He was on a new medication. His work was less stressful because he had brought in a partner. My mother was promoted to a supervisory position, and overall, there was more money in the household. And I had become a certified lifeguard and had a weekend job at the local Y as a lifeguard and swim instructor.

Then one night, I woke up at two in the morning to my mother screaming. I ran into my parents' bedroom. There was my father, half sitting on his bed. He looked wrong, like a wax dummy version of my father. He was not conscious. He was not breathing. He was holding his nitroglycerin pills in one hand and the telephone in the other: my guess was that he had been trying to call 911.

As a lifeguard, I knew CPR, but I hesitated for a fraction of a minute because giving my father CPR felt intimate and weird. He smelled bad. I lost my focus. Was I supposed to do three rescue breaths and then thirty compressions or two rescue breaths and twelve compressions? I pulled myself together and started the process, yelling at my mother between breaths to call an ambulance.

The mouth-to-mouth resuscitation was the hardest part. I remember the taste of my father's mouth and the rubbery sensation of his skin, which now I know meant that he had been dead for a while. But I kept going. Pushing. Prodding him back to life. Nothing.

When the paramedics came, they literally had to drag me off his body because they needed to administer defibrillation. Eventually, they gave up. I remember screaming at them not to stop. But he was gone.

At the funeral, everybody was talking about the fact that I did CPR on him and how much he had loved me. One uncle called me a hero, and I wanted to yell "You're lying!" I knew that I didn't save him. I had failed.

What is your acute trauma story? Was there one incident of trauma in your life that you can point to? If your life was a movie, that would be the moment when the suspense music would start playing.

Part III

Post-Traumatic Stress Disorder (PTSD)

I started having flashbacks. My flashbacks were unusual because they contained both an auditory and a tactile component; the more typical flashbacks are visual, like a scene from a movie superimposed on whatever you're actually seeing at the moment (I've treated patients who have been in car accidents and they keep seeing the car accident in their mind's eye). Then there's a complete flashback, when you have such a strong flashback that you are in an alternative version of reality, like the well-known story of the Vietnam vet who shot his wife after he heard a car backfire, because he believed he was back in Vietnam, taking enemy fire.

I would have flashbacks in school or sometimes when I was lifeguarding. School was particularly triggering because right after my father died, a girl in my school had an aneurysm. I was the only person who realized how dangerous the situation was. I remember begging a teacher to go to the office and call the ambulance, and when she froze, I actually shoved her toward the office. I was a lifeguard, but I didn't have major advanced life support training: all I could do was take her pulse, make sure she was breathing, and wait for the paramedic. I remember that loneliness of being the only person who realized that she was dying. Her eyes were empty, just like my father's had been. The two incidents became conflated in my head. I could be sitting in chemistry class and concentrating as hard as I could, and suddenly I'd be having a flashback. I remember thinking, *Oh no, it's happening again*, and noticing that everyone else was having a normal high school experience. And I am in this alternate reality. I could feel my hands pressing my father's chest, and I would have that awful rubbery sensation. I could taste his breath in my mouth. It could last anywhere from a few seconds to as long as fifteen minutes. Usually, it wasn't noticeable, but sometimes it was obvious. Once my friend got very upset. I was having a flashback and she yelled at me, "You do this all the time. You just check out and it's really scary and it's weird, and people are going to think you're socially off and I hate it. It creeps me out and you need to stop."

I thought I was crazy because the flashbacks were so immersive. Had they just been visual, I probably would've thought I was reexperiencing a memory. But what I had didn't feel like a memory at all: it felt real. Today, the analogy of what I experienced might be a really good 4D virtual reality movie. The funny thing is, I've been triggered by the sound of sirens, even though there were none when my father died, because the ambulance came in the middle of the night. There was no traffic. I can't imagine the ambulance came careening down the street blaring its siren. But I associated the sound of ambulances with my father's death, my schoolmate's collapse, and my failed lifesaving attempts with each.

My only ability to understand what was going on was thinking that I was schizophrenic, because I had a distant relative that was schizophrenic. My parents used to invite him over for a meal sometimes, so I had seen delusional behaviors up close. I was also volunteering at a nursing home where there were people with dementia and mental illness. No one who was around me—my relatives and my teachers—knew what to do. In so many ways, I seemed fine. No one knew about my flashbacks. After my classmate died, my school arranged for some crisis counselors to come talk to us. I spoke to the counselor, and she did not see my PTSD, even though I shared that I was having flashbacks. I used to describe the flashbacks as dreams because I didn't have the words to explain them better.

I had a teacher who functioned as the school guidance counselor, but she had no formal mental health training. She suggested that I could pray away the demons in my mind; she was a big believer in the power of positive thinking. She really tried to help me, but she kept doing this whole mind-over-matter thing that a lot of untrained people who don't understand real psychological dysfunction do. So, I tried harder, went to bed earlier, ate healthier, tried to keep a positive thoughts journal. She made it my responsibility to get better, but as hard as I tried, nothing changed. Once again, I felt like a failure. Why couldn't I just will the flashbacks away?

Meanwhile, I was trying desperately to pretend that I was fine. I felt so bad for my mother: she had just lost her husband and now her daughter's schizophrenic. That enormous guilt was the worst of all the traumas, because the guilt made me responsible for someone else's heartache. How could I let my mother down this way? I was the bright spot in her life. She had enormous expectations for my future. We had a shared interest in psychology and I was going to go on to become a psychologist, as well as a wife and a mother. All these dreams would go away if I were crazy, and she'd have to take care of another sick person forever.

The truth was, my mother would've been the perfect person to help me with all this. Had I confided in her, my mother would have known whom to ask for help. She would've called colleagues or friends who were psychologists. But I never said anything. And I did things to hide my flashbacks all the time. I remember digging my nails into my palm to make a tactile flashback go away, because I didn't want my mom to realize. I just hoped that I could let her live in the illusion that she had an okay daughter for as long as possible.

Part IV

All Research is Me-Search

I was always drawn to the field of psychology because my mother was a guidance counselor. I used to listen to her stories of utilizing therapeutic techniques with students and think, *I'd love to study why those techniques work and maybe invent some of my own.* Now I know that *all research is me-search.* Without really realizing it, I was on a journey to figure out this essential question: How do you give kids a normal childhood if you didn't have one? And each twist and turn I took, like the kind of kids I was interested in treating, the hospitals I wanted to work in, the researchers and professors I wanted to learn from, were choices that were made by me just trying to answer this question.

I first learned about PTSD as an undergrad studying psychology. I remember raising my hand during the lecture and asking the professor, "Does this only happen to Vietnam veterans?" He said, "Well, no, PTSD can result from any experience where you felt like you were close to death or you witnessed death." That's when I realized, "Oh, that's what I have." At the time, PTSD research was in its infancy. Now I know that there are so many more causes of PTSD other than death, even though his definition was appropriate for me.

That's when I went to get help for my PTSD. I went to the college counseling center, and a counselor there was being trained in this "new, kind of weird" therapy (as I recall her describing it). I was treated with a very early form of eye movement desensitization and reprocessing (EMDR) when it was just referred to as EMD. They hadn't quite figured out the R yet. It really helped me with the flashbacks because it allowed me to go back into the memory, explore it more deeply, and separate the physical sensations from the memory. And it allowed me to feel my body more fully, understand what was happening during a flashback, and recognize it for what it is.

Even that therapist—who was providing a PTSD treatment—hesitated to diagnose me with PTSD. I remember asking her about it, and she said, "You're just too functional. People with PTSD aren't honor students who are taking full courseloads, double majoring, and working full time. You just had one traumatic experience you need the skills to process better, that's all." Of course, we now know that the characterizations of hyperfunctionality often go hand in hand with PTSD; in fact, there are a whole lot of very productive, very traumatized people. Sometimes, trauma teaches us to be more independent, productive, and motivated than everyone else. But behind that productivity and that hustle is a whole lot of pain.

I call this way of being a "duck." At first glance, a duck appears to be so serene as it floats on the water. But under the water, the duck's feet are paddling madly. It's working so hard just to appear perfect on the surface. I was a duck—I looked perfect on the surface. If we use Freud's definition of success—to live and to work—I was perfect. But under the surface, my legs were peddling madly, trying to make sure no one knew that I was crazy.

Are you one of those very productive, hyperfunctional people? Are other people amazed at how much you can take on at once? Have you ever asked yourself, How can I be traumatized if I'm so capable?

Once I understood what PTSD was, I could tell when I wasn't present. I also learned about myself and the fact that for my whole life, I had taught myself to *dissociate*: to separate yourself from the present moment and go so deeply into your mind that you're not in the world. It was the reason that I could get great grades in school even though I was living with the trauma of absence and then with the acute trauma of my father's death. It was the reason why during my undergrad studies (which I completed in two years, not four), I got married, had my first child, and then went straight from undergraduate to not only graduate school but also one of the most prestigious programs in the country. Even today, I could be in the most pressured situation and I am calm as a cucumber. But you can't parent that way.

I started thinking that my PTSD was affecting my parenting when my oldest daughter turned five (perhaps not coincidentally, the same age I was when my father's sickness began). I was in my fourth year of graduate school. I was doing research with Sandee McClowry, a brilliant child development researcher and a truly wise parenting expert. I was really happy in her lab. I had a lot going on at home and at work.

It was the morning that my daughter was going to her first day of kindergarten. I did all the first-time rituals, packing her backpack, taking pictures, walking her to the bus. As she got on the bus, I called out, "Have a good day. God willing, I'll see you later."

And then I thought, *And if God doesn't want, I won't see her later.*

I went into the house and had a panic attack. I froze. I sat at the kitchen table. I was supposed to be taking my twin boys to the babysitter. And I had to get on a bus to get to work and deliver a very important dataset to Sandee. Yet I was sitting at the kitchen table, frozen. I was in a completely dissociated state, in a total panic attack. I could barely talk. And I quietly said to my husband, "Text the office manager at NYU that I'm not coming. I'm sick. You'll have to take the kids to the babysitter." And I literally sat, unmoving, at the kitchen table all day long until the panic attack passed.

I remember thinking, *This is ridiculous. I need to get up. Let me go make myself a cup of coffee. At least if I'm home, let me do some laundry.* It was as if there were two "mes" in my head. One me was pleading, "Get up. Do something. Start moving." And the other said, "Stay put."

And then it passed. Suddenly, I was fine.

But I knew that something was seriously wrong, deep down in my psyche. That's when I realized this thing that I'm dealing with is going to impact my parenting. And then I put a pin in it. I decided not to think about the entire incident again. It was too big for me to deal with.

Years later, when my second son was about ten, he told me that he didn't like it when "I go away behind my eyes." By then, I thought I had my flashbacks under control. His comment triggered the memory of my high school friend who had said something very similar all those years ago. I knew I couldn't purposefully dissociate any longer: there was a real problem I had to address. But what was I going to do about it? I knew the dissociation was a problem, but I also knew that it was my coping strategy, and I didn't have another one. It was as if my son was telling me that even though I was five feet tall, life would be better if I was six feet tall so that I could reach everything on the top shelf. I thought there was nothing I could do about it. Was I supposed to go through my day and feel my feelings? Not an option, because that would be terrible.

Did your trauma leave you with psychological scars, like panic attacks, intense anxiety, or insomnia, that interfered with your everyday life and now affect your parenting? Did your trauma teach you certain coping skills, like dissociation, that prevent you from having the relationship you want with your kids?

Sometime later, I was teaching a court-mandated parenting class as part of my doctoral internship. It was for parents of kids with disruptive behavior problems. The goal was very progressive: rather than criminalizing the kids and their problems, let's give their parents the tools to help their kids understand their emotions that lead to bad behaviors. The parents came from a complete mix of socioeconomic groups, and it wasn't parents who had abused their children. So I was surprised when in the middle of the first parenting class, a woman raised her hand and asked, "How would I know what's normal parenting? I know I did not have a normal childhood like you see on TV. How can I give my kids a stable childhood when my life is such chaos?"

In that moment, I decided to abandon the curriculum. I asked the class, "How many people in this room feel this way? Because I know I do." I looked around: everyone had raised their hands. And then we began to share our stories: bullying, social exclusion, abuse, parents in prison, toxic home lives. No one realized that their traumas were underlying so many of their parenting challenges. In fact, while each of the parents had a different traumatic experience, parenting their children led to feelings of confusion, insecurity, and hopelessness.

I could totally relate. For me, parenting was another chore on the list. I was a very good technician of parenting. I did good story time. I'm good at playing with kids, yet when I was playing with my own kids, I didn't feel the deep connection I wanted: it felt more like I was playing with a patient in my clinic. I was organized about suppertime, bath time, and bedtime, but I wasn't living parenting. I looked calm, but I was not connecting. Now I see myself during those years as if I were the duck, seemingly functional on the surface, lots of turmoil underneath.

Soon after that meeting, I decided that I would specialize in trauma-informed therapies so that I could focus on treating both parents and children with trauma. I could clearly see that the coping skills I used to deal with my own trauma were interfering with my parenting. I then did the work to accept, integrate, and make meaning of my own trauma.

That last sentence may seem flippant, but it took me more than a decade of intense therapy, self-discovery, journaling, and processing. It was like the training montage in the *Rocky* movies—where he morphed from loser/bullied/out-of-shape status into winner/champion/hero. Living that training montage is torture, and you don't know what the payoff will or won't be, while you're going through it. You just know it's a journey you must take.

I often tell my patients that parenting is a mirror, a map, and a motivator out of trauma. The way I interacted with my children was like a mirror that let me see how trauma was affecting me. Learning how to be a better parent provided the road map to health for both myself and my children. And parenting provided the motivation for me to embrace the discomfort of my trauma and learn new skills and practices for the sake of my children.

I realized that I had to undo my dissociation so that I could be more present for my family. Now I can remain present when my kids are acting up or when my own stress is starting to increase. I figured out stress-coping tools that work for me and realized that if I lower my stress before my kids come home from school, then the stress never rises to the level where it gets the best of me. I learned to set intentions for my behaviors and how I was going to interact with each child so that they each had a sense of secure attachment. I learned how to better communicate with my children. And most importantly, I learned to let go of the shame and blame and to break the cycle of how I was parented.

While I still have flashbacks, I know my triggers, can recognize when they come up, and make sure they don't affect my parenting choices. What I am most proud of is that I can now parent in accordance with my values; I have deep, meaningful relationships with all my children, and I have been able to help thousands of parents do the same.

Welcome to the Post-Traumatic Parenting Community

If you connect to my story or have ever had the thought that you are broken, damaged, or simply not "normal," then you're normal in our community. We've all had those thoughts too.

Here's the thing: the *D* in PTSD stands for *Disorder*; it implies dysfunction. I know that PTSD is a part of me, and it is how my brain functions, not how my brain *dys*functions. Since I've operated in "dysfunction" this long, it has just become how I function. The same way I know that I'm an extremely light sleeper: there's nothing I can do to change that. And my dysfunction is actually my superpower. So now, instead of running from my diagnosis, I can embrace who I am.

I've also realized that I can't shut off my triggers or will myself to not get triggered. I can tame triggers, I can manage triggers, I can handle triggers, but I can't surgically excise them.

Last, I learned that caring for myself is important. I found joy in movement and in the adrenaline release that accompanies physical empowerment. And I can see that my younger children have really benefited from my shift. Once I understood my trauma, I was no longer the focus of my life, and parenting stopped being a job. It was a relationship. My perfectionism also went away. I didn't have the need to be checking off all the boxes every night of "the right way to do things." And I didn't burn out as much because the whole experience was joyous.

Getting you to this same point is the work we will do together in this book. I'm going to lay out exactly what trauma is and how it affects our deepest sense of who we are. The goal is not to make you feel worse but to define our starting point. It's okay if you have been traumatized, because trauma can be transformed into a superpower of growth, resilience, and wisdom.

There is an ancient Japanese art called kintsugi. It's the art of taking broken vessels, piecing them back together, and joining the pieces with gold. The finished product is breathtakingly beautiful and so much more valuable for having been shattered and repaired. Legend has it that a kintsugi vessel cannot be re-broken on the original seams, because it is stronger now. The concept of kintsugi has always resonated with me, and I have a piece of kintsugi-themed art in my office for that reason. Trauma is like that. We are shattered. But when we pull ourselves together, we become something infinitely more precious.

How This Book Works

"I start every day with such good parenting intentions and go to bed filled with shame and regret," says every post-traumatic parent (PTP) at some point. Trauma sounds like damage. Saying out loud that we are traumatized might make us feel like we're a defective product, a broken doll, the one that's marked down 50 percent. But trauma doesn't mean that you're defective. It means that certain psychological functions in your brain have been rewired, and you need to reclaim them for parenting. That's what this book is about: I'm here to give you the tools I've created that are based on the best trauma and parenting research. I'll share dozens of anecdotes from people I've met so you can find yourself on these pages. I believe that a well-crafted children's tale can really tell us everything we need to know about the world, our own challenges and struggles. That's why you'll see many movie references; they provide useful examples of the universal issues we're facing. I've seen my program work every day in my clinical practice, in the online post-traumatic parenting community, and in my personal parenting journey.

Imagine that you could take all the psychological resources that you have been using to manage your trauma—the cognitive capacities that you use for overthinking, the emotional intelligence that goes into people-pleasing, the exertion wasted during a rage spiral, and the sheer effort of trying to keep it together—and put all that energy into your parenting. Imagine going to bed feeling like your kids got the best of you, not the rest of you, like your kids felt seen, heard, and connected. Imagine that internal Greek chorus of "You're a terrible parent, you did this wrong, you're a loser" transforming into an adoring crowd chanting, "And the Parenting Oscar goes to . . . you. For your incredible commitment, hard work, and progress."

If you've ever read a parenting book and felt inadequate, shamed, and blamed or like you've done *everything* wrong, you're not alone. I know I've felt that way. It's not that the advice in the books is wrong—all the recent techniques for mindful, conscious, and responsive parenting are valuable. It's that we can't follow all that excellent advice until we understand the way trauma intersects with our parenting and affects our lives. In other words, we need to clear our own slate so that we can be open to giving our children—no matter their age—the very best chance at a healthy adult life.

In part I, I explain why trauma blocks our ability to parent and provide specific exercises and journal prompts to help every parent see trauma's invisible influence on themselves as well as on their relationships with their children.

Part II showcases the five typical parenting defaults that result from trauma and how to undo them. You will learn how to refashion your trauma residue and turn your past into a parenting superpower. Parenting will become a true, authentic, powerful healing journey.

Part III focuses on what to do to become the kind of parent you want to be. My AIM model is a trauma-informed approach that combines the best of several treatment modalities that I have both studied and experienced in psychotherapy. I'm not good at rigidly adhering to any one protocol. By nature, I'm an integrationist. This model is based on the pieces I took from my journey that may be helpful to you because they have been helpful to others. We will draw on concepts like dialectical behavior therapy (DBT), acceptance and commitment therapy (ACT), internal family systems (IFS), eye movement desensitization and reprocessing (EMDR), polyvagal theory, and interpersonal neurobiology. And yes, you will be able to understand what each of these theories mean and how they affect you as a PTP.

The first step in my AIM model is a radical acceptance of the parent's own trauma. We waste a lot of our psychological resources trying to mentally undo our trauma, trying to ignore or subdue our emotions, and trying to manage our triggers without learning from them. Acceptance allows us to reverse counterfactual thinking and helps widen our focus beyond survival. Unaccepted trauma trains our brains to think only about surviving. Parenting properly is all about thriving. We need to reclaim our psychological resources from trauma so we can focus on our parenting.

The second step of my AIM model is integration. This practice allows us to fully integrate the parts of ourselves that we tend to ignore or dismiss, such as our inner child or unresolved childhood trauma. Our inner child can't raise a child, but a healed inner child can help us connect to our own children with delight. That way, all parts of our psyche can work together toward the common goal of better parenting.

Finally, you will learn how to make meaning of your trauma, using tools based on the third wave of psychoanalysts, including work by Viktor Frankl and Edith Eger. When you make meaning of your suffering, you can then control it, instead of it controlling you.

Then, I will review the specific challenges of the PTP. My system is called "R2 Parenting"—Responsive and Responsible Parenting. My parenting philosophy is that responsive parenting must also be responsible, and this duality is particularly necessary for PTPs. Many of us never had proper parenting techniques modeled or monitored—we never learned how to motivate a dreamy, unfocused child into putting on their socks by turning it into a game, how to start a discussion about anxiety by reading a picture book about a character with a similar dilemma, how to use shoulder-to-shoulder activities like baking together to teach children skills or get them to open up. Many of us were never taught how to connect to children with delight while also teaching skills—we never saw it, or we lost it because of trauma. R2 Parenting teaches exactly those skills. In your hands, a picture book, game, or toy will become much more than a pleasant way to pass the time; they'll become the medium through which you connect with, communicate with, and care for your child. What's more—you'll both have fun. (And your inner child might finally experience some crucial nurturance it's been craving.)

I will focus on both the "what to do" and "why it works" information so you can adjust your techniques and strategies to the ages and issues of your children and act in accordance with your parenting values. These lessons can be applied to the different stages of child development: young children, middle schoolers, high schoolers, and beyond. The truth is, it doesn't really matter what stage of child you're parenting. What matters is understanding how your trauma interferes with what your child needs from you and what to do about it. Right now, you may be reading this thinking, *I wish I read this ten years ago, my kids are teens now.* All is not lost: no matter where you are on your parenting journey, you can fix your relationship with your kids, and you can be a better parent going forward. You'll learn more about this, but the research shows us that it's never too late to repair.

If this sounds too ambitious, I get it, and at first, I felt the same way. But when it comes down to it, what I'm sharing is really a set of skills, and I believe that anyone can learn a skill. I've worked with thousands of PTPs who have been able to forge new and better relationships with their children while healing their own inner child. We all did it, and you can do it too.

Let's begin this journey.

Part I

It's Not You; It's Your Trauma

CHAPTER 1

Understanding Trauma

We think we know exactly what trauma looks like. It's the ripped-from-the-headlines incidents: the near misses with death, school shootings, war, starvation, violence, or abuse. These tragedies all feel legitimately traumatic to those who experience them as well as to those who hear about them. In my psychologically driven world, we refer to these examples as *acute* traumas: a single, discrete incident that anyone can point to and say, "That was the day my life changed."

Acute traumas that happen during childhood or adolescence are referred to as adverse childhood experiences, or ACEs.[1] They include the following:

- experiencing physical, sexual, or emotional abuse
- growing up in a household with instability due to divorce or separation
- growing up in a household with mental health problems
- growing up in a household with substance abuse
- having a family member attempt or die by suicide
- having a relative who has been sent to jail or prison
- experiencing physical or emotional neglect
- witnessing violence in the home or community

Yet there are other instances in life, even deeply disturbing ones, that we don't automatically categorize as traumatic. You might think, *I know that I still dwell on what happened to me when I was a kid, but I don't consider my experience traumatic. Lots of kids are bullied, live in poverty, or are scared to walk down their street.* You might remember when your parents viciously fought or gave each other the silent treatment for days on end. You might have been scared of a sibling or had unrecognized learning issues. These experiences may feel less "legitimate" than acute traumas because you can't identify just one moment of pain or suffering. If your life was a movie, there wasn't that one moment where the scary soundtrack would swell to point out, "There, that was it! That's the moment I was traumatized."

The truth is, these are all examples of traumas, and they are referred to as *chronic*, because they can be ongoing. I call chronic traumas the *s-ACEs*: the *secret* adverse child experiences, because they can develop invisibly and cumulatively:

- being parented harshly
- being bullied
- facing rejection
- having a psychological disorder
- living in a family impacted by a chronic, serious illness
- growing up neurodiverse—an alternative learner—in a world that expects neurotypicality
- growing up in a consistently invalidating environment
- or living through a myriad of other experiences that can leave their mark and result in chronic traumas

I define trauma as any experience that was too big for your brain to break down, or metabolize, that rocks your sense of security in the world. While it's true that our culture overuses the word *trauma*, I believe that if your experience meets the above criteria, you have been traumatized, regardless of whether others would consider your experience traumatic. And if you have children, you are part of the post-traumatic parenting community.

In my experience, the cause of your trauma isn't nearly as important as the effect it had on you: acute traumas are not "bigger" than chronic ones. For instance, being verbally bullied can be just as traumatic as being physically assaulted. And sometimes, one trauma morphs into another. My friend Samantha lost a parent to cancer when she was ten years old, and the other kids in school didn't know how to act when they were around her. They treated her as if cancer was contagious. Slowly, their discomfort became ostracism, and the ostracism became outright bullying. Samantha was dealing with both acute (loss of a parent) and chronic (bullying and neglect) traumas at the same time.

When psychologists like me are trying to distinguish trauma from other forms of upset, one aspect we look for is a persistent feeling of aloneness. Trauma is often something that you felt alone in your efforts to try to cope with, and without the necessary support, healing did not occur. In my own story, even though I had a very empathic, supportive mother, I chose not to share my trauma with her. That's a decision so many people make, thinking, *I don't want to burden anybody with my problems.* Samantha felt alone and confused at school: her friends didn't know how to talk to her, and her teachers didn't know how to listen to her. The only solace she found was food. Emotional eating led to weight gain, and the kids at school found another reason to tease or avoid her. Samantha felt completely alone, and her aloneness with an overwhelming experience was a secondary trauma in and of itself. Some of you may have been actively told to keep quiet, not to share your experience, which often happens with children who were abused or intentionally mistreated (again, the s-ACEs).

Often, even acute traumas are not what cause lasting psychological damage. Instead, trauma can continue to affect one's sense of self long after the event or events occurred. Experiencing trauma makes us draw certain conclusions, either about ourselves or about the world. Those conclusions continue to impact us as we grow up, becoming self-fulfilling prophecies, like believing the world is not a safe place.

The way we view ourselves and others is then unconsciously passed down to our children. It's also going to affect how we parent them. For instance, if you believe that you can't do anything right, your interactions with your child are going to reinforce that impression and make you feel even worse. What's more, the guilt we feel about the parenting mistakes we've made is on steroids compared to the guilt connected to other mistakes we've made, because the stakes are higher. We all have expectations of how we should act as parents and how our children should behave. Some parents feel so guilty, triggered, and overwhelmed by parenting that it almost becomes a new trauma in and of itself.

Trauma is also what didn't happen *for* you, as a result of what happened *to* you. We can call this the *trauma of absence.* This might look like teens who missed hours of school or were chronically late because they had to care for younger siblings in the morning when there weren't adults at home. Or children who were persistently bullied didn't have the capacity to develop close friendships. It's hard to master reading comprehension on an empty stomach or follow along in math class when you're worried about what you'll find when you get home from school.

Trauma Poker

So many of my adult clients share some variation of the following when we first meet:

> Dr. K—I was only fat-shamed and bullied. My friend Michelle had childhood cancer, and my husband Anthony was beaten by his stepfather. Next to them, I don't think I have the right to call myself post-traumatic.
>
> Dr. K—I don't think Tanya should be in this group. She is only an immigrant. That's not as traumatic as losing both my parents in a car accident and being raised by my toxic, narcissistic aunt.

These comparisons are like a game of "Trauma Poker." We play it with our friends or even with ourselves. Imagine sitting around a table, raising the stakes of your trauma: "I see your bullying, and I raise you having a sister with disabilities." "Oh yeah? Well, I see your sister, and I raise you growing up with a mother who was addicted to cocaine and tried to kill me."

The trauma of absence never makes its way onto the poker table. It's an invisible card that you can't play because there are so many things that you may have missed that you can't categorize them with just one card. And while it's a card that doesn't go on the table, it counts in your own psyche.

Trauma poker is a worthless game, because we can't judge the traumas of others. And the words we choose to describe our own traumas are often inadequate. What I mean by saying "I was bullied" and what you might mean using the same sentence can be very different. For me, being bullied meant relentless teasing in a lunchroom. For Tamara, it meant that the most popular kid in the class didn't invite her to a much-anticipated birthday party. For John, it meant enduring daily beatings at the hands of upper classmen while the other kids watched and laughed.

Trauma Occurring in Adulthood

Traumas can also occur for the first time in adulthood. Maybe you were married to a narcissistic partner or were forced to work for a toxic boss who shattered your self-esteem. Maybe you lost a family member, had a near-death experience, or recovered from a serious illness. Many of my patients were traumatized by the COVID-19 pandemic. They are also overwhelmed with thoughts about climate change, war, school shootings, and more.

I often tell my post-traumatic parenting patients that childhood is written in pencil and adulthood is written in pen; the challenges we face in adulthood are harder to recover from. As adults, we have other people—often our little humans—depending on us, and when we lose our bearings, the consequences can be disproportionately higher. A teenager who lives at home and loses their job can be disappointed. Getting fired as a single parent whose kids depend on that income is a whole different level of stress, which raises the firing experience to the level of traumatic.

Many ancillary emotions also come along with handling an adult trauma while trying to parent. When we "lose our cool" with a friend, we might lose a friend. When we "lose it" with a child, they don't stop loving us, but they stop loving themselves. We instinctively know that our damage can damage them, but in the moment of stress we don't see it, or we see it and don't know what to do about it.

I have also found that if you typically have a disproportionate reaction to stressors, your reaction may be pointing to a hidden traumatic event in your past. For instance, if a parent is traumatized by the idea that nuclear war is a real, present danger, they may have a *sublimated memory* or have been through something that felt similar even though the event was actually quite different. Maybe they were separated from their parents in an unfamiliar place and felt like the world was unraveling. Maybe they were once caught in an overwhelming storm or a car accident. No matter the cause, their brain translated that incident into a more globalized fear that surfaces in adulthood or around parenting.

Gisele Wasn't Lazy

Gisele was in one of my parenting classes. One day, she told me she didn't do her homework because she was "too lazy."

I was perplexed: Gisele is the least lazy, most productive person I know. I also know that Gisele has experienced a combination of ACEs and s-ACEs. She had immigrated to the US at a young age, and her parents had to start a new life from scratch. As an adult, she became a single mom when her husband was killed in a tragic accident. She is

The Trauma Controversy

People think that trauma is overdiagnosed nowadays, but I don't believe that's the case. I believe we are just scraping the surface of what people experience and are now willing to talk about. That doesn't mean that all challenges are traumatic.

You may have gone through some very challenging moments in your childhood, but you've never thought of yourself as traumatized.

Here are three quick questions to ask yourself: When you think about what happened to you, was it something that you would go to any lengths to make sure it doesn't happen to your child? What happened to you in adulthood? Was it something that you wouldn't wish on your child?

If the answer is yes, congratulations. You're traumatized.

However, just because you were traumatized doesn't mean you aren't resilient or that you weren't resilient then. It doesn't mean you're broken or damaged or that you haven't been doing the best you can. Yet there may be a better way to handle some situations, and that's what this book is for.

now an attorney who put herself through law school at night and also has her own start-up company.

Yet Gisele had been called lazy throughout her life. In her early years in school, her teachers called her lazy because she couldn't read English; they told her that she wasn't trying hard enough. Her parents told her that she was lazy when she spent more time studying than working in their dry-cleaning shop. Her parents expected her to contribute her physical labor for their business, but she just wanted to do well in school. These shaming voices left Gisele with a core belief—she is lazy. By the time she was in middle school, her teachers were constantly praising her academic achievement, but the damage was done.

Post-Traumatic Stress Disorder and Post-Traumatic Parenting

The brain's attempts to understand or make meaning of trauma can lead to physical or emotional distress or both. Have you ever experienced

Journaling Exercise: What's Your Trauma?

I don't specify any particular or best way to keep a journal: any way that works for you is great. You can record your thoughts as video or audio, or you can type, write, create art, etc. I'll suggest writing and journaling prompts throughout the book, and I invite you to take those to the modality that works best for you. If you feel blocked at any time, switch modalities: swap out a written journal for creating a voice memo on your phone. Do what works for you, thinking about the following questions:

- What was your acute traumatic experience? If we were watching a video of your life, it's that experience that would be shown with dark, sad, or dramatic music.
- What were your chronic traumas? What were the ongoing struggles you had to deal with every single day? In a movie, chronic traumas are those reflection montages, where you see scenes quickly spliced together: someone gazing at a loving family, then being in an orphanage, or crying while holding a photograph.
- What traumas came after an acute trauma? What happened as a result?
- What were your traumas of absence? What do you believe that you never got that other people had and that you desperately craved? In a movie, traumas of absence are often shown as an empty seat at a table or a child having to take on adult responsibilities.
- What were the traumas that occurred in adulthood? If you can't think of any, think of a pervasive worry or fear you have, something you can't stop thinking about no matter how hard you try. Behind every "what-if" is likely a trauma.
- After you've generated the list, write down one word that encapsulates each trauma. For example, if there was the chronic trauma of living in a family with food insecurity, write down *poverty* or *lack*.
- Now, think of your biggest parenting challenge or mishap: the parenting mistake you wish you could rewrite, the situation that you still cringe at when you think about how you handled it. Look at your list and bring up that memory at the same time. Can you see how your trauma could have influenced your behavior and that you didn't intentionally cause harm? Then you can say, "That behavior

wasn't me; it's my trauma, and I can learn to handle my trauma and parent better." Try saying that last sentence out loud in front of the mirror.

Remember, understanding why you did something doesn't make it okay. We're not giving ourselves permission to engage in that behavior again. In chapter 10, we're going to learn exactly what to do when we need to repair with a child regarding that "cringe" memory. The goal of understanding it is to give yourself the space to be an imperfect human, precisely because you never want it to happen again.

flashbacks, persistent thoughts that won't go away, a constant sense of threat, or an inability to relax? These are some of the most common symptoms of post-traumatic stress (PTS).

People make a big deal about psychological diagnoses, but they're not so mysterious. A psychological diagnosis is simply a list of symptoms that appear together. Depending on the intensity and frequency of those symptoms, as well as how they interfere with your life, they may rise to the level of a disorder, which is then referred to as post-traumatic stress disorder (PTSD).

It doesn't really matter whether you qualify as having a true disorder. The only time psychologists like me care about whether someone meets the criteria for a true disorder is when we are taking either health insurance or medication into account. Since there's no medication that treats PTSD, having a firm diagnosis is pretty much meaningless.

This is not to say that your experience isn't valid. Don't gaslight yourself, and don't doubt yourself. These symptoms are real and can affect your parenting. Not all people will have all of the following symptoms: everybody's experience manifests differently.

- panic sensation, fear, or anxiety during incidents that remind you of the traumatic event
- avoidance of stimuli associated with the traumatic event (not going outside, staying away from external reminders)
- delayed expression of emotion
- dissociative reactions (daydreaming, losing track of time)

- dissociative symptoms, like depersonalization and derealization
- exaggerated startle response
- flashbacks
- hypervigilance
- inability to remember important aspects of the traumatic event, like dissociative amnesia
- irritability
- persistent and exaggerated negative beliefs or expectation about oneself, others, or the world ("I am bad." "No one can be trusted." "The world is extremely dangerous.")
- persistent inability to experience positive emotions, like happiness, satisfaction, or loving feelings
- persistent negative emotional state, markedly diminished interest in or participation in significant activities, feelings of detachment or estrangement
- persistent, distorted cognitions (inaccurate thoughts that lead you to the wrong conclusion) that lead you to blame yourself or others
- presence of recurrent, involuntary, intrusive, distressing memories
- problem concentrating
- reckless or self-destructive behaviors
- recurrent distressing dreams, insomnia, or disrupted sleep

We really don't know exactly why PTS symptoms occur. Is the brain trying to restore safety? Or are the symptoms a reflection of the traumatic experience? Is it a memory that got stuck? Is the brain's entire network of memory in some way tainted by the fact that a memory was traumatic? Is it an emotional reaction that your body can't process? Or is it something else?

My psychodynamic training—a modern take on psychoanalysis—suggests that these symptoms might be a part, or an aspect, of yourself that you don't want to recognize that is trying to get your attention. You wouldn't be having dreams, memories, and flashbacks if your brain wasn't trying to tell you about something that happened, because what would be the point?

Bessel van der Kolk's *The Body Keeps the Score* shows that trauma doesn't always come back as a memory; it often comes back as a physical reaction. That's why Lisa Feldman Barrett has stated, "The body doesn't keep the score. The body is the scorecard."[2] What she's saying is that embodied memories are not creating your distress. Instead, embodied memories can create physical symptoms, reactions, or distress, which then become problematic in and of themselves.

Your PTS symptoms may never go away. However, you can learn how to manage them, recognize when they're coming (you'll see in part II), and create a toolbox of tricks (like I've provided in part III) for what you can do to avert them.

Chronic Traumas and Complex PTSD

Some researchers believe, as I do, that personality disorders stem from chronic traumas or the traumas of absence. They link symptoms like a persistent inability to make friends, or a persistent lack of desire for social interaction, to chronic experiences like being parented harshly, being neglected, or being bullied. If you have been told that you have elements of borderline personality disorder because you are "needy" or "pushy," you may have been misdiagnosed. Instead, you may be experiencing complex PTSD (cPTSD).

Here's how it might work. If you grew up in an invalidating environment, and you've never experienced the sense that somebody truly understands you, you might take any sign of acceptance from another person the way a drowning person grabs a lifeline—and react with an overwhelming sense of attachment. This is the logic underlying a "trauma bond"—when you finally have a relationship that provides essential attachment needs, that relationship becomes crucial. Within that relationship, you felt safe, seen, soothed, and secure. You'll then do whatever it takes to get that sensation to recur. This kind of behavior doesn't mean that you are manipulative or evil, and you're not "addicted to relationships." You're addicted to the sensation that someone's attention gives you. This could happen with a friendship. This could happen in a marriage. It's like you've been craving salt your whole life, and then you are given a giant bag of pretzels: you are going to hungrily gulp it down. And what happens when you don't get that feeling from the person with whom you've trauma bonded? You lash out just like a toddler who doesn't get their way.

There are other personality disorders that are linked to chronic trauma. Another is schizoaffective disorder. Someone who was bullied, belittled, or demeaned as a child might develop tendencies that are unsociable to the point of dysfunction. If you were raised by a narcissistic parent who had unattainable expectations of you, you might develop a very shaky sense of self or your own narcissistic personality disorder.

For instance, Juan was a gawky, nerdy child who was bullied at school because he wasn't good at sports. At home, he was the complete focus of his mother's attention. She would constantly praise his intellectual achievements and brag about them to her friends as if they were her own. Yet he and his father butted heads: his father was critical of Juan, who wasn't a compliant child.

By the time Juan got to high school, he had grown out of his awkwardness. He became tall and strong and suddenly could dominate in sports. The boys in his class started giving him positive attention instead of the constant teasing, and suddenly Juan felt "Finally, the other boys like me."

Juan was now surrounded by praise: at home he was still his mother's favorite; at school he was getting accolades from the boys and attention from the girls. He became narcissistic, with a desperate need to dominate in sports and be the loudest, smartest voice in every room. Deep down, though, he couldn't shake his feelings of worthlessness that the bullying had left him with. He couldn't shake the hurtful criticism his father doled out. He still felt like a worthless loser. His solution was to prove to the world that he was a winner. Anyone that got in the way of his stardom had to be shut down. The girl who just wasn't interested, a teacher who dared call him out on his behavior, or a friend who reminded him of his elementary school self became an existential threat, which he felt that he must take down publicly. The bullied became the bully.

PTSD and Its Effect on Parenting

Once you know where your thoughts are coming from, they will not be so scary. If you have any of these thoughts, you may be experiencing PTSD:

- *I start out my day planning for everything to go well, to be the mom in those commercials who is romping in the grass with her baby, totally present and really connecting. But by the end of the day my behavior was more like the Incredible Hulk—something triggers me, and I lose it.* Can you see the "irritability" and "exaggerated startle response" symptoms of PTSD that we mentioned above?
- *I'm just blocked as a parent. My daughter has always been more challenging than other kids, and the teenage years don't help matters, but I can't figure out how to handle anything. Sometimes I feel so disconnected from her.* Can you see the "persistent inability to feel positive emotions—like love and connection"—that can occur with PTSD?
- *I don't know why my wife just gets my son and can instantly intuit what he needs and what he's not saying. I just can't do that. I feel downright incompetent at parenting. I'm good at everything else—people at work think I'm a rock star—but parenting makes me feel like an idiot.* Can you see the persistent and exaggerated negative beliefs or expectations about oneself, others, or the world?
- *I can't seem to get this parenting thing down pat, and I'm always playing catch-up. I'm always forgetting the dentist appointment or the spare gym uniform or starting homework time way too late. The other moms don't seem to have these problems. I've been disorganized and spacey my whole life, so actually, why did I think I could take on the responsibility of another human?* Can you see the problems concentrating, the dissociation/daydreaming that are associated with PTSD?
- *I need to provide my kids with everything I didn't have. They want to spend more time with me, but I work all the time to make sure we have enough money. No matter how much I earn, it never feels like enough.* Can you see the hypervigilance, the sense of being on the edge of disaster?
- *My baby won't stop crying because she knows she has me for a mother, and I'm not good at anything.* Can you see the persistent, distorted cognitions that led to self-blame, when the truth is that babies don't have these types of

sophisticated thoughts? Babies are limited in their thinking to *I'm hungry, wet, cold, or content.*

- *I'm an angry, explosive person, and if I spend too much time with my kids, I'll ruin them. I leave parenting to my wife to keep my kids safe.* Can you see hypervigilance, an exaggerated startle response, and persistent negative beliefs about the self?

The Result of a Traumatized Brain
The Trauma App

The part of the brain that responds to trauma is the amygdala. When a traumatic incident happened, it jogged your brain to respond, and the brain created both the PTS symptoms and a way of dealing with those symptoms. The amygdala is an incredible problem-solving machine, but it doesn't always know the difference between perception and reality. It can't tell the difference between the illusion of safety and real safety. It forces us to make decisions that make us feel safe, not that would actually make us safe. So, in the moments when your trauma occurred, you were likely left feeling powerless, and the amygdala kicked into high gear and came up with an explanation for why your trauma was happening. This explanation then created a behavior pattern that you could use in the future to give you the illusion of control if that same threat happened again. This behavior pattern becomes your survival instinct, or your stress response.

I like to think of this response as *the trauma app*. The moment you were traumatized, your trauma app was created. Like an app on your phone, the trauma app does only one thing and runs on your own personal algorithm based on the rules "if X, then Y." *If* you are triggered, *then* your stress response behavior activates, and you will fight, flight, freeze, or fawn. These behaviors could be people-pleasing (fawning), dissociating (flight), aggression (fight), control (fight), or perfectionism (fawn). The exact behavior doesn't matter, as long as you feel safe. If I'm perfect, then no one will criticize me. If I control every single aspect of my kids' lives, then no one can harm them. If I people-please, then no one will bully me. If I lash out whenever I hear someone say no, then no one will bully me.

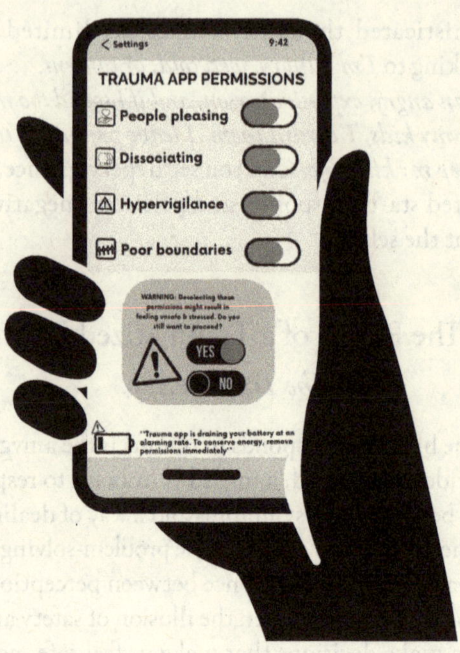

The trauma app creates an effective illusion of safety so that you can get on with your life. It's a necessary adaptation to a terrible circumstance. If every time I got into my car I worried that someone had cut my brake lines, I would be afraid to leave my house and would never go anywhere. If there had never been trauma in my life, I could get into the car without thinking about the brakes, because I would have an inherent sense of safety and think, *My car has never let me down before, why would I think it will let me down today?*

Yet trauma pierces our illusion of safety so that we forget that we're usually safe. With trauma, I start to believe that it is possible that my brakes could malfunction, and every time I get into my car, I worry that I will crash. Or perhaps, I engage in a safety behavior—maybe I crawl under my car every time to see if the brake lines are intact, call an Uber instead of driving myself, or decide I didn't want to go anywhere after all. If I did that, I'd feel safer—but would I actually *be* safer? I'd waste a lot of time, energy, and resources. In some ways, I'd be less safe—if I decide I don't want to go to the doctor for my annual physical, because my car feels unsafe, in the long run, that could kill me.

This is where the trauma app comes in handy. Its entire job is to restore our illusion of safety so that we can function. It comes up with a strategy that is only tangentially related to survival. But whatever it uses, it's going to feel very important to us. In this instance, the trauma app might say, "I don't really need to drive." In the moment that decision feels safer, but in the long run, it creates a very constricted and small life. It solves the immediate problem but creates other problems that you will have to overcome. It makes us believe it is a positive influence, but in fact it gets in the way of our ability to live our best, safest, and healthiest lives.

The trauma app is always on, scanning your environment. And often, your trauma app becomes your superpower. The fact that I can disassociate, become intensely focused on my work, and quickly finish my task is my superpower. This strategy worked for me in college and in graduate school and is great for running my business. I know I have it and I also know that I developed it in response to my trauma, when I didn't want to think about my father's illness or his passing and instead focused only on my schoolwork. I can become so absorbed in my work, I can literally work through an entire day and night and not notice time passing. People talk about it being hard to enter a flow state. For me, it's hard to get out of one.

Think of any superhero movie: the superpower is great in the one situation it's needed, but it always causes other problems in the rest of the hero's life. Can you see how my superpower presents a problem for parenting? If I can't leave a task to attend to my kids, I'm never really present with them. Even if I'm physically with them, a corner of my brain is not.

Exercise: What is Your Superpower?

What is your powerful habit, behavior, or action that is meant to prevent trauma from reaching you again? Think about your superpower. The very thing you get praised for at work, in your family of origin, or by your friends. That same skill is probably the thing that blocks you from parenting well. When people praise you and say, "You're so [fill in the blank]," that's your superpower—that's the blockage.

The Trauma App at Work

Our brains are hardwired to look for validation of what we already believe. This process is called *confirmation bias*, and it's how the trauma app keeps itself in power. For instance, a child who was constantly criticized by their alcoholic parent might learn that if they are super quiet and helpful—a real people pleaser—their mother criticizes them less. As a result, people-pleasing starts becoming how they restore their sense of safety. The trauma app reminds the adult to people-please every time they are in an uncomfortable situation, and then they start believing that they must people-please in order to be safe.

The Trauma App's Limitations

Even at their most efficient, the amygdala and the trauma app can't tell time, and they can't interpret every experience we have in real time. This is why certain *triggers*—any thought or event that elicits a reaction—can make you feel like you are experiencing an old trauma right now, even though it happened twenty years ago. The technical term for that experience is an *emotional flashback*. The trauma app cannot tell the difference between your male boss criticizing you this morning and the time you were physically assaulted at a mall fifteen years ago. The trauma app doesn't care. If your ten-year-old says something snarky to you, your trauma app responds as if you were being bullied when you were a kid. It doesn't decipher that the kid that's right in front of you is the one you love more than the whole entire world. It recognizes only that the sensation of being bullied, which must stop. This is why parents overreact, pressure their kids, or take on too much: all these reactions stem from the trauma app.

Another thing about trauma app is that it tells us the truth, and it also exaggerates. At the core of its algorithm is a nugget of truth, derived from your original trauma and the confirmation bias that grew up around it. It *is* true that pushing back when someone tries to bully you can be self-protective. And it's also true that lashing out at your child when you feel bullied by them isn't effective parenting. Whenever the trauma app initiates the "no one bullies me" program, suddenly you're reflexively responding to feeling bullied. In that moment, you are no longer thinking/acting like a parent; you are executing the trauma app's command. Just because you are the parent doesn't mean that in every moment you are *parenting.*

And the trauma app does not differentiate between discomfort and danger. While it may be true that any threat can make you feel uncomfortable, it is untrue that every discomfort is dangerous. It is true that my discomfort could have repercussions, but it doesn't mean my life will be over if I endure it. Problem is, the trauma app can't tell the difference.

While your superpower and your trauma app may have worked for you in the past, they both derail your ability to parent. Superpower skills do not have the subtlety, nuance, and flexibility needed to be a good parent. If I use my superpower—that I can focus on a problem and solve it—with my child, I will see my child only as a problem that needs to be solved. I lose sight that they are in fact a person, not a problem. So, the same skills that work to keep my office running smoothly are not great skills to have when I'm dealing with a young child learning to read.

You don't want an algorithm parenting your kid—you want to parent your kid. Once the trauma app takes over, you are no longer in the driver's seat, and your parenting becomes inconsistent with your values. When you end the day asking, Why did I start yelling again? When will I get a handle on it? know that your trauma app took over.

When a child becomes "bully I must shut down," or for that matter "threatening person I must people-please," "problem I must solve," or "stressor I must dissociate from," the trauma app has a solution for that. If you're a people pleaser, it's hard to say no to anyone. It's doubly hard to say no to a child you love. But kids need to hear no sometimes. If you know that stress causes you to lash out, so you dissociate instead, you're not parenting with presence. It might feel like dissociating is "better" than yelling, but honestly, is it?

What's more, the trauma app overwrites our parenting instincts. When people say, "Trust your gut," they mean your instincts. I happen to think the concept of "maternal instincts" is a bit romanticized. Or maybe it's just that I'm a post-traumatic parent (PTP). For people who aren't traumatized, there's probably some truth to the idea of "instincts" or "trust your gut," because normative, healthy development can train your gut. Your gut is supposed to send you a warning message when something is truly off. Personal safety expert Gavin de Becker talks about personal intuition in his book *The Gift of Fear.*[3] You might know that as your "uh-oh voice," the inner protective voice that warns you to not get in the car with that stranger, that this girl is acting like a friend but is going to talk about you behind your back, or to not stay after the holiday party to chat with your very inebriated boss. Normative development can really hone that voice.

Traumatized people, though, have a gut instinct that is either way too reactive (seeing everything as a threat) or way too desensitized (not seeing legitimate threats as dangerous). We are left believing that we are naturally bad at parenting or that we don't have that mysterious maternal instinct everyone else seems to have.

The trauma app blocks you from hearing what your gut is trying to tell you, and instead it sends another instruction, in effect saying, "Forget about your gut. I'm right, and you have to listen to me." This means that your parenting instinct could be very right, but the way you react to your instinct can be very, very wrong. For example, one of my favorite movies is *Inside Out* (2015). If you haven't already, please watch it! In one scene, the main character, a young girl named Riley, comes home from school, and even though she says that "school was great," she rolls her eyes and her parents can see that something's wrong. Her mother's emotions are more controlled, but her father is triggered by the eye roll and immediately makes a show of force and sends her to her room. The dad's response was very algorithmic. He was not seeing Riley as a person; he was seeing Riley as a problem. The dad's gut instinct was correct. Riley was rolling her eyes at him. But the action that he took based on his gut instinct was wrong. Riley badly needed emotional support, validation, and attachment in that moment. What she got was punishment.

You can learn to develop that parenting gut instinct, but first you have to shut down the trauma app.

Exercise: What Is Your Trauma App Protecting You From?

Here's an exercise in trauma app algebra: If I consistently try to do X, but Y happens, what is Z, the thing my trauma app is trying to protect me from?

Fill in for each variable:

- My most predictable parenting fail, when I try to do X, but Y happens, what is Z?
- My most predictable life fail, when I try to do X, but every single time, Y happens, what is Z?

Neuroplasticity Isn't as Great as It Sounds

Neuroplasticity, which is the brain's ability to change itself, is frequently touted as good news. However, I see neuroplasticity in a different light: if the brain is malleable, anytime you repeat a certain pattern it becomes more ingrained. If the saying "neurons that fire together, wire together" is true, then neurons firing together repeatedly, over years, get welded tightly together. So instead of the old adage "practice makes perfect," what is really happening is that *practice makes permanent*. The fact that your brain is neuroplastic is why you are the way you are right now—trauma created a behavioral response that has become solidified. You are not lazy or weak-willed if you can't change; you are simply well rehearsed.

The more frequently the trauma app is used, the more likely that your response becomes engraved into your brain, and the harder it is to replace it with a new behavior. That's why the trauma app is so hard to turn off.

I can't say it enough: this is hard work, and don't beat yourself up or blame yourself or believe that you are a terrible person when you see other parents who seem to function calmly and easily and with joy and delight and you can't. You can absolutely change your behaviors and turn off the trauma app, but it's going to take time. It's going to take a lot of intentional effort in order to be a better parent.

The Real World of Post-Traumatic Parenting

Whether it's the PTSD symptoms that are directly affecting your parenting or the trauma app, it doesn't matter. Most PTPs have both. Sometimes, the symptoms are easier to handle, because you can (and probably have) created a work-around for them. For example, if you're prone to panic attacks, maybe you choose not to venture far from home. But if a belief you have about yourself or the world is governed by your trauma app, you might not know how to manage your life if you have to change your behaviors.

Trauma is going to pinpoint our every flaw and make us believe that those flaws are catastrophic in terms of our parenting. Any criticism we've received—no matter how invalid—is going to flash before our eyes as we parent. It doesn't matter what those flaws are, whether we're being told we're self-centered, lazy, or inadequate. A sense of being a bad person, a misfit, or unworthy of love. The instant parenting becomes challenging is the instant those old self-beliefs will awaken.

The voice of trauma is exhausting. It eats up our emotional resources, leaving very little energy for parenting. So many parents feel incredible guilt when they snap at their children, hear themselves using the same harmful statements that their parents used, or disengage from parenting because it feels so impossible or they are so exhausted.

For Gisele, trauma taught her an effective lesson: having a good work ethic is a great way to transform your life. But it also lied, teaching her to internalize this sense of herself as "lazy." Gisele's not lazy, but her trauma app will tell her so, over and over again. And where will the shaming voice strike the deepest chord? In her parenting.

Gisele's default is to overwork herself to the point of exhaustion, because there's this voice in the back of her head that's reminding her that she's lazy. She knows that she is the sole financial supporter for her children, and she feels like she always has to hustle. The fact that her company is doing incredibly well is irrelevant. Her trauma is telling her overworking makes her safe, but in actuality it's making her less safe because she is always exhausted. And her relationship with her children is suffering because she never takes a break to spend time with them.

Gisele knows that there's something wrong with the way she is interacting with her children, but she doesn't know how to fix it. Luckily, we've been able to work together, using the same tools that are in this book. She has come to understand that her trauma app is keeping her busy and away from her children. But she can't see a way to stop.

Freud said that *to know the good is to do the good*. Yet with apologies to the great man, there is so much real estate between knowing how to behave the right way and implementing that behavior. We have all had the experience of our kid coming home and pushing our buttons, and we try so hard not to overact, yet we end up losing our cool.

Just knowing that you have a trauma app is not enough to shut it down or change its permission settings. You must also understand another concept, which is the wounded inner child. In the next chapter, you will learn how to locate your inner child and see how it is persisting to influence your behaviors by the way it reacts to your trauma app. If your wounded inner child continues to experience pain, it will work against your adult self, and every time you try to turn off or change the settings on your trauma app, your inner child will turn them right back on.

CHAPTER 2

Your Inner Child Can't Raise a Child

SARAH'S EIGHT-YEAR-OLD DAUGHTER, Penny, gets overwhelmed whenever her teacher gives her an instruction that she can't complete exactly the way her teacher asked. Sarah told me that one day, Penny was just about to get on the school bus when she realized that her homework folder was missing. Penny was supposed to have Sarah sign her homework. "I need to go back in my room and get my folder! My teacher said I have to bring in my homework folder, and you have to sign it!"

Sarah had just heard from the teacher that Penny's frequent lateness was disruptive to the class and that Penny shouldn't be the exception to the rule: she needed to make the bus with the other children every day.

Penny threw a tantrum, and so did Sarah, who later told me, "In that moment I lost all of my compassion for Penny. I started yelling, 'You're embarrassing me! Why can't you just get on the school bus! You're always late! Don't be such a baby.'"

As Sarah retold the story, I could hear in her voice the exact moment when she was traumatized. Inevitably, the trauma shows up as a person's wounded inner child. Suddenly, instead of talking to an adult client, I'm talking to someone who is using the language of a teenager or an eight-year-old. When Sarah said, "Don't be such a baby," or when she spoke in absolutes, like "You're ALWAYS late," I knew that this language represented a wounded inner child: it didn't sound like adult language. And I also knew exactly where her language was coming from. Sarah had already shared that she was dyslexic and her childhood was filled with being shamed, blamed, and told she was dumb and lazy. She was always a bit late, a bit out of step, confused by things other kids found easy. She was always trying to hide her essential incompetence.

Penny triggered Sarah's wounded inner child, who couldn't read when everybody else could. All Sarah could hear was that voice inside her saying, "The teacher is going to tell me again that I'm a bad parent. I cannot let a teacher tell me I'm bad. I cannot tolerate a teacher making me feel like a dummy." Meanwhile, Penny was refusing to get on the bus because she didn't have the folder, but Sarah's inner child couldn't let Penny *not* get on the bus in order to save herself from shame.

I explained to Sarah that her trauma app and wounded inner child were working together to block her from being able to respond to Penny appropriately. Her wounded inner child could not accept being criticized by the teacher, and her trauma app had a solution to avoid that: force Penny onto the bus. As much as Sarah had been trying to remove permissions from her trauma app, during stressful times, her wounded inner child was turning them right back on.

The first thing we needed to work on was healing Sarah's wounded inner child.

Where Does the Inner Child Come From?

Can we open up our brain and find our inner child, crouching there, coloring or playing with Play-Doh? Of course not. The inner child is a metaphor for unresolved developmental stages, unprocessed grief, and other developmental trauma that has become stuck in our psyche. We need the metaphor because we can't see the inner child directly, but we can see its effects: when we respond to something in an inappropriate way as our younger self and not like our adult, present-day self.

Yet as neuroscientist Lisa Feldman Barret says, all metaphors are helpful, and all metaphors are wrong. The metaphor makes conceptual sense because we can imagine how we sound like a younger version of ourselves. When Sarah's telling Penny, "You're such a baby," it sounds like a six-year-old talking to a sibling, not a mom who's coming from her true adult self. Think about when you're around your family of origin and all of a sudden you are acting like a socially awkward eleven-year-old again.

However, the metaphor doesn't work consistently. Lots of therapists use the metaphor of the inner child with different intentions. For example, the book *Healing the Child Within* by Charles Whitfield, MD, is all about this idea that the inner child is an essence of health and that we have to restore it to health. Other psychologists use the inner child metaphor as a wound that we have to reprocess. There are experts who will talk about embracing your inner child and others who want to "raise" or "dismiss" it. We're left to wonder, Is an inner child an asset or a problem that has to be resolved?

There are two ways in which a wounded inner child can be created. The first involves attachment, which is our inherent survival system that keeps us close to our primary caregivers.

Our attachment system operates like the baby bird in the classic P. D. Eastman book, *Are You My Mother?* It's always asking, Are you Mother, or are you Other? If you are Other, am I safe with you? If you are Other, where's my Mother? When the baby bird finally finds its mother, then all is good and it continues on in the world. But when we don't get what we need from our attachment figure, our attachment system prevents us from continuing on: if you're not my mother and I can't find my mother, then I'm in distress, and I'm going to keep searching.

Attachment is all about surviving: it's comforting, but in the moment, it isn't necessarily comfortable for either the parent or the child. Anything hardwired to keep you alive is meant to be a loud, intrusive signal. If our safety and security needs aren't met, and if our protest behaviors (whining, complaining, crying, etc.) when we're separated from an attachment figure (mom or dad) don't restore safety, then our attachment system keeps searching, and that searching creates psychological distress.

The second way a wounded inner child is formed involves the way we transition through a series of psychological developmental stages. The famed psychologist Erik Erikson believed that as we mature, we have to resolve an essential psychological conundrum at each stage in order to move to the next.[1] I believe that if we don't resolve that psychological conundrum, or if we resolve it in an unhealthy manner, this creates a wounded inner child, a little version of your infant self, or your five-year-old self, or your fifteen-year-old self, who is still desperately trying to reconcile what the world sees as "normal" vs. their own perception. I also believe that if a trauma occurs in childhood and we don't receive the proper support to process and understand it, that can create an inner child who is frantically trying to process that trauma and restore safety.

A lot of people learn about the basic Eriksonian stages in Psychology 101, but what we don't usually learn about is what happens when a stage isn't resolved. His theory involves the development of certain "virtues" or "character strengths," which are created as each stage resolves.

The first stage, trust vs. mistrust, occurs during infancy. The essential questions each of us are faced with are, Can I trust the world? Is the world a safe place? Will I be nourished, protected, cared for, responded to with tenderness when I have needs? If the infant is responded to in a good-enough fashion (to quote the work of D. W. Winnicott, another child development theorist), they establish a sense of hope.[2] With hope, even if life isn't going perfectly, the infant can trust that the world is a safe-enough place and move onto the next developmental stage. Without it, a wounded inner child will be created that's always trying to resolve trust and mistrust.

The second Eriksonian stage is autonomy vs. shame and doubt, and it occurs in the toddler years—ages one to three. The essential question of this stage is, Is it okay to be me? At this stage, the toddler is learning how to navigate the world independently. They learn to use the toilet, to explore the world, and to start using language to meet their needs. They also start noticing the world, expressing their interests and preferences. If resolved successfully, this stage leads to the development of "will." Without it, a child will develop extreme self-blame or extreme passivity.

If the parents allow for the child's need to explore, play, and learn, while being tolerant of mistakes, and are also protective (I know you want to climb on that ledge, but it's too high. Here, I will hold your hand and help you . . .) the child learns that they can handle life on their own and can move to the next developmental stage. Have you ever seen the absolute joy on the face of a toddler who uses the potty successfully, manages to "flip" on their own coat, or successfully slides down a playground slide? That's autonomy! If parents demand too much, too soon—if they expect perfection and don't make space for little hands and little bodies to mess up—the child develops a sense of profound shame and doubt. So, if you walk around feeling essentially flawed or feel guilty for situations that fail yet aren't under your direct control, you might have an inner toddler, still trying to figure out the essential question: Is it okay to be me?

The next developmental stage marks our entry into school and socialization. It's from ages three to six, the stage of initiative vs. guilt. The essential question of this stage is, Is it okay for me to move, do, act, and make things happen in the world? Successful resolution of this stage is a sense of purpose: "There are tasks for me to perform, and I know how to perform them reasonably well; I have wants/desires/interests, and it's okay for me to act on those."

At this stage, a child is learning how to master the world. But when a child is frustrated, their stronger emotional system but relatively weak executive functioning means they'll act out their anger. "Stupid bike!" a child might yell, throwing it down on the ground, forgetting that they really love that bike. Parents have to strike a balance between not making a children feel "bad" for their intense anger, frustration, and mistakes and teaching them how to manage these feelings. If the adults don't allow for increased independence or if they punish strong emotional reactions, the child is going to feel guilty. If you struggle with your emotions or say/do things you regret, you may have an inner three- to six-year-old, still trying to resolve the question, Is it okay for me to do, move, and act? Is it okay for me to have my own preferences and interests?

The next stage, ages seven to ten, the primary school years, is when the child fully moves into the social and academic world. There are a lot of opportunities to succeed and a lot of opportunities to fail. The stage is called industry vs. inferiority, and when it's resolved, the child attains a sense of competence. The essential questions are, Can I make it in the world of people and things? Am I as good as the other kids? These are the years of self-comparison—the awareness of "self" and the idea that other people are "selves" too—and the realization that some selves can do things better than others. If you feel "less than" other people or believe that you have to constantly try to hide your incompetence, even if other people praise your work, you may have a wounded inner seven- to ten-year-old.

The next developmental stage occurs during the ages eleven to nineteen. The essential questions of this stage are, Who am I? What can I be? The adolescent is figuring out identity vs. role confusion. Adolescents are very much aware of the need to fit in and the need to have a distinct, unique identity. Adolescents are capable of a lot, yet they are also dealing with adult-strength emotions and hormones with an underdeveloped brain that's more similar to a toddler's than we would hope! They understand the world, but they're also egocentric and impulsive. Parents can become threatened by a teenager's need for independence, their need to explore different identities and opinions, and their impulsivity, and they can react harshly in an effort to control them. Parents are often concerned with long-term implications of behavior—if you party instead of studying for the SATs, what will become of your future? Teenagers are more concerned with immediate exploration of their world and identity. If you walk around feeling afraid of the social world or find yourself with controlling bosses, romantic partners, or friends who have strong opinions, because you're not really sure of what to do, you might have an inner wounded teenager. If you walk around feeling extremely rebellious, ignore commonsense rules, or engage in risky behavior, you may also have a wounded inner teenager.

A healthy response to an inner child acknowledges a feeling of discomfort but is able to understand that discomfort is not an emergency. For instance, when my friend Blake was in nursery school, he got on the wrong bus at the end of the day. He became upset, the bus driver noticed, and eventually took him home. Blake can remember this experience as *uncomfortable*, but it never felt like a life-and-death scenario. He's now left with an inner child memory of an uncomfortable experience that he can tap into and use to relate to his own preschooler. Because he experienced appropriate support—both from the bus driver and his parents—Blake didn't develop a wounded inner child. Had his mother shamed him, saying, "How could you get on the wrong bus? Are you lazy or stupid? No one else in your class ever made a mistake like that!" Blake's inner child might have been wounded. He might have seen himself as less industrious and capable than the other kids. Had the bus driver been angry (or worse, exploitative), Blake might have developed an inner child that saw the world as inherently untrustworthy. But because both the bus driver and his parents were supportive and kind and helped him recover, Blake's inner child is healthy.

You could also have a healthy inner child experience from age eight and a wounded inner child experience from when your trauma started at age twelve. I've met plenty of parents who resolved certain stages very well, yet when their child is at a stage that wasn't resolved, their own wounded inner child shows up. For instance, I remember confessing to a friend of mine that I felt a sense of dread for no apparent reason. She reminded me that I had just celebrated my oldest daughter's sixteenth birthday. "I wonder if there's a part of you that sees sixteen as a very dangerous age," she mused. "I think there's a little Robyn inside of you who is shrieking, 'Sixteen is when daddies die. Sixteen is when you develop PTSD. Sixteen is very, very dangerous.'"

However, an unresolved childhood trauma can undo any developmental stage, just like a sweater can unravel. If you grew up thinking that the world was always safe and then when you were eight lived through a catastrophic earthquake, that experience might undo the infant-stage resolution of trust vs. mistrust, because suddenly your home and community wouldn't feel safe anymore. If your trauma occurred after you went through all the developmental stages, it can take you back to any aspect of development, depending on what the essential trauma was.

And if a sense of safety was never established, it's a lot harder to create one, because the original sweater never existed. We don't even have a ball of yarn. Instead, the child must move onto the next stage, even if their questions are unresolved. Each time a wounded inner child is formed, it will impact the next stage, which might mean that another wounded inner child will form.

Don't despair, what was unraveled can be reknitted. According to Eric Erikson, all therapy provides a way to literally move through and resolve each of the developmental stages.

The Wounded Inner Child and the Post-Traumatic Parent

Theoretical psychologists like Erikson have informed my thinking, and my clinical experience has shown me how the concept of an inner child fits into the context of post-traumatic parenting. I believe we all have at least one inner child and there's nothing wrong with that. If you "raise" your inner child or try to get rid of it altogether, you can't access earlier versions of yourself. And if you can't access earlier versions of yourself, you will lose a valuable tool for gaining insight into what your own child is going through.

Your inner child is a powerful resource that's critical for healthy parenting. I recently found my journals from sixth grade. As I was reading them, I could clearly remember the incidents I wrote about, as well as exactly how I felt at that age. Being able to tap into this information helps me parent my own children when they are that age. Your inner child can also help you understand other adults. A healthy adult who remembers that time they were crying because they had to start at a new school can develop the compassion to be kind to a new coworker.

However, a wounded inner child is the opposite: it can derail our parenting. The way I see it, a wounded inner child is a ghost version of ourselves from each stage, existing inside of us. It goes unnoticed until we are confronted by its unresolved essential questions, and then it can wake up, take over, and frantically restore permissions to the trauma app.

For many PTPs, their wounded inner child is still trying to make sense of the world but is frozen at the stage of life where their trauma took place. Sarah's wounded inner child developed when her teacher labeled her as *the dummy of the class*. And because she's carrying that trauma today, it's affecting her relationship with Penny. Penny is becoming a threat to Sarah's wounded inner child. Her inner child must pretend to be competent and must succeed. Her inner child simply cannot tolerate being criticized by a teacher. Every time that Penny is late and misses the school bus, Sarah tenses up. She doesn't see Penny as a five-year-old who needs to learn from making her own mistakes. She sees her as a threat—a potential for criticism. She can't risk that. She also might unconsciously be reinforcing Penny's need to execute her teachers' instructions perfectly, because she feels that same pressure. And if Penny starts to struggle academically, it will be catastrophic for Sarah. Even if Penny has a mild reading setback, mistaking *bab* for *dad* (something that's typical for first graders), Sarah is going to panic. She might reinforce Penny's fears about school being too hard. She might push Penny to study or perfect her skills with way too much force, simply because of her own unresolved competence fears.

The wounded inner child and the trauma app work together, keeping us stuck in patterns that feel safe but are ironically counterproductive. When Sarah pressured Penny and Penny got on the school bus, Sarah felt a sense of relief, but she was also upset about the interaction. And in the long run, making Penny feel small is going to have some serious repercussions on their relationship. Sarah knows this—and knows that pressuring Penny is inconsistent with her parenting values—yet she can't seem to stop.

The worst case is when that inner child is constantly in the driver's seat, taking over your life. In these circumstances, it's very clear that you may not know the difference between your motivations and responses and those of the wounded inner child.

A Wounded Inner Child and the Trauma App

Sometimes when you feel triggered, you are reawakening a wounded inner child. That's when the trauma app kicks in, locking you in some sort of defensive posture, mediating what your wounded inner child needs in order to feel safe again. Here's how it works: when your

Exercise: Who Is Your Inner Child?

Let's get in touch with your inner child. By tapping into it, you will have new insights into why you are the way you are and why your inner child is trying to get your attention. The ability to access an inner child is one of the reasons why we like nostalgic music or television shows. When I was a child, I used to feel odd whenever my mother met her old school friends. They'd start to sing their alma mater's song or the theme to their favorite shows, and all of a sudden, they would be giggling and acting like teenagers. I used to roll my eyes and try to pretend that I didn't know my mother—because I was feeling confused about seeing my mother's teenage self. But being around her friends and singing those old songs brought an earlier version of herself to the surface.

The following statements offer an opportunity to tap into earlier versions of yourself.

1. As a child, I used to daydream about__________.
2. As a child, I always said I want to grow up to be__________ because _________.
3. My favorite game, book, movie, or music from my childhood was __________.
4. As a child, what I loved to eat was __________.
5. My biggest fear as a child was __________.
6. My biggest source of self-consciousness as a child was __________.

For the following, I'm reframing the "I" statements to "you" questions. The reason is that I want to put some distance between you and your memory. You are the narrator, or observing self, of your own story.

7. Do you remember a time in childhood when you were joyful, uninhibited, and not self-conscious? (It's okay if you don't; not everyone does.) If you do, what happened to change that?
8. What is your very first memory?
9. What did your childhood bedroom look like? What did it smell like? What sounds could you hear as you were in it?
10. Did you have any collections or favorite possessions as a child? What were they? What happened to them?

Now, let's see if you have a wounded inner child.

1. Was there a significant life experience that interrupted the resolution of a childhood developmental stage as listed on pages 26–28? What was going on in your life at that time? Do you have specific memories?
2. Do you lack specific memories but know from family stories that something serious was going on? If you don't have specific memories of a trauma, can you remember times in your childhood when you fantasized about having a different life? If you're watching a sitcom on TV where the parent lovingly talks a kid through a mistake and you're thinking, *I wish I'd had that*, think of how old you were when you first had that feeling. There's a wounded inner child there.
3. If you have absolutely no memories of your childhood, that's a pretty strong indicator of trauma. Try to find photos of yourself as a child. If you've kept mementos from your past, look at them. Listening to music and watching the TV shows from your childhood can bring up memories.
4. You know when your wounded inner child is guiding your decision-making whenever your reaction to your children is disproportionate to the problem.

wounded inner child pops up, it tells you, "Make this stressful situation stop." The trauma app responds, "Okay, I got this." The trauma app starts up its to-go stress response. For Sarah, that meant "get Penny on the bus. She cannot be late. I cannot be criticized by the teacher."

Because the trauma app always comes up with the same solution, so does the wounded inner child. Sarah couldn't even conceive of a world where it would be appropriate for her to call the teacher and clarify what Penny should do if the homework folder was truly missing. Sarah couldn't advocate for herself and Penny, because her trauma app removed all flexibility from her parenting repertoire.

A wounded inner child cannot help you raise a child. How can an eight-year-old raise a twelve-year-old? If you have a belief about yourself and the world that's being influenced by eight-year-old you, it will very likely be distorted. The eight-year-old is going to keep its stranglehold on the trauma app, assessing danger based on its understanding of the world, so the trauma app needs to be left on and at the highest power.

When Sarah can learn to be more flexible, her wounded inner child will begin to heal. The teacher may still be judgmental and she still may criticize both Sarah and Penny. Yet Sarah will be able to relate to that criticism in a more flexible manner. She may think, *From the teacher's perspective, it's important that Penny get there on the bus. But I know what my child needs, and I can advocate for myself and for Penny. Maybe we're more competent than I thought.*

When my daughter turned sixteen, my trauma app wanted to make me safe, but it didn't need me to feel soothed. Quite the opposite: my wounded inner sixteen-year-old needed to keep the trauma app scanning for danger because my daughter was sixteen. After discussing my dread with my friend, I understood why I was feeling unsettled. Once I had that conversation, my wounded inner child could take a breath because it realized that adult me was ready to keep us all safe. This time, when I removed some permissions from the trauma app, they stayed removed.

Healing the Wounded Inner Child

All Parenting is Reparenting

Our important work as PTPs is to heal the wounded inner child. But we need only to heal the wounds. We don't need to undo the memory of our trauma: we don't need to pretend it didn't happen. Instead, we need to expand our understanding of what happened so that the wounded inner child can relax knowing that there's a trustworthy adult in charge (you), who can figure it all out and keep us all safe.

Sarah felt terrible about that morning at the bus stop, and she knew that the scene she made would keep happening if she didn't get a handle on her behavior. She knew that her bad experiences with school were coloring Penny's. Yet Sarah felt stuck because it was too painful to revisit her childhood years.

The only way I could get Sarah to do this—to enter back into those horribly painful years—was the incredible love she has for Penny. We needed that love as our resource: we needed to manifest it, think about it, and transform it into the energy we needed to go there. We didn't go there for Little Sarah's sake. We went there for Penny's sake. For

An editor helps a writer focus on what's important. Parents can act as an editor and shine a light on how our kids can reframe their thinking. It's not our job to write their story.

Penny, Sarah was willing to talk about those days, even though they were so painful.

In order to heal Sarah's wounded inner child, we first had to access her, letting her inner child know that she is not alone, even when life feels big and overwhelming. As we will see later in this book, parents are not the authors of their children's lives—as much as we'd sometimes like to be—but we can be the editors. We can't control what happens in a child's day, but we can control how the child interprets it.

When Sarah came into my office, we brainstormed ideas about her wounded inner child. What did it feel like to have a reading disability in first grade? What words would her inner child use to describe itself? *Dumb*? *Lazy*? *Spaced out*? *Embarrassing*?

Then, I had Sarah look at her inner child from the vantage point of an adult—a loving, caring parent. What words would the adult use to describe that child? *Trying so hard. Earnest. Eager to please. Kind. Softhearted. Artistic. Creative.*

Sarah's homework was to write a letter to her inner six-year-old, as Adult Sarah, telling Little Sarah how she understands her struggles, explaining the concept of dyslexia, and pointing out all the wonderful traits that Little Sarah has.

Dear Little Sarah:

You are not dumb. You have a condition called dyslexia. It means you're an excellent visual spatial processor, and you will eventually learn how to read—but you read differently than other kids.

You're not spacey and dreamy—you're just very creative and artistic, and you have a rich fantasy life.

I'm sorry that you have to keep going back to school, and I'm proud that you kept trying hard—you are so brave and resilient. Also—your teacher is WRONG. She should not be bullying you and calling you a "dummy." That's not how responsible adults talk to kids. Her response says a lot about her values, and absolutely nothing about you.

Love,
Big Sarah

Next, we worked on reparenting Sarah, giving her the support that she should have gotten all along. The method was to build on her own parenting skills with Penny.

I asked Sarah, "Let's imagine that you are coaching Penny through something painful. What would you compassionately say to Penny?"

Sarah responded, "I know it's scary, but we can do this. It'll be better afterwards. I will be there with you the whole time."

Then I said, "Now I want you to hug yourself and I want you to say that to yourself. Say to yourself the exact words you would say to Penny."

Sarah's inner child heard, "Maybe I'm not globally incompetent. Maybe I was feeling so bad about myself because Penny wasn't prepared, and it reminded me of the time when I was being bullied by my teacher. Not everyone was rejecting me. It was that one teacher. It's true, I couldn't read. But it's also true that my teacher should have known about dyslexia. She was wrong to call me names in front of the class. I can see why calling Penny names isn't the answer. Instead, I can help her with compassion."

When Penny is late for school and Sarah talks to her without panicking, we know that Sarah's wounded inner child is no longer accessing the app. When Sarah can be flexible in her responses, that means Adult Sarah, not Little Sarah, is in charge.

You're always going to have a wounded inner child that's going to remember the pain of that traumatic experience. It's going to create a scar, but suddenly you have a capacity to draw on because the wounded inner child reminds you just how painful that feels. The wound never fully goes away, but we can recruit it and use it as a point of strength, a healthier version of an inner child. Sarah's inner child is now available to provide her with useful information. If Sarah is compassionate with

Exercise: Self-Parenting

You can parent your inner child while parenting the child in front of you by using the following self-talk. First, find a picture of yourself as a small child or an item from your childhood that's evocative of that stage. You can also talk to yourself in the mirror.

Then, read aloud the following before you see your child for the first time each day:

> Today, I am going to be present with my child.
> Today, I am going to make my child feel seen, felt, and heard.
> And, as I do that, Inner Child, I want you to pay attention to this message from me to you.

You can customize this script so it's perfect just for you. Here are some inner child wounds you might want to choose from (there could be many more).

I felt the following:

- incompetent
- unseen
- shamed/blamed/criticized for things that weren't under my control
- imperfect
- broken
- too needy/clingy/loud/much
- awkward
- stupid
- lazy
- unworthy of love

I was afraid of the following:

- being abandoned
- being judged
- being essentially bad, that I should have been "good" or "selfless"
- being abused or hurt more
- being hungry/deprived
- encountering a scary person
- being bullied
- causing harm

people who are struggling because she remembers what it was like to be a first grader who's struggling, that's tapping into that inner child in a beautiful, transformative way.

More importantly, when Sarah can access her inner child, she has other tools to parent Penny besides her trauma app. She goes from the robotic, algorithmic responding of "Penny MUST make the school bus, or I'm a bad mom. I can't be a bad mom, because I can't be incompetent." to "I can talk to Penny compassionately through her morning. Even if she misses the bus, I can tolerate being judged by her teacher. That doesn't mean I'm incompetent."

Dear Little Me:

As you watch me parent [Name of Real-Life Child], you're going to see me making them feel seen, felt, and heard.

You're going to think, I wish I'd had that.

There's going to be some sadness attached to that.

That's okay.

You might feel some other feelings, and that's okay too.

It would have been so nice if you'd had that.

It would have been so wonderful to be seen, supported, and heard back then.

It wasn't your fault. And it's okay to feel however you feel about it.

Right now, I am going to do that for [Name of Real-Life Child].

While I'm doing that, you're going to experience the sensation of being seen from the aspect of the person doing the seeing.

Today, one of the children is going to make a mistake—mess up—fall down—and they're going to need to be soothed.

And I am going to soothe that child.

Inner Child—as you feel me hugging that child, I want you to feel hugged.

As I soothe, you can tap into the sensation of soothing.

You're going to tap into the sensation of what "seen-ness" feels like, what "felt-ness" feels like, what it feels like to be heard, supported, and cared for.

And that's going to help—a little.

I'm inviting you to tap into that experience.

Love,
Adult Me

When Your Inner Child is Envious

As they heal, some of my post-traumatic patients express that their inner child is envious of their current children. Their comments often sound something like, "I wish I was my kid." If you think about that old refrain "I walked uphill both ways in the snow to get to school," that sentiment is really coming from your inner child's envy of your current kid having it easier than you did. It's not saying, "You don't have the grit that I developed," even if people think it does.

This envy is normal, and it's okay. Sometimes, we try to dismiss, downplay, or deny our envy, because we think it's unbecoming to us. How can we be envious of our own child? Does that mean we love them less?

The problem is, when you try to deny an emotion, it generally means that this emotion has a hold on you. Anything that's unaccepted is unexaminable. When we act out against our child because we're unconsciously jealous of them, that needs to be examined.

Let's take the classic "toy aisle in Target" scenario. (I always feel like the toy aisle in major stores should be accompanied by the kind of soundtrack that generally plays when the psycho serial killer shows up in a horror movie, because all the most horrific parenting scenes take place there. The candy aisle and the treats in front of the checkout lane should also be similarly equipped.) Your five-year-old son, Aaron, is demanding a new toy when you're in Target shopping for a birthday present for his cousin. He wants you to buy the same present for himself. He wants you to buy ALL the presents for himself. Right now. As you are rolling the cart down the toy aisle, you're hearing, "Buy me this" a thousand times. And when you say no, Aaron melts down. You have a feeling that this interaction is not going well, because it's not a "perfect parenting moment" like what you see on TV or on social media. You know that you should talk him through the meltdown or create a compromise, but when Aaron starts crying, your inner child gets triggered. You start thinking, *I'm not getting him anything. He needs to learn that he can't have everything he wants. He's already spoiled enough. I never got any toys when I was growing up and my mother never took me out to a store for anything. How dare he.* And then you act on those thoughts and start saying no.

Can you see how your inner child is teaming up with your trauma app, leading you to think that the cause of Aaron's problem is a lack of education, as in, "He has to learn that he can't have everything." With each passing minute, your inner child is going to get meaner and act out in some way because it's feeling envious.

But what if you flipped the script and thought about how it would feel to be that five-year-old in a toy aisle: Is your inner child envious?

A "no" response comes from one of two places. The first comes from a true connection to your parenting values, as in, "I know you REALLY want that truck. It's so hard. Right now, Aaron, I need you to say yes to no! Today, we're buying a small treat from the treat aisle for you, and a present for Daniel." Then, you as a parent stick to that no because it's a boundary. You know that Aaron doesn't need the toy, and he needs to learn to take no for an answer sometimes. You feel good about that decision, even if Aaron is struggling with that no.

The second no is almost a survival mode response, because saying no is always easier than saying yes. When our brain is overstressed and we're trying to conserve resources, saying no lets us stay in control. Yet sometimes, an automatic no to a request should be checked to see if your inner child's envious of your current child. If they are, you have to proceed with caution. It's okay to say no to your child—even in the toy or candy aisle at Target—and you should stick to that "no" boundary even if your kid is upset. But a lack of empathy as your child struggles with the no is the sign of an envious inner child. Getting angry at the child for their meltdown or labeling them as spoiled is your wounded inner child talking.

Understanding that you could be envious of your own child is actually a sign that you are on the road to healing, because you have a better understanding of who you are. You can recognize that your judgmental, punitive thoughts are coming from a wounded inner child.

In this scenario, you are envious of Aaron's ability to ask for an abundance of stuff and get it and his uninhibited freedom to have a meltdown in Target. You value your children feeling safe enough to come to you with big emotions. In practice, right now, it's feeling uncomfortable. But if you can focus your attention on your real-life child, not your inner child, you can say (out loud to Aaron or to yourself), "It's so hard to see all the toys in Target. Today, we are picking

Journaling Exercise: Where Is My Envy Hiding?

It's okay to feel envious of your child at times: it just means that you want something they have that you couldn't have. It doesn't mean you're a bad person.

I am envious of my kids because ______________________.

Now, validate the envy for your inner child: Yes, it would have been nice to have ______________________________________.

out a toy for Cousin Daniel's birthday. I can take a picture of the toys you like. Then, when it's your birthday, we can look at all the pictures and pick one. Today, we're buying a small treat for you, and that's it. I see that it's hard for you. That's okay."

By focusing on your value—allowing Aaron to have strong emotions, even uncomfortable ones and being kind and supportive rather than judgmental—you raise your empathy and keep your wounded inner child from intervening.

Sometimes when I watch my husband be a healthy father with my kids, I am so jealous that they are able to experience a healthy father relationship. In the past, I would get so consumed with jealousy that I would withdraw completely: the whole family would be laughing and roughhousing together and I would pull back and go somewhere else. Or I'd get angry with them and yell, "It's bedtime! She hasn't done her homework yet! Why are we wasting time?!" Today, when I have those feelings, I know that I need a minute to acknowledge my feelings, and when I can stay in the moment without having to leave, I can join in and revel in the play.

Finding Your Parenting Values

You have parenting values; you just don't know you have them. You value something that you believe in providing, something that you know is essential and that you're willing to forgo other things for.

For example, Sarah had really wanted supportive kindness from her parents and teachers. She wanted someone to say to her, "Sarah, reading is hard. You're doing your best. Take a deep breath, give yourself some time to recover, and try again." When she learned that she could provide supportive kindness to Penny—even when that costs her time or criticism from Penny's teachers—she was acting on an important parenting value for her.

The first place to look for your values is your envy! If you're envious of something you're providing your child (ample food and clothing, attention, supportive care when they're feeling big emotion, extracurricular activities) you are looking right at your values.

One of my parenting values is to create opportunities to have spontaneous joy with my little humans. When I was controlled by my inner child, I couldn't participate in play. But once I took the control away from my inner child, I realized that I could be the fun parent too. I can experience it by giving it, even if I didn't experience it by getting it.

Do you see how an emotion you didn't want to acknowledge—envy—can actually be the roadmap toward your parenting values? If you're envious of it, you value it. If you value it, you can have it, even if you have it only by giving it.

As you give it, your inner child gets to experience it. And that's how we keep our inner child intact but also keep it from parenting our children.

CHAPTER 3

How Trauma Shows Up in Parenting

Triggers and Responses

NOW THAT YOU have a deeper understanding of how your trauma has affected you, let's unpack how these same traumas affect your parenting choices and decisions. To do this, we have to go back to the basics of human biology and understand how every person, post-traumatic or not, responds to their world.

The truth is, humans are simple creatures. Pop quiz: What's your brain for? Remember learning "I think, therefore I am" in philosophy class? Sorry, Descartes! You were wrong. Actually, our brains exist to do one thing: keep us alive. Everything else we do—from interior design to car mechanics to songwriting—is directly related to that one simple goal.

Our brains keep us alive by activating pattern analysis, which tells us that a berry with a certain shape is always safe to eat; that a stick, used in a particular fashion, can help us protect ourselves; or that this bumpy terrain can cause us to fall, so we'd better take precautions as we walk. That same pattern analysis is also what allows us to use our past knowledge to write music, follow fashion, and make parenting decisions (*last time I didn't bring snacks on the long car trip and the kids had a meltdown—don't do that again*).

Pattern analysis is also what creates our response to triggers. Even with our sophisticated ability to navigate the world, there are lots of things we wish we could control that we know we can't, like the weather. And there's an even greater list of things we think we actively control but in reality are determined by our biology, our thoughts, or the behaviors of others. The perfect example of this are triggers. Triggers are an automatic association—any thought or event that elicits a reaction. They lead to a response or change in our behaviors or our feelings. Your stomach grumbles and you recognize that you are hungry and are triggered to go get something to eat; you feel sleepy so you make your way into the bedroom. Or you watch a sad movie and you cry. Or you think about your trauma and you dissociate. Or your child (or even a perfect stranger) does something that triggers a reaction.

Triggers happen, and there's virtually nothing you can do to stop them. Sometimes you are content with your reaction to a trigger: *Yes, I was hungry and needed to eat lunch; thanks, trigger!* And sometimes you are deeply ashamed of how you reacted: *I'm so embarrassed by the way I gobbled up those ribs so messily in front of my coworkers, but I couldn't control myself.* Sometimes, you may be bewildered by your reaction and can't make the connection between your response and the trigger: *Why did I eat an entire pizza after I just worked out and was proud of myself for being so healthy?*

For PTPs, triggers affect the way we relate to our children. Anything a child does can be triggering. And any thought you have about your child, or yourself as a parent, can be triggering. In fact, some of the most triggering thoughts can be all the ways that we judge ourselves as parents. You might feel like you're not cut out to be a parent, because how can a good parent be touched out, or dissociate, during parenting? You might be triggered when you wonder how a good parent can be envious of their own child. You're likely to be triggered when you yell at your kids, especially if they break down in tears right after.

You might think that if you loved your kids more, you wouldn't get triggered by them, but that is simply not true. Remember: triggers are automatic and cannot be controlled, no matter how much you try. The table includes some of the most common triggers PTPs share with me.

So now you get it: triggers provoke a response. Trauma interferes with interoception—the ability to accurately read and interpret triggers or warning signs from our own bodies. This means we can sometimes miss our stress levels rising and then suddenly snap at a child. We can ignore our body states (our need for the bathroom, our hunger, our thirst, or our need for rest) until we melt down. If we can't read our own bodies, how can we help our kids read their bodies? Interoception is also the origin of our gut instinct—when we have that sixth sense that something is up with a child and we should intervene. If our brain isn't decoding the triggers from our body, that's a serious advantage that we're giving up.

Deep in the brain, we all have various operating systems running, just like with the trauma app. In fact, the trauma app is happening specifically because of a trigger. But in between the trigger and the trauma app, there is a critical pathway that causes the trauma app to fire up: the default mode network (DMN).

Your Child's Age Range When Triggers Typically First Appear	Triggers Caused by Your Child's Behavior	Triggers Caused by Your Thoughts, Feelings, and Behaviors
Infant-Toddler (0–2 years)	• A dangerous situation (toddler dashing into the street) • Sudden loud noises • Sudden touch • Meltdowns	• Feeling "touched out" • Feeling incompetent as a parent • Being shamed for your parenting by a spouse, a family member, teachers, or strangers
Preschool (2–5 years)	• Stubbornness • Separation anxiety • Bullying/abusive behavior • Getting in trouble with teachers or authority figures • Fighting • Being unkind to others • Emotional turmoil • Failure in reaching a developmental/health milestone	• Your separation anxiety • Feelings of sadness/grief when you realize how young you were when you experienced trauma • Fear of being unable to play joyfully with your kid • Oppressive need to do parenting perfectly or "right" • Being shocked by your intense rage • Feeling overwhelmed • Being embarrassed by your child's behavior
Early School (5–10 years)	• Acting less mature than their age • Poor social skills, shyness, or excessive exuberance • Obstinate behaviors, like talking back to you • Intense emotional reactions • Unending demands and needs	• Distress of watching children grapple with "competence" and the social world that reminds you of internalized shame/self-doubt • Your impostor syndrome as children begin to compare you to their peers' parents and your need to make the right decision

Your Child's Age Range When Triggers Typically First Appear	Triggers Caused by Your Child's Behavior	Triggers Caused by Your Thoughts, Feelings, and Behaviors
Middle School (10–14 years)	• Not talking to you/avoiding you • Any behavior that reminds you of your wounded inner child at that age	• Processing your traumas of absence, what you are providing to your children that you didn't have • Fear of loss as peer group becomes more prominent • Fear for a child's future as they make independent decisions that you might not be comfortable with • Fear as you watch your children display personality characteristics that you have—that may have gotten you in trouble, bullied, or turned into traumatic situations—and realizing those characteristics are not flexible and may be hardwired
High School (14–18 years)	• Any attempts at separation, especially when they are coupled with anger or rejection	• Interpersonal trauma coping tendencies, like extreme reactions to being pushed around or people-pleasing • Becoming aware that the child is going to leave the nest • Fear for the child's future, particularly if they are making choices that seem unwise

Neuroscientists used to think that the DMN operated like some sort of screen saver, because it's a network of brain cells that operate when we're not engaged in task-related thinking. It's what is engaged when we let our mind wander, like when we find ourselves several exits down the highway with no conscious memory of having driven. However, neuroscientist and psychologist Lisa Feldman Barrett discovered that this interpretation was seriously wrong. Her research in her book *How Emotions are Made* showed that the DMN is what your brain defaults to when it's not actively trying to do something else.[1] That default creates an action instead of inaction.

If you were raised in a household where loud voices meant being playful and enjoyable, the sudden sound of a child shrieking just for the sake of making noise will sound good, or at least tolerable, and your DMN would stay silent. But if you were raised with a lot of loud arguing and yelling, you may not be able to handle the sheer LOUDNESS of your kids and you'll react to their noisiness. That reaction doesn't mean that you have a lack of love for them; it's your brain defaulting to "loud equals danger."

Every time you witness an event, your brain defaults to an assumption to make sense of what you are seeing, based on your memories. In the movie *Inside Out*, Riley is trying to sleep the first night in her new San Francisco house, and she hears all these unfamiliar sounds. The emotion Fear starts wondering if there is a bear nearby, because Riley is from Minnesota, where bears are a problem. Even though there aren't any bears in San Francisco, her brain goes directly to bear, because a bear is the scariest thing it has come across in her memory.

You have no control over what the DMN does: it's your brain's default that has been programmed because of your trauma. If you are a PTP who suffered from physical abuse and your toddler runs to hug you, the unexpected touch might be a trigger for you. Your DMN recognizes "touch" as "danger."

And this is really important: you cannot blame yourself for your reactions to your triggers. It's like blaming yourself for gravity. Gravity is Earth's operational default. If I drop a ball, it's always going to fall to the ground. Your DMN operational default is "the world seems threatening." So when a PTP mother judges herself, as in, "How can I get so enraged by my kids running around being loud, when I love them and

Do Your Triggers Have a Where or When?

Is there a time of day that's hard for you? For the next seven days, track where you are and the time of day when you feel most challenged or experience a change in your behavior.

Does this place or time relate to certain difficult daily activities, like getting your kids to bed or out of the home and to school on time?

Does this place or time remind you of your trauma?

they're so little?" it's her DMN reacting to whatever her trigger in that scenario was—loud noises, erratic behavior, etc.

Triggers Push Traumatic Memories and Flashbacks

Triggers can also provoke the DMN into feeling as if you were reliving a memory. Ask any PTP and we'll tell you trauma memories don't feel like memories—they feel like fragments of the past that are intruding on the present. Let's get something straight: the term *traumatic memories* is a misnomer.

For people outside the PTP community, this is a hard idea to wrap their heads around. Luckily, new research points to what we have always known. An important 2023 study showed that traumatic memories don't activate the memory centers of the brain—the hippocampus and amygdala—but rather activate the posterior cingulate cortex (PCC)—the part of the brain that processes internally directed thought, like introspection or daydreaming.[2]

The PCC is a part of the brain that isn't very well understood. It seems to process internally directed thought—the kind of introspective thinking we might have when we witness an event, as in, *Who am I, in the context of what happened?* It's the part of the brain that is formulating a story of what happened as it happens. The authors conclude in their paper that "traumatic memories are not experienced as memories as such," but as "fragments of prior events, subjugating the present moment." This means that our brains are processing traumatic memories as though they are currently happening, even if it's something that happened twenty years ago.

For those of us who have been traumatized, this makes sense. The sensation of "What just happened? Who am I again? What does this mean for me in the world?" feels very familiar to those of us who have been in that dreamlike, altered state of extreme shock. This self-referential thinking—when we get caught up in our thinking, lost in thought—that's what activation of the PCC feels like.

And guess what: the PCC is part of the DMN. During DMN activation, no new learning is occurring. The brain just goes back to its default. So, if a trigger is pushing you to keep experiencing the same emotions—shock, fear, terror—you're training your brain to evoke a PTSD response, to instantly go to dissociation, flashbacks, or panic as a way to deal with the current stressor. To our brains, a flashback isn't "Oh no, I remember when that happened!" It's "Oh no, it's happening right now." We're not recalling; we're reliving.

You don't have control over your DMN, but you can retrain it. But the fix is not just recognizing that you love your child, because loving your child alone can't change the fact that your brain has an automatic response. The trick is to learn how to turn off your DMN by turning on another operating system, your executive control network (ECN). Executive functioning is your brain maintaining focus on the task at hand. It is also the ability to control your internal thoughts and remain in the present moment. When your brain is actively engaged in this kind of purposeful thought, by definition, it's not in default mode. It's in a proactive place instead of a reactive place.

Experiment

Turn On Your DMN

Have you ever had a moment of panic, a disproportionate response to something that you later realized wasn't that big of a deal? When this kind of panic happens, your DMN is turned on. Some of us have panic attacks and flashbacks all the time, some have them less frequently, but almost all PTPs have experienced them. This exercise will show you what's happening with your two operating systems. All you need is a straw.

Run in place as fast as you can with your hands over your head while breathing through a straw. You are restricting your oxygen supply and raising your heart rate at the same time. This physiological reaction will feel exactly like you're in a state of acute danger. When you feel panicky, stop running.

Now, notice how out of breath and panicky you felt.

- Can you remember the first time in your life you felt this exact way?
- Can you remember the worst time in your life you felt this way?
- How about the most recent time?
- Did you notice that being in this state reawakened those memories as sharp and intense?

Now, look around your room. Say out loud three items that you can see that are red, two that are blue, and one that is yellow.

Notice your heart rate slow down.

Now, think back to one of your "first, worst, or most recent" memories. Is the sharpness of the memory fading? Is your breath back to normal?

Your DMN was activated when you started running; you may have felt trapped in your panic. But when you activated your ECN by focusing your attention, you automatically shut off the DMN response and came back to the present moment.

We have so much more control over flashbacks and panic attacks than we think: we can learn to respond appropriately.

My Mother's Flashback

I was almost seventeen when the neighbor's gardener killed my father.

I came home from school one spring day. My mother was sitting at the kitchen table, sobbing like she would never stop.

I froze. I didn't know what to do. I wanted to go to her. I also wanted to go to my bedroom and pull my covers over my head. I wanted to cry like a baby. I made a noise, and she looked up and registered my presence.

Later, I found out what had triggered my mother. The neighbor's gardener had cut down my father's rosebushes.

Years earlier, when my father had first been diagnosed with his heart condition, the cardiologist wanted him to switch to a less stressful line of work, eat healthier, stop smoking, and start exercising. Among a host of other changes, he took up gardening as a way to both de-stress and get some exercise (or at least some fresh air).

No one thought he'd stick with gardening. My high-powered, intellectual, always-on-the-go dad, kneeling in the dirt, waiting patiently for things to grow? Didn't seem like a predictable choice. But he stuck with it. First, a rose of Sharon tree in our front yard. Then, seed catalogs started appearing in our mailbox, and he'd let me choose the flowers. We needed tulips because our front yard was shady, and there was something to do with the quality of our soil. I got to pick the colors. To this day, purple tulips are my favorite flower.

And in the backyard, in the one corner that wasn't shaded by our enormous cherry tree—rosebushes. Apparently, rosebushes are the highly sensitive people of the plant kingdom. They need a lot of care and attention, and my father lavished it on those roses. However, the neighbor's gardener didn't like that the rosebushes would shed petals onto their property. When my father was alive, he would prune the rosebushes, so only a few stray petals would end up on the neighbor's lawn. After my father died, pruning the rosebushes was not on my mother's priority list. But every afternoon, she'd come home from work and drink her coffee while looking out at them. It was a way of feeling close to my father.

And one day, she came home from work, went to their bedroom to drink her coffee, and the rosebushes were gone. The neighbor's gardener had gone into our backyard when she was away at work and I was at school and uprooted all of them. When my mother saw, it was like my father had died all over again.

She wasn't responding to the memory of my father, and she wasn't having a flashback to her feelings the night he died. She was reexperiencing her trauma as if it was happening in that moment. She had an emotional flashback: that feeling of being out of control, of the enormity of her loss.

Parenting While Flashbacking

When it comes to how we relate with our children, the stress they inadvertently create doesn't just trigger a traumatic memory. It triggers a reaction to our actual traumatic experience. Let's say your teenager is mad at you and you're a people pleaser. Your DMN goes to default mode and recognizes their anger as a threat. The trauma app interprets the threat and responds with its preprogrammed stress response, "Someone's mad at me, and whenever someone's mad at me, I need to people-please." So even though your teenager is refusing to finish their homework, you give them your car keys. Now, people-pleasing and giving into every whim of your teenager is not consistent with your parenting values. After the incident, you're sitting there thinking, *What the heck did I just do? I was going hold firm. I meant to say no. How did yes come out of my mouth?*

What happened? You were triggered, the DMN responded by default, and it engaged the trauma app to find out which threat you are dealing with. Then, it provided the algorithmic response for how you always best respond to that threat. Your trauma app reacted to *an emotional flashback.* The circuitry involved in the original trauma activated and you responded automatically. And once the flashback circuitry activates, we have even less choice about how we're going to respond. Our brains default to the "it's happening again mode" and to that very rehearsed response that's been honed over years.

The challenge for post-traumatic parenting is uncoupling emotional flashbacks from parenting decisions. We need to keep the trauma app out of the driver's seat. The trauma app co-opts our sense of self, our interoception, our ability to be present, and our internal voice. We need to be able to be guided, but not controlled, by our stress response. We need to be able to remain present in a stressful moment rather than relate to that moment as a situation that must be escaped. The trauma app cannot limit our reactions to only algorithmic responses like "When someone upsets me, I snap at them," "When I'm intolerably stressed, I dissociate," or "When someone is mad at me, I people please" because those algorithmic responses aren't parenting. Parenting means intentionally acting in consonance with our values, keeping the needs of the developing little humans as the primary consideration. Parenting is teaching children the ultimate skill—*How to Human*—in zillions of tiny little steps.

The Five Post-Traumatic Parenting Defaults

I've identified five distinct post-traumatic parenting defaults. These are the typical ways of responding to your triggers, based on how your trauma app operates to restore your sense of safety. If you can recognize these parenting defaults, you'll be able to predict how you will react to different triggers so that you can make a more intentional choice in the moment.

Each person may respond to the same trigger differently because of their defaults. For example, when some people travel, they need to take medicine to calm themselves down because of their anxiety about flying. I have the exact same fear, but because I'm hypervigilant, I need to stay ready for action. I would never take medication that would put me to sleep on a plane. My trauma app would forbid that and would probably defeat the medication by doubling down on adrenaline production. Yet the same emotional valence—feeling unsafe on a plane—would cause a different PTP to act in the complete opposite way and take the tranquilizer.

Both are trauma app default responses, because they're both algorithmic. Neither response is serving us well.

In internal family systems (IFS) therapy, we talk about "parts" as in "parts of the self." We're all composed of different parts. Each part is a default mode. If you've ever said, "Part of me wants to yell at my child, and part of me wants to hug him," you are instinctively thinking in terms of parts. And just as you can recognize that you have different parts, you can recognize that you are moving between different default parenting modes. Can you see yourself in any of the following? Don't think in terms of the "what" of your behaviors, think in terms of the "why."

- Are you the *entangled* parent that is so caught up in your own trauma that there's no space for parenting? Instead of connecting with their children, these parents are so triggered by their family of origin, their narcissistic ex-husband, or their toxic workplace dynamics that they are constantly being pulled back into that initial drama. This is the parent who wants to be responsive but ends up snapping reactively at their children and then feels incredible shame and guilt about it.
- Are you the *perfectionist* parent, so focused on doing parenting "right" that you lose sight of what you and your children really need? For instance, my patient Kendra and her husband both suffered from traumatic childhoods.

They don't want their kids to be raised the way they were, and they're so focused on being perfect that they are always looking for signs that the other may inadvertently be traumatizing the kids. They also want to give their kids all the experiences that they would have loved and needed, yet they are frequently disappointed because their kids don't respond well or want to engage in those activities.

- Are you the *disengaged* parent who appears unmotivated but is actually protecting the children from the biggest danger you believe they are in: a relationship with you? Disengaged parents aren't always neglectful; they shut down and don't engage. For example, my friend Amy was a workaholic and, consequently, was very wealthy. She would hire people to do everything with her kids and tell me, "My staff is better at parenting than me. The tutor is better at doing homework with my kids than I am." When we unpacked her responses, she saw that her workaholism was the barrier she created because of her ingrained fear that she was going to harm her kids.
- Are you the *paralyzed* parent who has a strong sense of what you don't want to do as a parent but no idea what you should do? Do you feel like you're operating on the edge of disaster all the time but have no idea how to fix that? I find that these parents are highly susceptible to criticism and the whims of parenting influencers. They frequently switch to the latest new parenting approach, only to find that none of them work the way they seemed to on social media.
- Are you the *survivor* parent, the one who can focus only on getting through the day, aware that you're not providing what your kids need but lacking the emotional resources to change that? Survivor parents are the most likely to have had a recent trauma as opposed to, or in addition to, a childhood trauma.

If you're reading this and thinking there are times you're all those things, part of you is paralyzed, and then another part is disengaged or entangled, your reaction is entirely accurate. It's okay if you don't fit neatly into any one category all the time.

However, one category is likely going to be the one you resonate with the most. That's the category that you should keep in mind first, and then you can learn about the other categories you fit into. Sometimes, moving out of one default slides us into another. That's a normal part of the healing process.

Once you learn more about your parenting defaults, it will be easier to see your triggers when they come up. If Kendra could say, "Hi, perfectionist parent default" when she's starting to get stressed, she could stop the trauma app from taking over and start thinking about other options. The goal is to change your responses and behaviors slowly and build new, better intentional parenting responses.

The Post-Traumatic Parenting Quiz

Read the questions in the first column of the following table and the choices of possible answers. Circle the response that would most closely match your own. You'll likely find that you are not the perfectionist parent all the time. You're not the disengaged parent all the time. But usually, you fall back to one style, because that's where the trauma app focuses your attention.

The column that has the most circles matches your parenting default mode. Read that chapter first. Then, read the chapter that corresponds to the second most circled column, and so on.

Even if you haven't chosen any answers in some of those columns, read those chapters anyway. I've found that as we address the issues in one parenting type, another default reaction might appear. The brain doesn't always heal itself; it often substitutes one not-so-great coping skill for another. So if you were an entangled parent and then started to set boundaries, you could transition into a paralyzed parent.

As you completed this exercise, you may have thought, *Wow, I'm doing a lot of parenting wrong. I'm triggered a lot; this can't be good.* Yet triggers can be a good sign: we're triggered because we care and because a particular situation is deeply important to us. If we're triggered by our own sense of incompetence at parenting, that also means we value parenting with competence. Now, let's create a plan to increase parenting skills. Whatever the trigger, there's a way to create a plan to not only manage it but also learn from it.

Most parenting books focus on trying to undo mistakes in parenting behavior: the "what I did wrong." These books don't work

Questions	Entangled Parent	Perfectionist Parent	Disengaged Parent	Paralyzed Parent	Survivor Parent
The teacher called a third time about your child. What do you do?	I get angry because now I can't focus on my own stuff.	I go online to start looking for a solution.	I call my child's therapist to take care of this.	I start looking up solutions on the internet but stop because it is overwhelming.	I can't even. I'm ignoring the call, and now I'm going to be stressed and on edge for the rest of the day.
Do you have addictive behaviors or tendencies?	There is a relationship I can't break free of. Is that an addiction?	There's alcoholism in my family, so I don't ever drink.	I sometimes drink too much or exercise too long, especially after a hard day at work.	I'm too scattered for anything besides lots of coffee.	I've tried lots of things to help me calm down. So far, none of them have worked.
How do you typically talk to your kid about tough topics?	I try to be as transparent as possible about what things feel like for me.	I have a script for handling tough conversations.	We don't really talk. I make sure they have someone to go to, though.	I try to avoid topics that will upset them. Sometimes, I use candy or screen time to distract/soothe them, to get through the moment.	When something upsetting happens, my kids end up comforting *me*. Sometimes, I pick a fight with them to shut the conversation down.

Questions	Entangled Parent	Perfectionist Parent	Disengaged Parent	Paralyzed Parent	Survivor Parent
What's your biggest parenting fear?	That I'm going to emotionally damage my kids. I'll raise kids who are just like me.	That I'm not good enough. That I don't have a plan for how to handle things. What if we have to go "off script"?	That I have no idea how to build a relationship with my kids. My kids will go elsewhere for love, or they won't have a felt sense of being loved.	That I am going to do the wrong thing or make the wrong decision, and it will damage them. My kids won't know how much I love them.	That my kids won't come to me when they need help. I fear the resentment of my kids—they entered into an already stressed system. It's not fair to them—or me.
What do you wish you had most from your parents?	More emotional safety and boundaries. Space to be.	Acceptance and unconditional love. To be seen.	That they spent more time talking with me—instead of yelling at me. Stability/safety. Modeling how to deal with big emotions.	Less criticism and more acceptance and support. To have been seen as essentially good/trustworthy. Not to have been compared with my siblings or peers.	I try not to think about my parents. Too painful. I wanted them to love me, not abuse me. To see me as a human with legitimate needs.
If you had a magic wand, what would help you do better as a parent?	Being able to better handle my own emotions, being able to put my past in the past. The ability to pause before reacting.	Confidence that I am doing a good job. The ability to be present in the moment.	Knowing how to engage better with my kids. Trusting myself enough to relate to them.	Having a game plan for what to do next, knowing that this game plan is good enough. Get rid of my shaming inner voice.	Time and space to breathe, so I can get a handle on the chaos. Energy. Motivation. Hope.

Questions	Entangled Parent	Perfectionist Parent	Disengaged Parent	Paralyzed Parent	Survivor Parent
What is your biggest parenting mistake (focusing on X instead of Y)?	I focus on the larger dramas in my life instead of on my kids. Focusing on everyone else's needs, not my own.	I want to give my kids what I would have needed. I should be focused on giving my kids what THEY need. Pushing achievement vs. growth as authentic humans. Focusing on appearing calm vs. being actually calm and present.	I want to protect my kids from their greatest danger—namely, me. I should be focused on helping myself become the parent they crave.	Focusing on doing it all instead of focusing on THEM. Focusing on their appearance/behavior/social judgment instead of on what they need. I want to do it perfectly. I'm looking for that gold star from the experts who know what the right thing to do is. Instead, I need to remember that I have instincts and that even if I mess up, I can repair. A course of action—even one that turns out to be a mistake—is better than no course of action.	I can only focus on getting through each day, managing my pain and my triggers. I haven't fully processed my trauma. I'd love to focus on my kids instead of on trying to keep it together. I'm in so much pain all the time. Focusing on their behavior rather than on what underlies it.

Questions	Entangled Parent	Perfectionist Parent	Disengaged Parent	Paralyzed Parent	Survivor Parent
What do you dread your children saying to you one day?	You didn't protect me. You didn't break the cycle. You were there for everyone else but me.	You failed me, and now I'm damaged.	Where were you when I was growing up? I don't even know you or feel a connection to you.	You messed up and now I have to live with the consequences of that. You should have done things differently.	You were such a mess when I was growing up—I needed a grown-up, and you were just another child. You made me feel like a burden/unwanted.
What is your dream vision for parenting?	My family of origin, my relationship drama, and my toxic friends are all peripheral to my central task of being there for my kids.	I'd feel like I'm doing a good-enough job—and that's good enough.	My kids and I could have a real relationship. I could relax into it and so could they.	I feel like I'm being that secure base for my kids, that awful fear of messing up is gone.	That I'd actually parent instead of survive.

for PTPs. The "what's" of parenting behaviors—play more, hit less, talk more, yell less—are meaningless without understanding the "whys." The truth is, you are behaving a certain way with your kids because of your particular parenting default. I tell my patients all the time: in therapy, we don't treat problems, we treat solutions. Your defaults are pointing you to unpack what your behavior is a solution for.

In the following chapters, you are going to learn all about your very specific whys. You're going to be able to see where your behavior is coming from. And then it is going to be crystal clear what is possible for you to do instead, so that you can be prepared with solutions that match your parenting values.

Part II

Post-Traumatic Parenting Types

CHAPTER 4

The Entangled Parent

"I FEEL TRAPPED, like I'm on a nightmare seesaw that's hovering over hot lava, where my parents are sitting on one side and my kids are dangling on the other. I'm trying desperately to maintain a balance where everyone is happy, but I can't figure it out. The only way to soothe everyone is to prioritize my parent's demands and my kids' essential needs and put myself last and pretend everyone is fine. I'm tapped out, and I know I can't sustain this balancing act forever. What's going to happen when I fall off?"

Esme shared these feelings with me in an email. I could resonate with her sense of frustration and desperation, and I immediately knew that Esme is an entangled parent.

When people hear the words *entangled* and *parent* together, they may think it refers to parents who are too intertwined, or *enmeshed*, in their child's life. And while that situation does exist for PTPs, I refer to that as the "perfectionist parent," which is covered in the next chapter.

"Entanglement" for PTPs can be more complicated. It involves a parent who remains heavily influenced in the present by their past relationships: someone or some people—including the family of origin, an ex-spouse, a toxic boss, or a frenemy—are still influencing their own sense of self, the deepest, most authentic part of them that tells them, "This is who I am."

There are two important schools of thought that explain entanglement: object relations theory and internal family systems (IFS). In the very confusingly named object relations theory, the "object" isn't a thing but the "object of our attachment," which is typically one or more of our primary caregivers. As we form attachments with them—or not—we develop our sense of self. As philosopher Hazel Rose Marcus says in *Pillars of Social Psychology*, *"You can't be a self—by yourself"* (my emphasis).[1]

According to object relations theory, if you feel nurtured, you will likely develop a healthy and secure sense of self, and you will be able to live according to your truest, most authentic values. But if your primary caregiver, or even someone later in life, is neglectful or abusive, your sense of self will be compromised. You might still understand your values, but you are afraid to act on them. You may see yourself as bad, deficient, and unworthy. You may become insecure, anxious, and desperate to hold onto any relationships, even knowingly toxic ones, in order to bolster your sense of self. You can then become entangled, where you are so deeply engaged with a particular unhealthy relationship that you can't see a way out, and you can't develop healthy attachment with your children.

As you learned in the last chapter, IFS explains how one person can hold different aspects of themselves. IFS suggests that each person is comprised of different *parts* that contain distinct emotions, thoughts, and behaviors. These "parts" can be categorized into two types: *managers* and *exiles*. Managers try to control our emotions and behaviors in order to protect us from pain or harm by forcing us to engage in behavior patterns that make us feel safe. Exiles hold our emotional pain or trauma away from us so that we can remain functional on a day-to-day level. Both managers and exiles can block us from authentic attachment with our children because they can separate us from the inner wisdom that emotions provide.

Your trauma app is similar to an IFS "manager" that keeps you stuck in old patterns of behavior that made sense in the context of your trauma but are no longer useful. Worst of all, the trauma app can block you from attaining true attachment with your children.

If certain feelings, responsibilities, or obligations keep you entangled in old relationships, old senses of self, old values, or goals that are no longer important to you and pull your focus away from your children and your parenting values, then you're entangled.

Entangled PTPs often feel a sense of anger, despair, frustration, guilt, or shame. They instinctively know that something about the situation is wrong and that it's affecting their ability to parent. They know their entanglements are stopping them from moving forward, toward their children, toward their values. But they can't break free of them because the entanglements feel too intrinsic to the parent's sense of self. They subscribe to the illusion that if they could just manage their time better or explain themselves more clearly, do more deep breathing or the latest stress-management hack, cut back on their own (selfish?) needs or recruit more support from their parenting partner, then they'll finally be able to manage their entanglements and parent the way they're dreaming of.

The confusing part of entanglement is that the entangled parent *can* say no but chooses not to, because the consequences of those noes are too great to bear, at least in the short term. They instinctively understand that noes are punished—not just with consequences like shaming but also with an internal sense of being bad, selfish, not good enough, not dedicated enough, lazy, disorganized, inept, unqualified, and so many more self-judgments. Sometimes what they need to do is say no to following an ex-partner's social media feed or responding to a message that's meant to be psychologically destructive. They *can* say no, but it feels threatening to do so. For these parents, it's just not worth dealing with those internal and external consequences.

Entangled parents want to model a different kind of relationship for their children than the one they had with their family of origin, but they end up stressed and snapping at the kids. For instance, you might be texting with your abusive ex about custody over the weekend or ruminating about a recent argument you had with your parents, and when your child says, "I want another bedtime story," you snap back, "Can't you see I'm tired? I need you to go to bed."

Entanglement and Women

Entangled mothers often don't want to say no to their entanglements because being selfless is socially reinforced for women and girls. Let's face it, being giving, kind, caring, and responsive are all considered particularly feminine traits and aspirations. When a woman is entangled, these traits are often the only source of her self-worth, especially if her selflessness was rewarded with praise.

Saying no is scary for most women; saying no when your whole self-identity has been built around saying yes is terrifying. Entangled women wrestle with this ultimate conundrum: *How can you bring your healthy whole self to parenting, if you've been training yourself to be selfless your whole life?*

What Entanglement Looks Like

Entanglement feels like a trap. It can look like the following:

- Emotionally charged fights with an ex-spouse's new partner over something minor, like a slight change to visitation schedules.
- Constantly being trapped in a cycle of drama with an ex-partner and their extended network.
- Watching the social media feed of an ex-partner, even when half of it is veiled attacks on you and it just makes you feel miserable. Still, you feel unable to look away.
- Being pulled back into the integral functioning of your family of origin by ongoing, predictable crises ("We need you to pick up your sister's kids, she's overwhelmed."), obligations ("You must attend every family get-together, even ones that were made up on a whim."), or role assignments ("You've been given the job of maintaining Mom's social circle and must visit her whenever she's feeling lonely."). You feel unable to say no to any of these roles or tasks.
- A friend who can be supportive at times and understands what you have gone through but who doesn't allow you to live in an independent reality outside of her own. A friend who can't hear, "It's not a great time, let's talk later." Sometimes, the friendship is referred to as a "trauma bond," someone who sees your trauma and validates it but doesn't see you in your entirety.
- Staying in a "golden handcuffs" job, where you are working for a boss who is powerful and somewhat of a mentor but who does not respect your other priorities or time limits. You know that you are losing precious psychological energy by staying, but the cost of leaving is too high.

Esme Was Entangled

Remember Esme? Here's more of her story. An entrepreneur with three children and a husband, she truly wants to parent according to her values but feels stuck in the endless loop that is her parents' drama.

Esme was eleven years old when her father was seriously injured, and her mother had to go back to work to make ends meet. The changes in Esme's family were subtle yet damaging: her mother became bitter and started drinking daily. Her father's inability to provide for the family left him feeling angry at the world, and his temper spilled over. What Esme experienced from then on wasn't one discrete or abusive incident. Her trauma developed like the "death of a thousand cuts," which is the case for many PTPs.

Ever since, Esme has played the role of sensitive peacemaker within her family. She is the one who is always trying to fix everything: to make her mother happy, to placate her father. Yet somehow, despite all her efforts, she was never good enough for her family. She was labeled the selfish one, even though she was the one who was constantly pitching in.

As an adult, Esme never feels good about herself unless her family is actively acknowledging her for being helpful. That's why she's driven to constantly do things for her own family and her parents and siblings: she wants to get that hit of appreciation, that momentary feeling of success, love, and accomplishment. The problem is that all this fixing is getting in the way of running her custom cake-baking business and, even more crucially, developing healthy relationships with her children.

Esme is constantly feeling torn between her old family and her new one. Every day she's attending to another crisis: her sister's kids must be picked up or she'll lose custody; her dad has a doctor's appointment and needs a ride. Her mother is very demanding and doesn't get why Esme can't drop everything and help her parents out all the time. In this entangled relationship, Esme's parents have set themselves up as the arbiters of her reality.

The result is that Esme is stressed out all the time: she's caught between her parenting values and her past. When she finally realized this situation wasn't sustainable, she set up an appointment with me. The first day she came in, she told me,

> When I feel angry or, worse, guilty, my parenting really suffers. I just cannot be present with my kids. I'm on edge, and I'll say things that I thought I'd never say, "Can't you see I'm having a bad day? Are you so selfish that you don't care?" When I read about cycle breaking, and gentle parenting, everyone always talks about not making our kids responsible for our emotions.

> And here I am, basically making my children the caretakers of my emotional state. It's been getting worse since my oldest daughter became eleven years old, which was when my own trauma started. I now have this temptation to lean on her like my mother did to me or say really mean things to her if her behavior isn't perfect. I get irrationally angry, much more than I should. There's this business expansion coaching program that I'm a part of and I keep missing their deadlines because of my kids or my parents and all their needs. And whenever I try to set boundaries with my parents, I get these texts from my mom or my sister telling me how selfish and lazy I am. I feel trapped and I can't get out. Can you help me? Teach me how to be a calm mother no matter how stressed I am. Or tell me what I can say to my mom that will help her understand that I need to protect my time and energy for my children.

I explained that Esme's desire to prove to herself and her family that she's not selfish or lazy and her trauma app's directive to protect her wounded inner child by keeping her family of origin functioning and healthy are both antithetical to what she really wants and values. The truth is, Esme isn't selfish or lazy. She never was. She should not be caretaking her family of origin, nor should she ever have been put in that role. It's not her job to "fix" her family of origin or even to shore up that system. It never was.

My goal was to help Esme see these truths and help her untangle her entanglements. As long as her family of origin is entangled in her sense of self, she'll never be able to move toward her own values, her own family, and her own dreams, desires, and ideal life. As long as Esme allows her family of origin to be the arbiters of her own reality—as long as she allows them to be the ones who determine if she's lazy and selfish or not, if she's a good enough person, if she's allowed her own time, or if she's allowed to stand down from her guardianship of them—she'll be entangled. As long as she focuses her energies on "fixing," she'll never break free.

The Power and Purpose of Anger

During our second session, Esme took a deep breath and said, "I'm so ashamed to tell you this story. A few days ago, I got really mad at my

Exercise: Notice How You Feel

Was your adrenaline pumping as you read about Esme's life? Do you resonate with the kind of stress she's under? Do you feel a sense of anger as you hear about how her family of origin treats her? Did you feel frustrated with her for not saying no?

Entanglement can create a visceral, physical reaction. Notice how you feel. Your reactions are going to be super helpful to you as you understand entanglement.

- Do you feel a sense of dread and a pit in your stomach every time a particular person calls or texts you, but you cannot ignore their call?
- Is there someone's social media feed that you know you should block, but you can't stop looking at it?
- Does the thought of saying no to this person's demands stress you? Congratulations, you have just identified an entanglement.
- As you think about that entanglement, notice what emotions come up. Do you feel guilt? Shame? Sadness? Anger?

eleven-year-old daughter. I had asked her to put the dinner I prepared in the oven before I came home. I guess I wasn't clear enough—she put it in the oven but didn't turn the oven on. When I started yelling at her that now no one will have dinner on time because of her, she burst into tears and said, 'Mom, I'm only eleven! I don't know how to cook!' I felt like the world's worst mother. I'm so angry at myself."

As Esme told me this story, I could hear a simmering sense of anger, fear, and frustration. Finally, she was voicing her anger, and I was so glad she did, because this is literally what anger is meant to do for us. Anger gives us the energy to act, focuses our attention to solve a problem, and is an important step toward breaking the entanglement cycle. Her anger over the cycle may feed the psychological energy she needs to create a new relationship with her family of origin.

Esme, like so many post-traumatic entangled parents, often feels a sense of anger simmering under the surface, and that anger tends to crop up as *mom rage* (I'm not sure why we gender it—dads can become enraged too). Anger has two jobs in our psyche: it identifies a problem, and it identifies a boundary. When you're feeling angry toward someone, especially when it's disproportionate to the actual event, or when you vent your anger with phrases like "You always . . ." or "You never . . . ," you are experiencing a boundary impingement: the true self, the most precious, tender part of you, is being threatened. Mom rage is almost always displaced anger: we are mad at our kids when we should be angry about some other part of our life entirely.

Anger isn't a primary emotion: it acts as a cover-up to other emotions, like grief, sadness, or fear. Esme is carrying a deep sense of grief over her own lost childhood and at the same time mourning the loss of her daughters' childhoods, even while they are living them. She is sad because she feels that she's valued by her family only for what she can do for them, not for being herself. She's sad that she's losing time and ground with her kids, trapped in her entanglements. And she feels a pervasive sadness for her own inner child, who wasn't parented the way Esme dreams of ideally parenting her own children. She also fears that she is losing touch with her true self, that she is moving further and further away from what she wants and values.

The problem is that anger distracts us from these awarenesses and creates new problems in its wake. When Esme communicates her anger toward her family, she lashes out, and that will become the next transgression she has to make up for. And at the same time, she's entered into a new cycle of guilt and shame.

Unlike many other mental health professionals, I'm not against guilt. It exists to tell us that we messed up, that we hurt someone, or that there's something in a relationship that we need to fix. Yet there is a difference between justified and unjustified guilt. When we feel guilty about doing something that violates our internal values, that guilt points us toward repair, and when we repair, the guilt resolves. When Esme feels guilty about snapping angrily at her daughter, her guilt leads her to repair with her daughter and to set measures in place to keep from snapping again.

Esme's family tries to make her feel guilty when they tell her that she should not have a life or goals outside of them, yet they're not telling Esme that she violated her own values. They're telling Esme she violated *their* values or expectations. Luckily, Esme no longer subscribes to that value system, so she doesn't internalize the guilt. She knows that since she didn't create the mess, she doesn't have to fix it. Now, she can use her anger for the actual purpose it exists for, which is to assert boundaries. And she can do so without guilt.

Exercise: Get In Touch with Your Anger

Get into a comfortable position, silence your phone, and try this exercise with an open heart and mind. It can feel a bit threatening to get in touch with anger the first time—we tend to relate to anger as a dangerous emotion, but it's really just there to show us our boundaries.

- Think about the last time your boundaries were violated. Imagine the situation. Do you feel yourself getting worked up, trying to ruminate over the situation and have that last word or make the person feel as much frustration as you were feeling? Do you feel yourself getting hot, flushed, fidgety, or tense?
- Now that you're in the situation, welcome anger in. First, notice it. How does it look? I find it helpful to visualize my anger as the little red emotion character from the movie *Inside Out*, but I've heard people give their anger all sorts of colors, shapes, names, and identities.
- How does anger speak? Ask it what it wants to tell you.
- Now, ask your anger these questions:
    - Which boundary was violated? What precious territory was that boundary guarding? Why is that a problem for you?
    - Go back to your past. What does this boundary violation remind you of? How old were you the first time this type of boundary was violated? When that happened, how did you make sense of it?
    - Imagine you live in a perfect world and this person was willing to respect boundaries. What would that respect look like? Would it be enough for that person to simply begin respecting the boundary, or would you also want them to acknowledge that it's always been okay for you to have this boundary, that there's nothing wrong with you for wanting it?
    - If it's not enough to have the boundary respected, if you also need that validation, congratulations. You have just identified one of your arbiters of reality.

Strong Boundaries Untangle Entanglements

Entangled parents need to understand how boundaries work and why they're important. The best way to unentangle yourself is to be able to set real boundaries. The problem is, most of us hear a lot about boundaries on social media, but we don't truly understand them.

Boundaries are—at their simplest—where you end and I begin. They are formed to protect the self so that you can say with conviction, "This is who I am. This is what I value. This is what I care about." Having a strong sense of self is incredibly protective. It's people with poor boundaries, and therefore a poor sense of self, that can be tempted, sidetracked, or pressured into behaving in ways that aren't consistent with their values. Having boundaries is a good thing. They are not, in and of themselves, aggressive in any way. We need riverbanks to keep the water confined, not spread out and cause a flood.

When I asked Esme what happens when she tries to set boundaries with her family of origin, she told me, "My mother says that talking about boundaries is ridiculous. People nowadays act selfishly and call that 'boundaries.'"

Esme's mother isn't entirely wrong. Boundaries are confusing for us, and they can be confused with other things, like *preferences*. I've heard people misuse the term *boundary* when they really mean *preference* or *comfort zone*. For instance, my patient Sheila tells me, "My mother-in-law wants to come and visit my baby again?! Hello, boundaries?!" Receiving a request to visit isn't a breach of boundaries. Instead, it's a *request*. A desire not to have the grandparents come over or to go and visit—is a *preference*.

A preference isn't a value; it's simply something we desire. Having a quiet evening at home is a preference that we can either exercise or not. When the lack of quiet evenings at home causes us to stress out, start snapping at our kids, and ignore self-care, staying home is no longer a preference. We have to set a boundary, which relates our value of putting calm parenting first.

Can you see the difference? Anyone can make a request. And we get to say yes or no. But the request itself is neutral. I call these requests "bids" because they are bids for our time or for our attention. Bids are usually neutral unless they're presented with inordinate psychological pressure. When a bid sounds more like "an offer you can't refuse," it's no longer a bid but an order.

Sometimes, a bid itself is neutral, but our inner child interprets it as an order. Your mother-in-law can make a neutral bid to visit, and your inner child can be afraid to say no. This can sound like, "If I say no, I'm a bad person because I 'should' be nicer, I 'should' make time for her, I should take responsibility for her emotions, and I know she's lonely." A child may make a neutral bid to be driven to school instead of taking the bus on a particularly busy morning, and your inner child is also afraid to say no. This can sound like, "If I say no, I'm a mean parent, and my child will think I don't love him." So, if either the external bid wasn't really a bid but an order or if our inner child doesn't know how to say no, we have a hard time acting on our boundaries.

There's nothing wrong with acting against our preferences. For instance, I *prefer* to spend time at home with my children, but it's my best friend's birthday party, so I'm going to choose to go. If making this same decision was based on a value or a boundary, I might feel differently. I may say, "My baby is up all night and I'm exhausted, I have a pounding headache, and going to this birthday party as a tired mess means I'll be tense and yelling at my kids the next day, so I'm going to have to pass." I still love my friend, and I truly want to support her, but attending the party is in conflict with a stronger value, that of caring for my children and preserving my health.

Boundaries are not the same thing as estrangement. In fact, boundaries are what prevent estrangement; ignoring boundaries is what creates estrangement. To be clear, I'm not saying that Esme needs to cut herself off from her family of origin, nor am I saying that she should *not* spend her time with her family. I'm not Esme, so I don't get a vote in what she chooses to do with her time. But then again, neither should her family. They can make a request or state a preference. They can even have emergencies. Yet Esme has the right to decide what to do with her very own time, and she can do that by setting boundaries.

Boundaries and relationships seem to be antithetical, because we think about boundaries as if they are walls, delineating separateness. The truth is, boundaries aren't about distance; they are actually about closeness. How close is too close? We're all going to have slightly different thresholds. The trick is to respect boundaries when we notice them, because there's no objective standard for them. There's no such thing as boundaries *against*. Ideally, it's boundaries *with*. And they may come with all sorts of subtle permutations:

- I love it when you visit, but please call first.
- You can borrow my Instant Pot whenever you want, but please knock before entering my home.

- I'm happy to show you my new coat or car, but I prefer not to tell you what it cost.
- Even if I'm okay with you looking at the price of my new car, I have to respect your desire not to let me look at yours.

It's not that one person is "correct" and one person is "too much of a pushover" or "way too uptight." It's that we all have boundaries that make sense to us. Most crucially, if we ignore them, we end up either distancing ourselves from others or overreacting. It's smarter to respect our own boundaries to begin with.

Objectification and Containers

Healthy infant attachment begins with *objectification*, when the parent's role is solely to meet the needs of the baby. Primary caregivers are the

Exercise: Visualize the Boundary

- If your boundaries were physical, what would they look like? Are they a fence? A force field? A stone wall? A moat? Outer space? What would they be surrounding? Your inner child? Your current family? Your time, your space, your home?
- Who would gatekeep the boundaries? A protector? A soldier, a door attendant, a secretary? A dragon? The most confident, capable version of you—your ideal self?
- Imagine yourself constructing the boundary. Visualize yourself adding one stone or one slat or more depth to the boundary each time you say no.
- Practice your stock phrases: "This is what works for my family." "I'd love to be the best employee possible, so I need to respect my schedule." "I'd love to talk, I'm available tomorrow evening."
- Practice repeating those phrases, and each time, imagine another layer added to the boundary. As you do so, imagine the health and joy of those within the boundary. Imagine your children flourishing, the time you free up, the resources you devote to self-care. Imagine those negative judgments—you're uncaring, lazy, selfish, spacey, unambitious—as outside the boundary, no longer entangled with you.
- Check in with yourself. How does it feel to have a boundary?

"milk provider," the soothing voice, the calming smell. A baby doesn't understand that their mother (and, to some extent, their father) is a discrete entity, living in a reality of their own. There is no expectation that the infant understands boundaries. "Mommy needs her sleep at two in the morning? I'm the baby, and I need food, so I'm going to cry." This objectification is healthy and expected. From anyone other than an infant, objectification is unhealthy because we're not being related to as fully human.

Objectification can be so confusing when entangled parents are parenting infants. Your baby's normal objectification can feel threatening and dangerous, because in every traumatic relationship we've had, it was. Suddenly, we are dealing with a new type of objectification—from our babies—which is good and normal but feels scary. Please take the time to say this to yourself: "Objectification from everyone else wasn't okay. My baby is allowed to objectify me. As my baby grows and matures, the relationship will become more mutual."

As our children grow up, they objectify us less as they learn about boundaries. They remain connected to us but know that they are discrete entities. This dance of connection and separation is part of healthy attachment. A sixteen-year-old can understand that while they may have the desire to blast their music as loudly as the speakers will allow at 2:00 a.m., that will interfere with the rest of the family's right to sleep.

Beginning in toddlerhood, the parent-child relationship transitions out of objectification. The parent takes on a new role, one of a container. News flash: toddlers are tiny bodies holding giant emotions, and it's our job as parents to help them. We do so by "containing" their emotions: we make their emotional response more manageable by reflecting their emotions back with language, we soothe them, and we resonate with their emotions. To some extent, we remain a container for our children forever, which is healthy and expected. And as Esme learned, we should never expect our children to be the container for us.

A full container doesn't have room for more. We cannot hold our family of origin's emotions, our ex-spouse's aggression, and our boss's stress and also be the container for our children. Something has to give. We have to set boundaries in order to keep the container available for our children. Entangled parents will be free when they can protect their container by saying, "My container belongs to my children and myself. I'm not responsible for holding any other adult's emotions."

It's Okay Being the Broken Object

When you relate to someone as an object, you don't think about their feelings. It would be absurd to ask a flashlight how it feels being turned on: it exists only to illuminate a dark room. Esme's family of origin treats her the same way, like an object. She exists only to fill her roles in the family. She is their "errand runner, the caregiver, the crisis first responder."

If Esme starts setting boundaries, her family of origin may at first increase their bids for her attention. They're going to double down on their criticism because in the past, this strategy worked. It's like flicking the switch on a flashlight that won't turn on, hoping that it will work again. But if she holds her boundaries firm, doesn't come running when shamed or blamed, and is brave enough to put her values and her own family first, those external bids will stop because her family of origin will realize their strategy isn't working anymore.

We have to be willing to hold our boundaries firmly, even when that means we are related to as the "broken object." The truth is, the broken object was never really broken, because you never were an object: you are, and always were, complete, authentic, and a very whole human.

Boundaries and Perceptions

A healthy adoption of boundaries involves understanding that there can be multiple perceptions of the same reality, because part of you ending and me beginning means we will perceive the same event differently. A holiday party can be a really fun event for some family members and a nightmare for others who are easily overstimulated.

This is something most parents have to balance. There have been times when I've had to say no to family obligations because I need to protect my time. Saying no to these events used to make me feel guilty and "self-centered" and I had a hard time with that. I know that there is an element of "self-centeredness" in the sense that I am putting my own needs first. But that doesn't make me unworthy, selfish, or any other negative word. It simply means that right now, in this context, I need to put my own needs first. It's hard to shake that sense of unworthiness, especially if there's an element of truth (and all the best lies have an element of truth). Now, when someone calls me self-centered, I can examine the evidence, knowing that I can hold several contradictory truths at the same time:

- I have the right to protect my time. And it's okay for others to ask for my time and attention.
- I have the right to plan ahead. And I have the right to keep my schedule open and flexible.
- I have the right to my emotional reactions. And I have the right to keep my emotional life private.

It's okay to be our own arbiters of reality. We're allowed to be ourselves. Just because someone is raised in a family that keeps schedules open and loose doesn't mean they are rigid or a control freak because schedules make them feel safe. Just because someone was raised in a family that shares all their life stories, emotional reactions, and information, doesn't mean they're a snob or cold if they don't want to share. You cannot compel others to see the world from your perspective; you can only disentangle.

Reflection

You Can Choose Again

- Ask yourself: Who is my arbiter of reality? Who has entered my sense of self to the extent that they can stop me from living my life according to my values?
- Envision you have a magic wand that would make this arbiter of reality see and understand your perspective. What are the details of how amazing your life would be? How would your parenting change? What would you be free to do?
- How much do you want this new dream? Can you get hungry for it? Can you see that you and your children deserve it?
- The truth is, you can't change your arbiter's perspective, but you can act in accordance with your values anyway. That's when you get to live a fully authentic life.

Setting Boundaries

Once we've delineated what our boundaries should be, if we get push-back and we are doubting ourselves, we have the option of running those boundaries by someone whose judgment we trust. Maybe that's a close friend, a therapist, or a spouse. We want someone who knows our life circumstances, who may be adjacent to them, but can see a situation with more objectivity and is willing to tell us the truth. Another opinion is especially useful if we're really unsure if our boundaries are a bit too rigid or too porous.

Even if you've vetted your boundaries with someone else, and even if they disagree with some of them, you get to make the final decision. Then, you have the right to communicate those boundaries kindly and gently to the people around you. In relationships, boundaries should be shared. If you call a friend or a neighbor to chat, do you want them to grit their teeth and remain on the phone with you, or do you want them to feel free to say: "Now isn't a great time, can I call you back tomorrow after my kids go off to school?"

At first, when we set boundaries, we might be a bit rigid about them. That makes sense—it's a new skill, after all! It's totally okay for boundaries to shift over time. For example, when our kids are little, we might be a bit less flexible about family visiting too close to bedtime, because too much stimulation right before bed could keep toddlers up for hours. But as the kids grow, we might be okay with later visits. We can also set up people who are exceptions. (For instance, I don't like answering questions about where I buy my kid's clothes, but Great Aunt Bertha is lonely and very curious about these things, so I'm okay with sharing. Normally, I don't lend people my car, but my sister-in-law is a very careful driver).

More and more, we live in a world that doesn't really respect boundaries. That's why it's up to us as parents to set them, reinforce them, and respect them. When our children see us establishing boundaries, especially ones that protect and nurture them, it will help them develop their own strong sense of self.

When Esme began to set her boundaries, I knew she was doing the right thing for herself and her daughters. She told me, "I could be working on this business deal all night, but eight o'clock is when I usually help my younger daughter with her homework, so I put my phone on silent mode for an hour." That boundary automatically communicates her values to her daughter, who then internalizes the idea as "I know who I am, I am a person that is worth focusing on. Seeing mom have boundaries means I can have them too."

When you know who you are, you also know who you are not, and that's the essence of safety. Setting good boundaries is what allows a child to make the crucial distinction between "I did something bad" and "I am bad." If a child feels "I am bad," they're not going to admit that to their parents. But if a child messes up and their sense of self

Exercise: Practice the Art of Saying No

Saying no can be terrifying, and it's a skill that most of us never learned. In an ideal world, "No" is a complete sentence. As you learn to set your boundaries, you can, at first, craft your response in a way that others will be more able to accept it. I'm not asking you to make your boundary softer. I'm suggesting that you make it sweeter.

You can communicate your most desired boundaries using positive language (tell them what you want them to do, not what you don't) and pair the ask with an incentive: what's in it for them (leaving the word *no* out). This strategy will soften the no and make it more palatable for the listener, and it will actually be easier for you to assert your no. The trick is not getting into discussions or debates. If the person starts to argue with your statements, repeat the boundary.

- "I love it when you come over. I need you to call first and to accept that sometimes, when you want to come over is not going to be good for me. This way, when you do come over, we can have an enjoyable visit."
- "We'd love to enjoy the party with you for three hours. This is what works for our family."
- "I want to be the best employee I can be. I need to leave on time so I can arrive refreshed tomorrow."
- "I would like to help you when possible, and I need you to take no for an answer when it's not possible. This way, you know when I'm doing you a favor, I'm doing it wholeheartedly."

Write your boundaries statements. Then, you can rehearse saying them until they feel and sound natural. Eventually, it will become easy and you will feel empowered.

allows them to think, *I did something bad, I need help fixing it*, they'll go to their parents for help. That's what will prevent that tiny slip of a mistake from becoming a slide into a disaster. I've met adults who were in exploitative, abusive relationships that started when they were young and felt that they couldn't tell their parents about a tiny lapse in judgment. I've met kids who could have avoided a full-blown eating disorder if only they could have discussed purging with their parents the first time they felt the impulse to do it. We want our little humans to know "I messed up, my parents will help" as opposed to "I messed up, my parents better never find out."

Recently, I took my kids bowling. It was a pretty nice day for the kids. It was pretty miserable for me. My baby was cranky. There were multiple diaper changes in multiple locations. The bowling alley was loud and bright, and I had that kind of instant headache you get in an overstimulating environment.

I definitely enjoyed some parts of the trip. The joy on my eighteen-month-old's face when his fortuitously dropped ball knocked down a pin and everyone cheered for him was priceless. I mean, when does Mommy cheer him for crashing things down and making a mess? Not often enough! My nine-year-old son said, "Mommy, this was the best day *ever*." And for him, it was. For me, it was mostly an exhausting hassle.

Is he right? Am I right? We both are.

I don't need to persuade my son that the day was awful. I don't need him to validate how hard it was for me. He doesn't need me to change my mind and make me believe that it was wonderful. I can reflect his joy and satisfaction, even if I didn't feel it myself. There is no one true interpretation of reality, and that's okay.

Boundaries mean we can each have our own interpretation of reality. He's allowed to have fun when I have a headache. I'm allowed to have a headache and not fully enjoy the experience. It is totally okay for us to have opposite experiences of the same event. That's not even slightly problematic.

Setting boundaries is the best way to get out of entanglements. We are all independent humans, existing in a reality that's adjacent to, but outside of, the reality of everyone else. In this story, my child's reality is very close to mine, but it's not exactly identical to mine. That's not only okay, but that's also the way it should be, because celebrating our similarities and differences is how we can forge authentic relationships.

New entanglements may come up, and now you have some tools to recognize them and reset your trauma app default strategy. If your PTP assessment in chapter 3 showed that you were firmly in the entangled camp, you can skip ahead to chapter 9 and learn about my AIM model, which will deepen your understanding of how to work with your daily triggers or your daily life experiences. If your assessment showed that you often responded with other defaults, head over to that chapter first.

CHAPTER 5

The Perfectionist Parent

IT'S NORMAL TO want our little humans to be healthy and happy. It's normal to want our kids to be safe. It's normal to want our kids to thrive and achieve excellence in whatever they want to pursue. But if you believe that with enough effort, you have the power to *make* your child happy, healthy, or successful, then you are a perfectionist. The truth is, we can only put our children on their path; what happens afterward is really not up to us. Yet perfectionist parents see the world through a slightly different, more fearful lens.

There's a difference between trying to be "as perfect a parent as possible"—whatever that means for you—and being a perfectionist. I see it as the difference between *I want* and *what-if.* I want my kids to have nice clothes, to have friends, and to be happy: these are reasonable parenting expectations. But if your fears about achieving those wants are expressed as what-ifs (as in, What if my child doesn't make friends? or What if my child isn't happy?), you will be guided by the imperative to head every potential mistake off at the pass. If you are constantly reacting to the what-ifs instead of being in the present moment and using your parenting tools, you are acting in accordance with your inner child's deepest fears and not parenting the child who is right in front of you. As you've learned, your inner child can't parent a child.

Whenever anxiety happens, there are two types of responses: you can either run toward it and fix it, or avoid the problem entirely and check out from the world. Perfectionist parents run toward their anxiety so that they can try to control the outcome. Ironically, it's actually a flight stress response, because they are avoiding the potential for danger. I met Allison in one of my parenting classes. Her baby had choked to death while sitting in a baby walker because he was able to pull off a piece of plastic and put it in his mouth. Despite being awarded damages in a class-action suit because of the equipment's defect, Allison is convinced it was her inattention that caused the tragedy. Now that she is parenting her second child, she doesn't allow herself to do anything that might distract her from watching her toddler Jason.

Can you remember back to before your child was born? You may have hoped that you were going to be a perfect mom or dad, like royalty in a fable, *the parent who never yelled*. When that dream fell apart the first time, and you realized that you're not perfect (or worse, that you will never be perfect), how intolerable was the very thought of messing up? A healthy, well-balanced person can recover from mishaps, even if they feel bad about their actions for a while. Eventually, they will realize that it's just not possible to do parenting perfectly every single day. But for the perfectionist parent, making any mistake has a litany of consequences. Simply put, a perfectionist has an intolerance for making a mistake. This feeling is often born out of a fear that terrible things will happen as a consequence of any mistake.

Perfectionist parents therefore go to great lengths to be perfect so that their child is free of physical or emotional pain. Whatever experience was intolerable for you as a child is the same thing you're trying to avoid for your child. Perfectionist parents worry about a slew of what- ifs. What if my kid feels left out if they don't get to participate in three sports? What if my kid's scarred for life if I yell? What if they're rejected from the college of their choice and it's all my fault? All these what-ifs were intolerable for me, so they will be for my kid. This is referred to as *experiential avoidance by proxy*. It's not "I want to avoid big emotions" the way a paralyzed parent sees things. It's "I want to prevent my kids from feeling big emotions." The problem is, it's difficult enough "controlling" our own emotions; controlling another person's emotions is exponentially harder. As Daniel Siegel so poignantly points out in his book *The Power of Showing Up*, "Your job as a parent is not to prevent them from experiencing setbacks and failures, but to give them the tools and emotional resilience they need to weather life's storms, and then to walk beside them through those storms."[1]

That's the essential paradox of healthy parenting. Kids need to experience a certain tolerable level of discomfort, fear, challenge, and disappointment to create healthy coping tools for these life challenges. Just like exposure to some dirt, mild childhood infections, and some germs can increase our physical immune system, these types of emotional challenges strengthen our psychological immune system. All healthy parents are uncomfortable watching their kids being uncomfortable. But just as we can teach our child how to tolerate discomfort, we know that we have to do the same for ourselves. PTPs, on the other hand, can't find any level of their child's discomfort tolerable. They can never get to "If my kid finds something intolerable, we'll figure it out together." They never let their kids get to the hard times, and that's a profound loss.

It makes sense that when my child is about to experience an emotionally challenging event—a crushing defeat, a friend dropping them, a bad grade—I might confuse my trauma memory with their real-time experience and see any of these as potentially traumatic. I might want to swoop in and save them, thinking that this will protect them from trauma. But typical childhood disappointments or butting up against a sometimes-unfair world are uncomfortable, not traumatic. Yet my trauma app doesn't know the difference. And it's so easy to swoop in and fix it—write that note, petition that teacher, cushion that blow. But this isn't me parenting; it's my trauma app trying to tell me that all discomfort is potentially traumatic and therefore must be eliminated.

Perfectionist parents know what they should be doing, but their behavior doesn't reflect their knowledge. There is so much focus on avoiding a parenting mistake of what "NOT" to do, perfectionist parents don't have the opportunity to figure out a better solution. In acceptance and commitment therapy (ACT), we learn that the only thing we can control is our attention. If my attention is on "Don't yell," my attention is focused on yelling and that means I'm more likely to yell. I worked with a classroom teacher who was trying to get a handle on yelling—instead of thinking, *Don't yell,* I had her think, *When I'm stressed, I'm going to sing my next instructions instead of speaking them.* Her yelling problem disappeared, and the students were much more cooperative. They would even sing along, which refocused them yet more! So if you're telling yourself "Don't yell" even though you know all the reasons why communicating gently, kindly, and firmly is good parenting, you can't access that knowledge because you forget that you have the tools. Inevitably, when "Don't yell" turns into a really LOUD conversation, the perfectionist parent will feel shame. *I know better—why did I not do better?*

Carol Dweck's research on growth mindsets, featured in her book *Mindset,* explains how this works.[2] When faced with a problem, a growth mindset will come up with "I can't do it—yet." A fixed mindset, like those of perfectionist parents, will arrive at "I can't afford to mess up," because mistakes are intolerable, and point to the fact that "I am a bad person" as opposed to "I made the wrong choice."

Perfect or OCD?

Perfectionism is like an obsessive-compulsive disorder (OCD). If you think about how OCD is depicted in movies as a solution to anxiety, the person with OCD comes up with the right solution to shut down their anxiety in order to keep them safe. If they worry about germs, their brain will create a default: I will wash my hands a million times. The reward for this behavior is a sense of control, because it feels really good to wash your hands perfectly. I'm safe and I've removed all risk of harm.

In the same way, if you find the thought *What if my child is damaged by big and overwhelming emotions?* and your trauma app comes up with the solution—I will make sure they won't ever experience those—it feels like you have control over an intolerable what-if. Yet by protecting them, you are hampering your own curiosity, which is a big parenting superpower. The child then gets the message that they are fragile, and the parent is stuck repeating the same behaviors and never learns new ways to navigate big emotions with their child.

What Perfectionist Parents Look Like

There are many ways to be a perfectionist parent, because every perfectionist parent has different interpretations of what perfect looks like. Some put incredibly high standards on themselves and their behavior, as in, "I must do everything perfectly." Interestingly, these parents are less focused on particular outcomes for their kids but insert themselves into their children's problem to meet the need to be "a perfect parent." The essential fears of these perfectionist parents are Will my kid be traumatized like I was? Will my kid be damaged by my damage? Therefore, I have to be so vigilant to do parenting perfectly so that they aren't damaged by me or other damaging influences.

Another type of perfectionist parent can be highly goal oriented because they are strivers. They were good students. They were the ones who were labeled *resilient trauma survivors*, *mature*, and *wise beyond their years*. Their trauma app creates the ideal of "perceived control": if they feel responsible for everything, they also feel safer. It makes sense that goal-oriented parents have good executive functioning: we have to be able to prioritize tasks so that our goals happen. But our kids need all of us, not merely our executive functioning abilities. Interestingly, even when we're hyperfocused—a typical trauma app superpower—we're not really fully present. We're only seeing the problem, not all the potential solutions or the emotions. We're not seeing our child in their full humanity. Our child is not a task we can cross off on a checklist.

Many perfectionist parents look much more "together" than other types of PTPs. If you walked into a paralyzed parent's home, it would be a literal mess, with everything strewn all over the place. In a perfectionist parent household, the home looks very functional, neat, and clean. This doesn't mean that all perfectionist parents are concerned about appearances. But when they are hyperfunctional, the home is just naturally going to be a little bit more organized (if my kid is going to be a top-level gymnast, I have to manage a lot to make that happen, and having the house being a mess is going to be a distraction).

Another aspect of perfectionist parenting is a sense of hypervigilance for keeping their little humans alive. While this is the most basic function of parenting, perfectionist parents take this responsibility to the extreme. Their trauma has pierced their illusion of safety in the world, and they cannot find the point where it's simply too much vigilance. It can't be sustained, nor is it helpful or useful. Many PTPs experience hypervigilance when their children are infants. My perfectionist parenting triggered for the first month of each of my children's life: nobody but me was allowed to touch the baby because I feared their germs, and I couldn't sleep because I had to make sure the baby was breathing. The one time my baby was in the NICU was great for me: I could totally doze off because he was being monitored so closely by the NICU staff, who would catch anything dangerous.

And then one day, my hypervigilance just passed. I could sleep again, and other people could pick up the baby. Yet for some post-traumatic perfectionist parents, it never does.

Some perfectionist parents can look like helicopter parents. Their essential fear is *regret avoidance*: *What if my kid misses out on an expectation or an experience? What if they are hanging out with the wrong kinds of friends? What if they don't get into the college of their dreams?* If it's *What if my kid feels bullied?* then I might have to hover in the playground. If it's *What if my kid feels criticized because they didn't get an A plus?* then I have to go fight with the teacher. But if you could take away the trauma app's permissions, you would realize *my kid's emotions aren't an emergency—not for them, and not for me. I can let them sort out their age-appropriate challenges on their own.*

Exercise: What's the Worst Thing? Identify The Fear Your Perfectionism Is Avoiding

When perfectionist parents come to see me and say that they're anxious about their child, I know almost immediately that the scenario they are presenting is actually not the core of their anxiety. I've found over the years that people do not come to therapy because of a surface fear like "my kid is going to fail their math test"; if someone is putting a disproportionate amount of fear, attention, or distress onto a somewhat typical problem, there's probably something lurking underneath. My line of questions helps me identify if I am dealing with perfectionism or not. And if the parents are perfectionists, it helps me determine what the intolerable fear really is and how it's affecting their parenting.

So, we play a game I like to call "What's the Worst Thing?" It's based on the concept of Socratic questioning. First, I address their anxiety by asking, "What's the worst thing that could happen to your child?" Then I say, "Tell me what happens after that." We keep going until we get to the absolute worst-case scenario.

How do you know you've reached the end of the game? Close your eyes and imagine what this scenario would look like. Your eyes might actually pop open as you start to envision it because you don't want to see it. I used to work with an anxiety specialist for supervision and she would say the worst thing always is "dead in a ditch." Other people get to "I'll be poor, and then I'll be homeless, and then no one will love me." If your "worst thing" is simply "I'll feel uncomfortable," then that's dangerous thinking. Life is often uncomfortable, and you're allowed to feel uncomfortable.

For perfectionist parents, a lot of times the "worst thing" has to do with their children's emotions, even though the first thing they say is only the surface concern. Here's an example of how we get to the real issue:

- If I lose control and yell at her, she'll be upset.
- And then what's the worst thing?
- And then she'll see that I'm out of control, and I'm the one that made her upset.
- And then what's the worst thing?
- And then she'll be really sad to realize that her mother could make her feel that way.
- And then what's the worst thing?

- And then she'll think I don't really love her.
- And then what's the worst thing?
- I don't know. She'll be all alone, thinking her mom doesn't love her. That is the worst possible thing.

Now it's your turn:

- Write down the worst possible outcome of the relationship you have with your child right now. What's the worst thing that can happen?
- Then, write down what happens after that.
- When you get to the worst possible thing, stop.

You have now located your biggest fear. Can you actually control that outcome? More likely than not, you can't, not for yourself or your child. All you can do is welcome your fear in, thank it for the information, and focus on what you can control.

Last, perfectionist parents are often burned out, depressed, and exhausted. They have lost any sense of joy in parenting and are just going through the motions in their efforts to do it perfectly. Think about a job where the standards are always too high, you're always on call, and always subject to both internal shaming and external blaming. Sounds like a recipe for burnout, doesn't it? In fact, in one study, researchers found that the higher the parenting perfectionist standards are, the greater the chance for parental burnout.[3]

Where Do Perfectionist Parents Come From?

When a child cannot control their environment, they will try to control themselves. Perfectionism is the ultimate effort to control ourselves to create some sense of safety within us. If trauma happened as an adult, the outcome is the same; it just relies on a more sophisticated understanding of the world. It's more specific, less global.

IFS therapy views the psyche as made up of various "parts," each with its own perspective, feelings, memories, and agenda. These parts all exist to keep a person safe. Parts are categorized into three types: managers, exiles, and firefighters. According to IFS, perfectionism often arises from the activities of "manager" parts, whose role is to maintain control of the individual's internal environment and external life to protect vulnerable "exile" parts that carry painful emotions and memories.

IFS suggests that the root of perfectionism lies in the fear that if things are not perfect, then something deeply bad or unworthy about the self will be exposed. This fear usually stems from earlier life experiences where we felt that love, acceptance, or safety were conditional on performing well or meeting certain standards. So, the manager parts adopt perfectionism as a strategy to prevent the individual from experiencing shame, criticism, or rejection, thereby protecting the more vulnerable exiles from being triggered and causing emotional pain.

Perfectionist parents may have also grown up in chronically invalidating environments. Marsha Linehan describes this as a home where you can't talk about how you're feeling inside, because your emotions are met by erratic, inappropriate, or extreme responses.[4] Imagine that you are crying because you just fell down and your dad yells, "Stop crying, or I'll give you something to cry about"; that's an invalidating environment. Or one day your dad responds totally differently, and he is super concerned about your welfare. Anticipating his response becomes really confusing, because you never know what you're going to experience. So you come up with the idea of perfectionism as a strategy to avoid being shamed and blamed.

The essential lesson that comes from an invalidating environment is that love is conditional. One solution to this dilemma is to develop perfectionism, thinking, *I need to be perfect to experience love. I need to meet other people's expectations or they'll reject me entirely.* And then you grow up and become a parent, and your inner child directs that same perfectionism toward your parenting. You translate your experience to *my kid must never fall down because they're going to feel so alone or feel shamed and blamed for crying.*

Goals vs. Values

Perfectionist parents often misinterpret parenting values and goals. So what's the difference? A goal is something that becomes a focus of your attention. A goal is inflexible: either you hit your mark or you don't.

Being goal oriented feels safe to your trauma app, especially when you were a kid, because a goal is a very distinct task that you can accomplish. If your parents set out the goal of "We expect you to bring home As on your report card," there's a clear measuring stick in front of you. When goals are created in an unhealthy manner, it may be about parental narcissism, "Your performance needs to reflect well on me," or it may be about fears of survival, "If you don't get all As, you won't get into the college of your dreams, and then your life will be over." If the trauma app says, "We avoid criticism by achieving goals," you're trapped in a perpetual perfectionism spiral, because there will always be another goal to meet.

I don't have a problem with goals, and parents need to set them for their children, especially if they are in service of a value. For instance, we have a family value about basic human competence. I have certain goals that all my children must attain, and achieving each becomes a little rite of passage into adulthood. My kids have to demonstrate to me that they can iron a shirt, change a tire, pump gas, sew a button, fry an egg, manage basic financial transactions, throw a punch, and break a choke hold. I'll admit the list is somewhat arbitrary, based on my own need for those skills at various times in my life! One of my kids didn't like eggs and didn't want to learn how to fry an egg. It was no problem for me to swap his goal from "fry an egg" to "make a bowl of pasta" because I wasn't invested in the egg. I was invested in the goal of "My kid needs to know how to cook for himself."

However, a goal in service of another goal isn't a great place to put your attention. Some goals are particularly difficult to attain. If your child doesn't get into Harvard but is welcomed with open arms to any other Ivy League school, then they haven't failed by any other human's perception except for your trauma app. And if they do achieve the goal, what comes next? Typically, perfectionist parents and their children find another goal to fill the void. You're simply keeping your trauma app on, because the app loves a checklist; again, it will always create more goals.

Values are as much about the journey as they are about the outcome. Values point to *Who will I become?* and *What's essentially important to me?* And values are inherently flexible, because they don't necessarily have markers of success. In fact, they kind of sneak up on you, particularly when you see them in action. I've had days when I can finally catch my breath and realize that it's been a few weeks since there was real drama in my house, so I must be living my value of talking to my kids calmly and respectfully.

If your family values are *athletics teach life lessons*, that's great, because there are lots of athletics to choose from. But if it's *all my children must be competitive gymnasts*, that's a goal, not a value. "Getting into Harvard" is a goal. "Finding the best school to support your child's academic needs" is a value.

Perfectionist parents have trouble when their children want to give up on previously important goals. For instance, Katie's thirteen-year-old daughter, Emily, wants to stop gymnastics, even though she is very good at it and has been doing this activity for three years. Katie automatically begins to worry, and the what-ifs come hard and fast: *What if she regrets her decision halfway into the season and feels bad? If she could give up gymnastics, what else might she give up? What else might go wrong? Aren't I supposed to be teaching her grit? Did I fail to teach her something essential?*

Perfectionist parents like Katie are accidentally undoing any striving toward grit with this line of thinking. The truth is, when a parent says, "I can't let my kid quit because I'm not teaching them grit," they haven't taught them grit in the first place. Angela Duckworth's *Grit* features a description that grit is *passion plus perseverance.* If Katie ignores the fact that Emily has lost her passion for gymnastics and forces her to remain on the team, she would not actually be teaching grit; she would be reinforcing perseverance without the passion, which is a sure path to burnout.

The real problem that Katie has is Emily's experience of freeness. To Katie, giving up on a goal is very scary. Her inner child is forgetting that children are meant to grow, change, evolve. And her trauma app and the inner child are working together, because the trauma app is sending a message that "bad stuff happens when children are free to choose their own goals."

In order to keep Katie's perfectionism in check but also honor her values around grit, I explained the difference between goals and values and showed her that gymnastics was a goal, but grit was a value. Then I taught her my rule for children and activities: no one quits an activity on a low. Whenever one of my children has a bad day doing the thing they usually love to do, we mark the date on the calendar and pick another day 3.5 weeks later. If they still want to quit, it's okay with me. The only exception would be if they're an integral part of a team that is counting on them; then they do have to finish out the season. I came up with this rule based on reading my journal of my martial arts training. I rarely had three bad weeks in a row. I also know that whenever you're learning a new skill, there's a progression: some days you will be better,

Exercise: Tell Me Why: Transform Goals into Values

Tell Me Why is my Backstreet Boys exercise. If you have a goal called "My kids must learn martial arts," ask yourself why as if you were talking to a friend. If your immediate answer is "My kid must have a black belt," you've identified a goal. But if the answer is "It's a good way to learn grit and resilience," you've uncovered a value.

It might take you a few tries to find the value, just like it took a few tries to find the core fear. Here's an example:

- My home must always be neat and organized.
- Tell me why.
- Because I was raised in dysfunction and it just needs to be that way.
- Tell me why.
- Because I don't want my home to be dysfunctional.
- Tell me why.
- Because a dysfunctional home makes kids feel unimportant, like they don't have a place to be themselves.

Can you see the beginnings of a value? Values are all about the "why," and goals are often about the "what." When the "what we do" part of the equation becomes too inflexible, it often loses the original "why." When we are flexibly enacting the goal of a livable, functional home where kids feel welcome, neatness is a part of that, but it's not an emergency. Occasionally, kids can finger-paint or make a mess. When we're rigid about it—and kids can't dare to play exuberantly, because we will freak out at the mess—the goal of "neatness" just blocked the value of "a livable home." Kids don't feel welcome to be themselves in an environment that's too rigid.

Can you see how the trauma app can turn a value into an inflexible goal and that can become counterproductive?

If you adopt the value "I want a livable, loving, healthy home," you can install some rules that align with your values: "We have cleanup time," "We keep the art supplies in the art corner," etc. Now you've identified a value that lets kids have a place to be themselves.

or enjoy it more, than others. This lesson teaches that today's passion might be missing, but they are using their grit mindset to keep going. What's more, while "perfect" can be the enemy of the "good," there is satisfaction in getting to "good."

Brian and Nikki

Too Perfect?

"Nikki, I thought we agreed. No screen time during family time." Brian rolled his eyes as he walked into the restaurant to meet his wife, Nikki, and their three young children. All three kids were perfectly dressed and perfectly behaved, quietly playing on their iPads. Nikki tensed up immediately. "The kids were really hyper and making a scene. It was a stressful day, and while I was shuttling them to all their activities, I seriously didn't get to eat even one bite of food or use the bathroom. I just needed to eat something, and then I was going to ask them to put the devices away. It was an emergency."

Brian shook his head and raised his voice. "But that's not what we agreed. Screens are not allowed during family time."

"We also agreed not to argue in front of the kids, but we're arguing right now." Nikki, visibly upset, got up and walked toward the bathroom, sobbing.

If you're wondering why I'm describing the scene as though I was there—I was, sort of. Turns out, their eleven-year-old daughter, Hailey, was recording them the whole time. (She was participating in a TikTok challenge where you stitch together your parents saying certain words to make it look like they said something else entirely. Her whole class was doing it, and it's funny, apparently.) Putting the whole "ethics of recording people without their consent" on hold, I had real proof and was able to ask my patients, Brian and Nikki, what was really going on.

"It's not a fight," Nikki was quick to say. "We've agreed that we don't fight. It's scary for kids when their grownups can't get along, so we don't do that."

I thought, *It sure looked like a fight to me!* And just so you know, there's nothing wrong with disagreeing, or having an argument, in front of your children. It's not the conflict that's problematic; it's the ratcheted-up emotions and hurtfulness that comes along with a fight.

But before I could bestow this parenting lesson, Brian interjected, "Dr. K, you spoke with us about parenting values. And this is a big parenting value. Screen time is terrible. It makes kids into unproductive monster zombies who don't know how to interact with other people and can't deal with any frustration in the real world. And we're trying to do so much to maximize their childhood—structuring their days so that they are full of family activities—yet they are still on their screens, and they get bored and fight. We're not making sure that they have the kind of childhood we dreamed of for them."

"Well, I can't do it by myself!" Nikki snapped. "How am I meant to manage them—the consequences we agreed on don't work, they don't listen when I reason with them, and the chaos is impossible. I don't want to yell and punish, and I don't want so much screen time either, but what do I do when they just won't listen?"

I could see that Brian and Nikki are both talking about what they don't want, but I wasn't hearing anything about what they do want. I asked them both to tell me about how they arrived at their parenting values.

Nikki talked about her parents and their sudden, explosive fights. They'd snark at each other, make pointed veiled references, slam doors, or give each other the silent treatment. She was witness to lots of screaming matches late into the night. When she was little, Nikki actually had a good relationship with each parent on their own, and she'd fantasize about them getting divorced and then feel really guilty about that fantasy, because isn't divorce supposed to be a bad thing? How could she wish it on her parents? So her parenting rule of "not fighting" became extremely important to her, alongside her own ability to remain calm with her kids. She also felt very overwhelmed by her children's reaction to their own big emotions (their overwhelm), projected that a gigantic meltdown or intolerable emotions were just around the corner, and that there was no way she could stay calm if all of them were upset. Nikki believed that if her children saw her and Brian fighting, or her reacting to anything with less than perfect calm, they would be irrevocably damaged. In Nikki's mind, that would be intolerable.

Brian spoke about a childhood where he felt like an afterthought. His parents both worked long hours in highly competitive careers. He just wanted to spend some time with them, but his parents were always busy, so they overscheduled his days with one activity after another. Yet he was always very lonely. Shy by nature, Brian didn't have much of a social life after school. He was gifted at academics and enjoyed reading, so school was a bright spot for him. "I once read a book where a character said wistfully, 'I want a life with people in it,' and that line always stuck with me. I want a life with people in it. And that's what I want for my kids." His perfectionism showed up in his penchant for overvaluing family togetherness at the expense of anything else.

The first problem was that both Brian and Nikki were mistaking goals for values. It's great to value family togetherness, but *no screen time* is a goal, not a value. Nikki's trauma app sees children witnessing conflict as dangerous, so it mandated that she present calmly all the time. The kids bickering in the restaurant—which prompted this whole interaction—felt so overwhelming that she had to give in to their demands. For Brian, the essential loneliness of his childhood is the worst thing possible. He never wants his kids to feel alienated, alone, and unwanted, the way he did. His perfectionism trauma app turned on when he saw the screens and got upset. If he was trying to create a cozy family memory, he actually did the opposite.

What Brian and Nikki are missing is that they are inadvertently trying to control their inner children's lives instead of parenting their three actual children. I explained that it's totally okay for Brian and Nikki to disagree. It's even okay to disagree in front of the kids, as long as the disagreement is productive, civil, and repaired in front of them. Brian's experiential-avoidance-by-proxy is all about his kids not feeling unwanted. He sees a child using any screen as being inherently alienated, being fed an electronic pacifier instead of a nurturing relationship. But there's a way to be "alone together." Brian never experienced it in his childhood, but it is possible. Some of my coziest memories of my own childhood involved reading at the kitchen table with my parents, who were reading as well. Ester Buchholz, one of my early mentors and author of *The Call of Solitude*, talks about the need for some alone time, some processing time, and some time to fantasize and how solitude isn't necessarily loneliness.[5] In today's world, screen time often replaces reading time and provides all the benefits of the "alone together solitude" Buchholz describes. However, screen time is like any other vice: there's an amount that's "way too little" and an amount that's "way too much," and it's not always easy to reach that Goldilocks level of "just right." And like sugary sweets or days off from school, there's a moment when these things can be relied on, not just as treats but in a pinch.

As Nikki and Brian discussed their values, the traumas that underly them, and where their values converge and diverge, I could easily help them find a more flexible family value. We did the Tell Me Why exercise and came up with some new insights. Brian realized he can't enforce a "no screen time" policy, so he has to let it go. Instead, he could still value family togetherness and come up with activities that the family can do together. Nikki realized that it's okay for kids to see that their parents are human and occasionally lose it or mess up—as long as they witness and experience repair.

The Relationship Between Rupture and Repair

Perfectionist parents fear making a mistake, which leads them to live in both the present and the future. They think that parenting decisions are written in pen when, in fact, they're written in pencil, and we can always erase and start over. Anna Kang and Christopher Weyant wrote a charming picture book called *Eraser* about an eraser who feels like she contributes nothing because all she does is wipe away mistakes. Throughout the story, Eraser learns that growth, discovery, and progress need an eraser. I often read *Eraser* with perfectionist parents to bring home this point—not only can we erase a mistake, but that erasure can also actually contribute to the overall beauty of the project.

In clinical terms, we call this "rupture and repair." Rupture refers to a breakdown or disruption in any relationship. This could occur due to a variety of reasons, such as misunderstandings, conflicts, emotional outbursts, or any behavior that causes someone to feel hurt, neglected, or unseen by another person. In a tiny rupture—like forgetting to buy a requested item—that feeling is barely perceptible, but it's still there. That's why we sometimes have that disproportionate reaction to something minor, like a spouse forgetting to buy milk or fill the car up with gas. There's a larger rupture festering already; the tiny rupture is the proverbial straw that broke the camel's back.

Repair is when we fix the rupture. We can acknowledge the issue, take responsibility, discuss it openly, and manage the emotional fallout. Every rupture can be repaired. This is something that people raised in healthy homes know because they've seen it modeled. They know that sometimes kids can be mad at their parents or parents can be upset with their kids, but whenever there is a rupture, they can talk it through and get to the repair. Nothing terrible would happen. They'd emerge from the conflict with hurt feelings at worst, and at best, they had the chance to have a productive conflict that allows both sides to understand each other better. What's more, when parents make mistakes, the child learns that they're allowed to make a mistake, because there's such a thing as repair.

Dr. Aliza Pressman uses a wonderful analogy to explain the normative process of rupture and repair in her book, *The Five Principles of Parenting.*[6] Relationships need small, manageable ruptures and repairs in order to grow. Think of how our muscles develop. When we work out, the muscle fiber tears, or ruptures, slightly. That's the soreness we feel after an intense day in the gym. Then, our body secretes more muscle fiber, which patches or repairs the tiny rip, and then the muscle increases. Relationships work on exactly the same principle: without ruptures, relationships stagnate. And when we've worked out too hard and we're too sore, we know that our rupture will need a more major repair. We've learned our limits, and we can also trust that we will get back to normal. The same is true for our relationship with our child. When a rupture gets too big, we'll know it will require a different kind of repair.

But if you are terrified of the sensation of rupture for either yourself or your child, you will never allow yourself or your child to make a mistake. The idea or the experience of rupture is intolerable because you don't believe in the possibility of repair. That's your trauma app talking. The truth is that ruptures do feel uncomfortable, but as I've said before, discomfort isn't danger.

The second error that most perfectionist parents make is to focus on trying to avoid the rupture when they should be focusing on how to create the best repair: when both the parent and child feel seen and heard. I can guarantee that you and your child will have hundreds of ruptures over a lifetime. And if you can keep in mind this principle, you can resolve each rupture with an appropriate repair.

The Fix for Perfectionist Parents

D. W. Winnicott introduced the idea of *the good-enough mother* in his book *Playing and Reality*. Back in the early 1900s, he was seeing a worrying trend toward perfectionism in parenting. His belief that "even the beneficial is toxic in the excess" shows me that our best intentions, taken to an extreme, are problematic. Not only is "good enough good enough," it's actually the ideal when you are bumping up against parental burnout or any type of perfectionism.

The overall lesson for perfectionist parenting is to remember the adage "The perfect is the enemy of the good." Given that in parenting, the gold standard—what we're shooting for—is "good-enough" parenting, we literally can't be "good enough" if we're trying for perfection.

When you hold onto perfection as the ideal, you lose the possibility of joy and serendipity in your day-to-day life, because every part of your day is prescribed. But you already know that life never goes exactly like the script, no matter how hard you try. We can't script the emotions that we feel or the responses our children will have. And the minute we try is the minute we are no longer present. Our children need our presence much more than they need our perfection. So, let's see how to break this habit.

No matter how your perfectionism comes across (among the different types discussed earlier in the chapter), these five steps work in sequence. The outcome may be different depending on what your perfectionism looks like. If your perfectionism is self-focused, "I must be a perfect parent," or your perfectionism is child focused, "My child must not feel disappointment," the way you apply these fixes might differ, but the underlying concept will be the same.

Step #1

Embrace the Idea That Not Everything Is Controllable

One of the universal truths about parenting is bad stuff sometimes happens. All parents want to protect their kids, and the imperative for protection, or vigilance, is even greater if you had trauma in your past. Remember, trauma pierces the illusion of safety in the world, and it's no surprise that you have tried to create as much safety as possible. But there comes a point where the Herculean efforts you're putting in place to make the world safe outweigh the perceived risk. Once you've taken commonsense precautions, you have to let go of the idea that you can control every outcome. You can't predict every possible danger, and that's okay. You cannot sit by your baby's bedside and watch them breathe twenty-four seven; at some point, you have to go to sleep so that you are ready to parent again tomorrow. In fact, if you don't your child is likely to be less safe the next day!

Great parents allow children to make mistakes and take risks, just like they allow for ruptures and repairs. We grow when we can learn from our mistakes. And just like emotions, mistakes happen. Sometimes, it's uncomfortable when mistakes happen, but that discomfort will pass.

We have to allow ourselves to make mistakes, to ditch the parenting scripts and the perfectly structured and optimized life, and allow ourselves to relax into our essential humanity. We waste a lot of psychological resources trying to control everything. That awful sense of indecision, when we simply can't figure out what the perfect solution is and our brains ping-pong between valid options, eats up our psychological processing power. In order to let go, I created a strategy that I call *pick and stick*. Remember Allison, who lost a child and then was caught in the web of perfectionism in an attempt to protect her son. I gave Allison the following instructions for making safety decisions for him: she can take one hour to do her research, and then pick one decision and stick to it. Once she googled the benefits of stroller A and stroller B and looked at their safety ratings, that was it. I gave Nikki and Brian the same advice: once they've decided on a day to have family time, or screen time, there was no need to overthink, analyze, and debate, because they had made a decision and could stick to it.

What decisions can you "pick and stick" to override your perfectionism trauma app? Fill in the blank in your own journal.

Step #2

Practice Self-Compassion

In *The Gifts of Imperfection*, Brené Brown points out that the essence of perfectionism is defensiveness that comes from our inner critic. The more we defend ourselves from these voices, the stronger they get, because when we defend against them, we give them credence and weight. I once took my kids to a zoo where there was a parrot trained to be an "insult comic." As each person walked by, it would say, "You're ugly." "That's a weird shirt." "You're the dumbest person I ever met." Everyone was laughing. Normally, insults like that are hurtful, so why were we laughing? Because the parrot doesn't have the ability to actually evaluate the stylishness of my clothes or my intellectual abilities. We're laughing because we don't actually value the parrot's opinion, so we're not going to argue with it.

How do we handle the parrot and its insults? We vote with our feet—we walk away. How do we handle our inner critic? The same way. Try this exercise:

- Think of the harshest criticism you say to yourself: "I'm so lazy." "I'm so stupid." "I am an emotional mess." "I have no self-control."
- Now, close your eyes, and substitute your child's name for your own: "Hailey, you are so stupid." "Hailey, you are so lazy."
- Did your eyes pop open? Did you have a hard time getting that sentence out?
- You've just met your inner critic. Ask yourself, would you allow anyone to speak to your child that way?

If you don't want that inner critic to become your child's internal voice, it's time to banish it. Let's use an ACT cognitive defusion technique. Cognitive defusion is a way of separating a thought from the person thinking it.

- Think of the sentence "I am so lazy." Notice what sensations that brings up for you.
- To gain a bit of distance, use your name and put the sentence in second person: "Nikki, you are so lazy." Does that feel any different?
- Now, think of the sentence "I'm having the thought 'I'm so lazy.'" Do you notice how the intensity of your sensations diminished a bit? That's because you put some distance between the "I" who is thinking, and the thought.
- Now, think of the sentence "I'm noticing I'm having the thought 'I'm so lazy.'" Do you see yourself becoming more curious about what sparked that thought? Can you access some compassion for the "I" who is thinking that thought? There's your self-compassion. As we access self-compassion, we start to see the inner critic as "part" of us, a "part" with one opinion rather than as blended with our sense of self.

Step #3

Focus on Repair

Perfectionism automatically interferes with presence because the minute you're monitoring how "perfect" you are is the minute you're no longer present. And you can't get to a repair if your attention is not in the same room with your child.

The essential fix for every rupture, large or small, is presence. Sometimes, a repair means having a postmortem, talking about a rupture that happened, and figuring out what went wrong and what to do next time. And sometimes, it's just about restoring your presence—sharing a favorite activity, making time to talk or play together, or doing something that makes you feel like two humans who are attuned to one another and value each other.

Some PTPs don't know how to apologize to a child because they never saw it modeled, or they believe apologizing will make their children more insecure, because they will think, *If my mom can mess up, she's not infallible. If she's not infallible, then I'm not safe.* But that's simply untrue. Parents are humans and sometimes mess up. And when they do, they should take responsibility.

It's okay to say "I'm sorry."

It's okay to admit to a mistake.

It's okay to own your emotions.

It's okay to say "I'll give you some space, and then we'll figure out how to fix this."

Step #4

Solidify Your Parenting Base

I have found over the years that perfectionists often marry each other, because clarity likes clarity. And one thing perfectionists have is clarity, especially about how they "don't" want to raise their children. Problems occur when their *don'ts* are not aligned. The two parents might have opposing values, or they might have the same values but have opposing methods for attaining them.

Two perfectionist parents can get into the rut of calling each other to task on the times the other wasn't perfect, without drawing attention to the other's parenting successes. The same thing happens in social media communities. As Jessica Winter pointed out in a *New Yorker* article, gentle parenting is ironically very harsh on the parents.

You can use the Tell Me Why exercise together to have a values clarification conversation until you hit a value you both can agree on. If you have strong values that aren't aligned, can you agree that the parent who wants a particular value has to "take point" in order to ensure its adoption? You can't outsource an unaligned value to the other parent. If Brian's value of "limiting screen time" gets refined as "being present during family time," he can't simply leave and mandate it for Nikki to enforce. Parents overvalue consistency, but in fact, children can easily adapt to the idea that parents can have differing values. They often appreciate the innate flexibility that allows them to try more than one lifestyle choice and see what fits for them, and they can understand that there are different rules for summer vacation or weekends vs. school nights. There can also be different rules when different parents are the parent on duty (POD). If one parent truly values cultural activities and the other parent would rather get a root canal, it's totally fine to have the point parent take on the ballet or museum visit. It's the same with food choices, slightly later or earlier bedtimes, or pretty much any decision.

Step #5

Remember, Your Child Has You

The intolerable part of trauma is very often the fact that you had to make sense of it alone. I once interviewed members of Survivors Path, an organization that supports survivors of mass shootings. One of the survivors, who was very young at the time of the incident, told me, "My parents did the best they could with the tools they had. I got a very strong message from them to move on and not think too much about my experience. There was no one for me to talk to about it. I was told to be grateful that I survived."

The way this survivor talked made it sound like she had suffered from two separate traumas: the school shooting and the feeling of being alone with her trauma. When I was growing up, there was definitely a mentality of "move on, count your blessings, don't dwell on it," and this was considered supportive. Now we know that advice isn't enough: our understanding of how to support young people through trauma has evolved.

Your child may go through many challenges in life. There will be ruptures—with you, with their friends, or with teachers. Your child may see your imperfection, and sometimes, they'll feel misunderstood by you. But they won't be alone with their feelings, because you've modeled talking together about problems. If they feel misunderstood, unsupported, or sad, they already know that you want to hear about it. What they won't be is alone. They will always have you for support, for validation, and for repair.

CHAPTER 6

The Disengaged Parent

I WAS ABSOLUTELY sure that I had my trauma and my triggers under control because I was *so good* at using my superpower of *adaptive dissociation*: the ability to emotionally distance myself from any stressful situation yet get the job done. This strategy had served me well for meeting deadlines and writing my thesis, but it turns out that it is not an ideal parenting strategy.

I learned that part the hard way. I thought no one was noticing that I was just going through the motions of parenting: after all, everyone was getting fed, I was reading bedtime stories, everyone's clothes fit, and no one was creating problems at school. But one day, my ten-year-old son just looked across the kitchen table at me as I was chopping up some carrots and said, "Sometimes you're not there behind your eyes. What happens to you? Where do you go? It's like you're talking and you're here, but you're not here. It's like someone else is here and it's not you, and I don't like that. And then when you smile, I don't see it in your eyes. I don't like that; I hate when you do that. Why do you do that?" Then he burst into tears. And so did I.

How come I could give a professional presentation to a thousand people in that same dissociated state and get nothing but compliments? How come I could do therapy with kids who were the same age as my own with my supervisor in my earbud and my classmates watching me, and no one noticed my dissociated state? I knew when I was dissociating and how good I was at it over so many years. Yet my ten-year-old saw right through me and it scared the heck out of him, and his fear terrified me.

I knew my dissociation was my trauma app's stress response. And I was also fully aware that I was terrified of parenting. I wasn't meeting my own expectations or deepening my relationship with my kids. On the surface, I thought everything appeared to others as "fine," but I knew there was something missing. I was carrying a family legacy of cultural beliefs about what "good mothers" are—we all carry a legacy. I knew that a good mother was supposed to be capable, feminine, relaxed, and always calm. I was also carrying a personal legacy of shame.

I didn't feel capable, was told I wasn't feminine enough, and I definitely wasn't relaxed or calm (hello, PTSD). So the fact that I knew what I was supposed to do and couldn't do it meant, to me, that there was something fundamentally wrong with me as a mother, as a person, as a human. And if I was so flawed, then I was going to somehow harm my kids. So I came up with the following reasoning: if I can keep my true self away from the children just enough to get through the day (a.k.a. dissociation), then they will be safe. I truly felt "I have to leave you to love you."

Can you see how my logic worked? Have you ever thought, *I'm a really shameful, flawed, damaged person. It's better if my kids get less of me?* This kind of thinking is legitimized when you do lose it—the times you yell, punish harshly, or overreact. Some of that mom rage is really about expressing repressed emotions from your childhood or recent traumas. Sometimes, mom rage is simply about the lack of support moms get and the unbalanced load they carry in the home. Either way, it's totally okay and normal to get angry when you've told your kid to put on their socks for the 377th time. That's your anger doing its job of telling you that there is a problem here. Mom rage is the disproportional response.

Social worker and YouTube commentator Patrick Teahan calls this type of mental gymnastics *sideways grief*. You are working really hard to repress your emotions, especially if you are feeling justified anger regarding what happened during childhood that you know you're not allowed to, or supposed to, get mad about. So you get angry at your kids instead. Remember that anger is never a primary emotion. There's always an emotion underlying it. Under anger is often sadness or grief.

For instance, I wasn't allowed to be mad at my father for dying, because that emotion would be shameful. So, I stuffed my anger down in an effort to disavow, or reject, it. Yet that anger was still there. Now I know that my adaptive dissociation was my way of dealing with my fear that my "mad" would come out as intense rage over silly or inconsequential issues.

Many emotions can come out sideways. You could be watching a commercial for allergy medicine with a mom romping around with her kids in a field of flowers and you're suddenly feeling furious. Or your kids will be having normal kid experiences that you didn't have the freedom to do and you feel intense jealousy of them. So you stay far away from your kids, whether by scrolling through Instagram or staying late at work, in an effort to protect them from your intense rage that could suddenly bubble out without warning or explanation. In essence, you are disengaging on two levels. You're separating yourself from your child in an effort to protect them. And you're separating yourself from your emotions that you judge as unworthy and unwelcome.

In IFS therapy, our personality is comprised of "parts." Right now, as I write this, there's a part of me that is really interested and engaged in what I'm writing about, a part of me that's anxious because I haven't written as many words in this chapter as I'd planned to, a part of me that worries that I'm not explaining this clearly enough and you will miss out on what I'm really trying to convey, and a part that wants to turn off my computer, take out a bar of chocolate, and play video games.

One of the key tenets of IFS is that "all of our parts are welcome." That means that even the parts I'd like to disavow—the "mom rage" part, the "jealous of my own kids" part, or the "actually, I'm not always calm and relaxed with my kids" part—are important. However, the parts that we try to disavow or rid ourselves of become "exiles." Ironically, by trying to exile these parts, we end up giving them more power and influence over us.

If you could accept that your rage is a part of you, you could then repurpose that energy for your benefit. My "rage" part could provide me with the energy for exercise, for creativity, or for finally organizing my kitchen, because we can tap into our anger as a source for problem-solving. But if I exile my anger, I can't use it for my benefit.

Sometimes, mom rage is turned on because we are so attuned to our children that their moods and intense feelings become contagious. That reaction is more about physiology—and brain chemistry—than it is about psychology. And that's actually a good thing. When your child's emotions become contagious, that means you care.

The Body Doesn't Just Keep the Score; It Also Calls the Shots

For many PTPs, our relationship to our bodies is fraught. Trauma interferes with so many biological needs and signals—sleep, time sense, proprioception, even how we process sound. So it makes sense that in parenting, which is the ultimate intersection of your need for the brain and the body to work together, it feels overwhelming. When you disengage, you leave the body in many ways. For many of us, the first time we feel that this disconnect is detrimental is when we are parenting.

The body feels like the source of uncomfortable sensations. The body is what I need to discipline, ignore, deal with, or feel intense shame about. After all, when I'm panicking, my body feels intensely uncomfortable. I remember having the thought when I was in high school, *I need to train my body to listen to me, not the other way around. I must be in charge.* This thought manifested in me not using the bathroom even when I really needed to go or not eating if it would disrupt my schedule. I thought my body was treacherous and needed to be kept strictly in line.

Sometimes that need included controlling my emotional responses. Do you know the sensation of trying to speak rationally, but tears betray you? For many PTPs who experienced narcissistic abuse, sibling abuse, or bullying, this is a familiar sensation. It feels like the ultimate betrayal—even my body isn't on my side!

If you can't trust your body, how can you trust your parental gut instincts? So it's no wonder that disengaged parents find the whole concept of parenting instincts confusing and threatening.

What Disengaged Parenting Looks Like

Disengaged behavior is a flight response from being present. Yet being dissociated or disengaged doesn't mean that you are pulling yourself out of your life in all aspects. That's the "adaptive" part. In fact, you might be very busy all the time. You might be highly successful and productive at work or are known as a really empathetic friend. Some disengaged parents use their busyness as a cover for presence and then try to outsource parenting, letting (or paying) others to do the tasks they feel they aren't very good at. In theory, it's not a terrible idea, and at work it's called "delegating," which is a strategy that's often praised. They might hire a homework tutor, turn to the youth pastors to give their kids the puberty talk, or ask a friend to take their daughter shopping. The tasks will get done, but the problem is you can't outsource presence. There's no substitute for you, and you can't outsource you.

Disengaged and Procrastinating

Being disengaged can also look like procrastinating, in that you're choosing not to engage when you know that you are supposed to be present. Procrastination is a great work-around for guilt, because you're not saying, "I won't attend to my relationship with my child." Instead, you're saying, "I'll be there soon. In five minutes. After this episode. When my task is complete. Tomorrow." The problem is, tomorrows add up. At work, when a deadline is looming, you can put off the work as long as possible, but eventually you have to do it. In parenting, there is no deadline to butt up against. In this case, procrastination isn't the thief of time but the thief of relationships.

Honesty has a way of making us take notice of what we're doing. When we're honest with ourselves, when we disengage and think, *I'm afraid that my damage will damage them, and my solution is I'm going to outsource my parenting* or *I'm just not good at this parenting stuff, so I'm not doing it*, we might feel a sense of guilt, and that guilt may guide us to revisit our decision. Procrastination is the lie that buffers our guilt, because we think, *I will definitely do it . . . soon.* This way, we satisfy the part of ourselves that values presence, that knows our kids need us, and that really does want to be there while also placating our terrified inner child, who is so scared of actually being present, of losing it and yelling, or of somehow contaminating our children with our own shamefulness.

Dissociative procrastination comes in a few flavors:

- Actively avoiding tasks perceived as either boring or hard. I'm not going to lie: parenting is frequently hard and sometimes boring. Avoiding it might seem like an excellent strategy. However, when we avoid parenting, we will feel some sense of shame, which then becomes a cyclical feedback loop. And then your strategy failed you.
- Inexplicably avoiding a task you enjoy because you are afraid that you can't do it "right." This response has elements of perfectionism—procrastinating starting dinner or going on a fun outing with kids, even though it's something you've been looking forward to.
- Scheduling procrastination/dissociation time. This is the parent who is constantly saying to their child, "I'll be with you (build Legos, read you a book, give you a bath, etc.) in five minutes."
- Disengagement disguised as self-care: "I'm taking myself out of the situation so I can take care of myself and not hurt anybody else."

Disengaged and Unproductive

Other disengaged parents are literally doing too little, sitting on the couch watching TV or scrolling through their social feeds while their kids are unsupervised. This is different than the paralyzed parent, who is busy being unproductive (starting a million tasks but finishing none). Disengagement is unproductive busyness (reading a cookbook instead of cooking).

My patient Louise relates: "I can literally sit on the couch, watching some celebrity chef demonstrate how to debone a duck, while playing a cooking game on my phone, and also be ordering pizza for my kid's supper, because I'm stressed out and I need to detach from the world. I know there's something off-balance about that, but I can't help myself. Why can't I just cook actual food for my actual children?"

The thought of shutting off the cooking show and her game is too stressful. I asked Louise what would happen if she turned off and tuned into her kids. She replied, "No way. Then my actual thoughts would come flooding in, and I would feel so stressed out."

Disengaged and Screens

Disengaged parents love screens and screen time for themselves and their kids. It's like having a babysitter for free! I was once getting a manicure and a mom walked in with her daughter, a very little girl, maybe five years old. Instead of sitting next to her daughter and chatting while they were getting their nails done—the activity—the mom set the girl up with a screen and walked to a chair farther away to get a pedicure, where she promptly put in her earbuds and began watching something on her phone. In essence, the mom disengaged twice in one beat: she separated herself from her child and then separated her child from the full experience of having a manicure. Ironically, I heard her tell the manicurist, "My daughter and I are having a girl's day." In structure, yes. In function, absolutely not. Remember the acceptance and commitment therapy (ACT) question, *Are you moving away from or toward your values?* Was this mom moving away from or toward her relationship with her child?

Watching a movie together can absolutely be a shared activity that moves us toward each other. Teaching a child to dissociate from what should be an exciting and bonding experience gives us the appearance of a "girl's day" but doesn't strengthen the relationship at all!

Ironically, parents like Louise are very busy; it's just a less productive busyness. Disengaged parents have learned to be *humans doing* and are deathly afraid of being *humans being*. Louise isn't any different from a workaholic who is avoiding parenting with a socially acceptable reason.

Disengaged Parents and Addictions

Disengaged parents are likely to have addictions because addictions are the essence of unproductive busyness: these parents are so busy seeking the addictive substance or experience that they are not engaging in their values or being present. For instance, people who drink a lot are often doing it to quiet their mind and avoid their stress.

When we think "addiction," we think substances. Alcoholism and drugs are indeed addictions. But there are many addictions that people don't view as such or view as relatively harmless. Some addictions, like workaholism or exercising to the point of obsession, are even praised. Yet in many ways, an addiction to work and an addiction to alcohol can be identical when we think of the function. Workaholism is a "respectable" addiction; the hustle mentality and the whole "I'll sleep when I'm dead" mantra sounds so productive and goal oriented. But what's the function? If the function is "to escape areas of my life that feel less successful," then working all the time is not all that different than getting drunk or high.

Busyness is a common engaged parent addiction. Many disengaged parents have low grade depression that feels like static in the background of their life: social worker Patrick Teahan calls this "refrigerator buzz depression."[1] When a disengaged parent is busy, it gives them a boost and keeps them from being present. They are the kings and queens of multitasking. But multitasking is a myth: you really can't focus on two things at the same time. It's an illusion that we are multitasking, but the brain is really switching between the two activities without ever putting its full attention on either. Disengaged parents tend to multitask as a validation of their existence, but parenting requires your full attention.

You could be a stay-at-home mom and be a totally disengaged parent, busying yourself with home decor or gardening. There are people who chronically underearn so that they can always be busy: they pass up or don't apply for promotions because then they would have more free time, so they stay in a lower-level job. Others feel that when they are busy at work, they don't have time to connect with their emotions.

You can even have an addiction to volunteering, thinking, *My kids don't need me; these people need me, and I won't harm them. No one can shame me for spending time away from my kids, because I'm doing something important.* This also can leave children with an uncomfortable legacy: *How can I object to my parent volunteering? I have enough to eat and she's off feeding the hungry.*

For some disengaged parents, there's a gray line between substance use and substance abuse. This is where mommy wine culture appears. It's having that extra glass of wine with dinner to carry you through the evening or a Benadryl with a beer chaser to help you sleep. You might think, *I need to take the edge off, because my edges are really sharp. My edge might come out and injure someone. I'm drinking to protect you.*

Disengaged and Tired

Insomnia or Phobia of Sleeping?

Disengaged parents often have sleep issues, because lying down still means you have time to think. Instead, they go to bed when they're falling down, exhausted. That was very much me for a long time.

I have three problems when it comes to sleep. I have a hard time believing in the possibility of tomorrow, so it's difficult for me to recognize that my day is done and any tasks left undone can wait. Some of this is an addiction to busyness as a way to avoid thinking, and some of this is true doubt in my future self, which is common in PTSD. I'm also incredibly phobic of my bed, because my trauma story revolves around beds and sleep. I was woken out of a sound sleep—by the sound of my mother screaming—to perform CPR on my dying father only to have him die in front of me. Beds became a rather triggering place. As a teenager, I couldn't understand why I had panic attacks the instant I would lie down or why my brain would play an awful highlight reel of my father's death as soon as I would close my eyes. I now know that this was my trauma app, warning me not to sleep too deeply (hypervigilance) so I could protect myself and my children.

I finally went for a sleep study and found that I don't actually have insomnia. It turns out that I'm an extremely light sleeper. In fact, once I'm in bed, I can fall asleep fairly quickly and I wake up again just as quickly. So I've put processes in place to make sure I can sleep through the night.

Does Your Body Feel Polluted?

Certain forms of trauma can make your body feel polluted, toxic, or shameful. This feeling might come from being parentified as a child, being bullied or sexually abused, or being the "glass" or "invisible" child in a family (where there's another child with more intense needs) or the scapegoated sibling of a "golden" child, any form of trauma where your body was in some way the source of the problem. It could be physical abuse. It could be fat shaming. It could be neurodivergence. It could be anything where you feel like there is something in your fundamental physical makeup that is wrong.

Our kids do a lot of pulling us back into our bodies—there are sticky embraces, the need to carry babies and toddlers, the need to physically care for kids when they're sick. They want to roughhouse, to dance with us, and for us to sit on the floor with them and play. When our kids try to pull us back into our bodies, but our bodies are the source of shame, then staying away from our kids as much as possible makes a lot of sense. Thanks again, trauma app!

Think about your own relationship with sleep. Do you truly have insomnia, or are you afraid of being "unbusy" or afraid of your own thoughts? Do you shame and blame yourself for procrastinating around bedtime, feeling like you're shortchanging your children (or yourself) of that rested, calm experience?

Amy and James Were Disengaged

I met Amy years ago at a women's entrepreneurship event, and we immediately became friends. Amy is one of the most impressive humans I have ever met. I feel impostor syndrome just reciting the story of her life. Amy came to this country from China as a teenager. She could not speak a word of English. Not only did she become completely fluent, but she also attended Ivy League schools for both her undergraduate and graduate degrees. Both Amy and her husband, James, are professionals, each with their own prestigious careers. Amy also founded a nonprofit organization for a cause she feels passionate about, helping underprivileged women start their own businesses. She's also gorgeous, an incredibly skilled tennis player, and a beast in the gym. Anything she does, she does not only well but also impeccably.

As much as I enjoy their company, I have never seen parents as disengaged as Amy and James. They have an eight-year-old daughter, Sonia, and a fifteen-year-old son, Henry. They have a slew of people they've hired to take care of their kids because they are always so busy. There is a homework tutor, a cook, a housekeeper, a professional organizer, and even a personal shopper. They never take family vacations, even day trips, because they're so overcommitted. It's just never a good time.

Over the years, I've become Amy's "parenting whisperer." I think I'm the only person she talks about anything imperfect with. One day, she confided that she doesn't have much of a relationship with Henry. She knows that he's a good kid, but he seems almost disinterested in his parents. While she chalked up his attitude as typical teenage boy behavior, she began to notice that she wasn't really connecting with Sonia either, and she was worried that Sonia would end up distancing herself from Amy, the way Henry had. Amy told me, "I can't believe how little I know of her life. She's closer to her homework tutor than she is to me—I always see them laughing together. But when I try to talk with her, I get nothing. The conversation goes nowhere."

Amy is the type of person who learns by doing, so I suggested that she needed to make some time each day to play together, even if it was just fifteen minutes. Immediately, her eyes lit up: she thought it was a great idea! She promised to check back in with me after the weekend to let me know how it went.

The following week, Amy and I met for coffee. I asked how the family game time went, and she said,

> It was a disaster! James and I decided to teach Sonia how to play chess. I was taught to play chess in China as part of our curriculum, and James was taught to play by his grandfather. We used to play all the time when we were dating. But Sonia wasn't interested! She kept fidgeting and squirming. She didn't like all my helpful feedback, and when I explained the rules for how each piece has a particular move, she kept getting frustrated and confused. When she was playing me and it was clear she was about to lose, she got up from the table, and I told her she needs to exhibit good gamesmanship and finish the game, even though she's losing. She exploded and threw her queen at me and stormed off. It's obvious I don't have the patience to be

> around little kids. That's why I hire homework tutors. Maybe I should enroll her in chess classes?

Sigh. There was so much to unpack here. It was clear that Amy knew that she had messed up and that her trauma app was doubling down on the solution—hire another teacher, disengage, outsource, and delegate yet more. I asked Amy gently if she understood what the function of game time was supposed to be. If it was very important that Sonia learn how to play chess, because it's a game that teaches life skills, math, or strategic thinking, then chess wasn't ever going to be a connection opportunity, and it certainly wasn't going to be fun playtime.

I explained, "Amy, when I said play with your kids, I meant to do something at their level. The function of playing a family game is being present together. Choose something like Candy Land, or baking cookies, or an age-appropriate puzzle. Any game that requires mastery is not play, especially with people who are competitive by nature. Chess is only play when you're at an equal level, or at least you are both very proficient. In the learning stages, it's never going to feel like play."

Amy started to cry. She said:

> I really don't know how to do this parenting thing. I'm terrible at it. I'm impatient and critical and I can be downright mean. I've heard that my whole life. As a kid, my parents would fight about me constantly. I could never make my mother happy. On the one hand, I had to reflect well on her, which meant succeeding and getting good grades. On the other hand, she hated my success, and she would point out all the flaws in me, and how they came from my father and his side of the family. She used criticizing ME as a way to needle HIM.
>
> I can't explain it, she was a good mother. In our elementary school, she won the "best parent award" every year. I'm so disloyal, making her sound bad. The only thing I'm mad at her about is divorcing my father and later, one of her boyfriends made me feel uncomfortable. When I told her about it, she took his side instead of mine.

I can't diagnose Amy's mother without meeting her, but it sounded like there were some strong elements of narcissism in her. It makes so much sense that Amy is afraid of her body and her sharp edges, her tendency to criticize, and her anger and frustration. It makes so much sense that Amy feels polluted, shameful, and in some ways, harmful. Of course, she's outsourcing her parenting—her trauma app taught her how to be productive, how to delegate, and how to dissociate with busyness. Deep down, she's protecting both of her children from the greatest danger in the world, herself.

How to Reengage

To remove this sense of being polluted so that you can reengage with your child, embrace the idea that neither you nor your body is problematic. You're actually not the biggest danger your child can face, you are not irredeemably damaged, and therefore, you do not need to be kept away from your kids. Actually, you're not all that special! In fact, you are surprisingly predictable.

Whatever specific trauma you experienced—in childhood or adulthood—the mark it leaves feels very unique, like a stigma. Yet as you go through a healing journey, especially on social media, or when you're reading a lot of self-help books, you may start to realize how predictable certain patterns are. In other words, you're not uniquely damaged and entirely toxic. You're having a predictable response to challenging life experiences—a normal response to an abnormal circumstance. So you aren't abnormally unfit to parent. Your children will be okay around you, even when you make mistakes. All they really want, after all, is your presence.

Try any or all of the following exercises. Some will help you get out of your mind and into your body, which is helpful because of the embodied nature of parenting. This allows you to undo that sense of your body as polluted, shameful, harmful, or wrong.

Fix #1: No matter what shameful thoughts or feelings you've had, all your thoughts are welcome. You are allowed to think your thoughts and feel your feelings. As we've seen in earlier chapters, you can acknowledge them and then move on as best as you can.

Fix #2: Fall in love with your body by arranging a "meet-cute" with yourself. In other words, get to know your body. Reacquaint yourself with the sensations your body produces: these sensations are meant to be helpful, not painful, and certainly not indicators that anything is wrong.

For me, getting in touch with my body coincided with the time my son told me he's scared of my dissociation. At the time, I was diagnosed as morbidly obese (I didn't exercise because I associated the sensation of a pounding heart with panic attacks, and my eating ranged from "not at all" to "highly emotional") and I was having some health challenges. I had a dissertation chair and mentor, Dr. Ester Buchholz, who had a lot of health issues herself. At one point, I was talking to her about an event I didn't attend because I had an asthma attack. She looked at me and said, "Robyn, you have asthma, arthritis, and digestive issues. Your body is doing its level best to kill you, which means it's trying to tell you something. When are you gonna listen?"

That was the wakeup call I needed to get into a healthier relationship with my body. The first way I reintroduced myself to my body was with exercise. When you're exercising intensely, your body will make itself known. Your lungs cry out for air; you get thirsty and sweaty and hot. You feel the pleasant ache in your muscles as they move in ways they're not accustomed to. Most importantly, your stress response becomes your friend. That adrenaline boost that gets you through the last set or the last mile, the slight elevation in cortisol that the adaptive stress of moving provides, the way your system is flooded with endorphins afterward, which pairs the stress responses with something pleasant. All this can be a way to meet your body again, to renegotiate your relationship with it.

The second way I made peace with my body was with sensation training. I learned to eat and drink mindfully, like sucking on an ice cube and tracing the ice-cold sensation trickling down my throat. The idea is to learn to tune back into body sensations, not just to turn them off as soon as you feel them.

Fix #3: Try progressive muscle relaxation (PMR). This is a technique for people who can't get to sleep, where you lie down and engage and release each of your muscles. This practice is pretty embodying because you have to feel all your body parts and welcome them as though you are loving a newborn baby. You're activating each muscle and joint, and it's also relaxing. When I first learned this method, I thought, *This is not going to work for me. This is never gonna put me to sleep.* But surprisingly, it does. It can take as many as ten repetitions of PMR before you feel the relaxation, so don't give up too soon. I've used PMR at bedtime with my children, which is an incredible way to create mirroring and attunement, help them relax and feel grateful for their bodies, and remind me how grateful I am for them.

There are many guided PMR meditations available online. Choose the one that works best for you. My website (drrobynkoslowitz.com) offers links to a few of my favorites.

Fix #4: In ACT, the chessboard metaphor shows how many PTPs think. Every time you have a good thought about yourself, or your relationship with your kids, an opposite and equally painful thought might arise. You might think, *I stayed so patient with my kids during that dreaded homework hour, even when my first grader had a meltdown about her homework.* Immediately, the thought *Yeah, but yesterday you yelled at her when she spilled milk all over your clothes and you were late* might pop up. These competing thoughts can go on forever: your brain is equally capable of creating as many positive thoughts as negative thoughts. But what if you realize that you are not only your positive thoughts or negative thoughts? You are the chessboard: your function is to hold the thoughts.

Let's engage in this metaphor as a journaling exercise. On a piece of paper, make two columns. In one, write down your love for your kids and the positive actions you've engaged in with them. Immediately, conflicting evidence is going to arise. In the second column, write down your shaming, negative thoughts. When you can see on a piece of paper your positive and negative thoughts, it makes the chessboard metaphor much more visible. You have love. You engage in positive actions. You also sometimes engage in negative actions. But you are neither. You are the chessboard. All the negative thoughts are just thoughts.

Fix #5: Play with your kids. Chapter 11 features play tips that are geared for each stage of development to get you started. For now, just know that even if you have no idea how to play, your kid will do all the heavy lifting. The truth is, you don't have to do a thing. You don't have to use your imagination. When you have a tea party with a three-year-old, they will script your every line. Your child may say, "Mom, now you say, 'More cookies, please.'" And you'll say, "More cookies, please," and your child will pass the cookies.

So many of my PTP patients don't realize that just like anything else, they can end play with kids. Some moms have even voiced the concern that they would be "trapped in a tea party forever." The truth is you won't, and more importantly, you can stop when you're ready to stop and schedule play and presence. Try this exercise: set your phone timer for ten minutes. Tell your child you can play for ten minutes and then the game is over. Your child might protest, and that's okay. It doesn't mean that you did play wrong; it just means that they were enjoying themselves. This way you've taught your inner child and your real child that there is always tomorrow.

Fix #6: Prescribe imperfection. I write an intentionally throw-away paragraph every time I sit down to write. Then I write what I want to work on, getting all my thoughts down. Rather than trying to create the perfect opening, I write the rest, and then I go back.

If the thought of being a perfect parent is holding you back, knowing that no one is perfect may open the door for you to just be yourself. You're going to make mistakes, and you're going to get over them. The best thing you can do is be present.

How Amy Reengaged

Amy and I discussed some options for her to become more available to both her children. I suggested that she set up scheduled time each day when she and Sonia would play and when she would touch base with her son. She's already an athletic woman, so I suggested that she renegotiate her relationship with her body with the help of a somatic therapist who understands how to work with trauma and the body.

Over the years, Amy's hard edges have softened. She makes time to play with Sonia—playing games that Sonia enjoys. She actually took an entire day off work to attend a pop music concert with Sonia, despite her own tastes running more toward the classical. She told me, "I didn't enjoy the music, but I didn't tell Sonia. But I loved watching how happy Sonia was. We bought matching T-shirts. We ate junk food. We screamed and sang. Having fun with her—that part was fun!"

Reengaging teaches you that you are not the problem, you are not the enemy, and you are not polluted. It will help you get back in touch with yourself and help you reengage in every aspect of your life. You'll be better able to bring your whole self into your parenting. And you'll see that when your trauma app is quieted, your whole self is pretty incredible.

If You Have an Addiction

If "mommy juice" isn't just taking the edge off or if workaholism, exercise, volunteering, shopping, or other substances are starting to become a barrier between you and your kids, take it as a wakeup call to get help.

For many PTPs, kids are the impetus to get clean, sober, and healthy. I've heard many stories—from the patient whose emotional eating and bingeing/purging made her smell so bad that her toddler didn't want cuddles to the patient who drove her kids while mildly inebriated and ended up in a car accident, the workaholic whose son said he shouldn't bother coming to his graduation because it's not like he knows him very well, and my own son, who told me that my dissociation was obvious and hurtful. That wakeup call is terrifying, but ultimately, it provides that moment of clarity that we need. If your kids have forcibly yanked you out of denial, stay there. Get help. There are so many resources available, and you'd be surprised how accessible and affordable they can be. There are also online and anonymous options. Remember, it's never too late to repair. And there will never be a better reason.

CHAPTER 7

The Paralyzed Parent

My patient Maria called me up in a panic. "Dr. K, when it comes to parenting, I know I need to do something, but I don't know what that something is. It's like there's secret information the other parents have that has passed me by. Most of the time I end up panicking, then I freeze, and don't do anything at all. Or I'm running around screaming at my kids and nothing about their behavior changes. I don't have any sort of plan for interacting with my kids. I never did. I just react all the time. The only thing I do know about parenting is that I'm doing it all wrong."

Whenever I hear this set of frustrations from my patients like Maria, I know that their trauma app is frozen. These parents are paralyzed—mentally, they're working very hard, but there's not a lot of purposeful action happening. Or they seem frantically busy, rushing around from task to task, tending to the loudest voice in the room, and perpetually in crisis mode. They don't look paralyzed; they look frenetic. If you look closely, you'll see a lot of effort but not a lot of effectiveness: flurries of reactivity and moments of frozen exhaustion. I call this type of behavior *glitching* because it's wonky, like a video that's not running smoothly.

Glitching results from an attempt to do two opposite things at the same time: running toward a child to smooth over the problem and running away from them in fear. And because these are two opposite reactions, we glitch and do nothing of consequence.

The paralyzed parents whom I've spoken to come from two distinct (and occasionally overlapping) groups: those who are terrified of "big emotions" and those who are terrified of their parenting instincts, because they were robbed of a sense of *discernment*, the ability to use good judgment to decide the best course of action in a situation.

Understanding Your Behavior

Paralyzed Parents Freeze and Fawn

To understand why paralyzed parents glitch, let's investigate Stephen Porges's polyvagal theory.[1] He realized that the prevailing understanding

What Does Paralyzed Parenting Look Like?

- Standing still or doing nothing when there is an upset or crisis
- Moving around a lot but ineffectively
- Half-completing actions with little or no follow through; making empty threats of punishment or unfulfilled rewards
- Constantly changing your mind, especially when reacting to children's protests
- Walking on eggshells as to not upset anybody
- Sticking your head in the sand; focusing on one aspect of a situation and disregarding other aspects
- Screaming, not as a form of discipline but out of panic, desperation, or frustration
- Playing whack-a-mole by inserting yourself into situations that you don't need to be a part of, to head off an imagined disaster
- Rapidly shifting focus that looks like a lack of focus

of trauma and its stress response was not always about "fight or flight"—when we're in a dangerous situation, we are programmed to either run or fight back. But what happens to children who face ongoing, chronic danger at home and that danger isn't a robber or a fire but Mom or Dad (or in adulthood, dealing with mounting bills or a toxic spouse)? We're not talking about the occasional fights with parents; we're talking about parents who are emotionally unstable or are easily provoked by normal child behavior, turning it into truly disproportionate and dangerous reactions. For some people, the nervous system goes to a different stress response, one that creates immobilization, where they either freeze or fawn to restore their sense of safety. Their trauma app develops a solution and creates a command: "When emotionally *dysregulated* people—the ones whose big emotions become everyone else's problem—are around, shut that dysregulation down." Sometimes, that involves freezing, simply not making a situation worse. Sometimes, that involves fawning, which is people-pleasing or placating—reactively calming the loudest voice in the room—with the goal of always keeping emotions small. Paralyzed parents most typically straddle between the freeze and fawn responses.

Freezing and fawning are both reactive responses: they are not conscious or purposeful. You're never moving the conversation or confrontation forward, teaching your child a new skill, or instilling one of your parenting or family values—you're only a barometer of an impending emotional storm, a receptacle of negativity, and soother of other's emotions.

You might be thinking, *Well, I'm definitely a people pleaser. I'm not paralyzed, because I'm doing something.* With fawning, even though you're actively people pleasing, you are still immobilized because you can only fawn based on another person's experience. When you're a people pleaser, the goal is to avoid troubled waters. The best way to ensure calmness is to shut down other people's emotional responses, starting by placating the most "threatening" person in the room—the one with the biggest emotions.

Your parent's behaviors were not your fault. But it is your responsibility to shift the lens from *Where did I learn this?* to *What would I like to believe instead? What capacities would I like to develop now?* Let's understand why your trauma app created this algorithm, so that we can deselect these permissions and expand our repertoire of coping responses. In order to do so, you have to understand what's triggering you in the first place. Paralyzed parents don't always have the same triggers, yet I believe they can be grouped thematically.

Trigger #1

Big Emotions

The paralyzed parent is often someone who grew up being very attentive to the emotional undercurrents in their family and got the message that managing everybody else's emotions was their job and their problem. And the truth is that in that situation, keeping everyone placated and making sure emotions stay small was a smart thing to do! It's very likely that there was overt abuse happening: physical or psychological traumas experienced by the person or someone else in the family. Perhaps they had an angry, abusive parent who took their stress out on the rest of the family, so from a very young age, they learned that angry people are dangerous and must be placated at all costs or that bad things happen when people express their emotions. They learned to be constantly on the lookout for emotional outbursts, but they may not have learned how to deal with them or make them go away.

When you're a child in this type of environment, you are trying to quash a potential situation before it happens, because you've seen what could happen if things get out of control. You take on the role of the person who is always smoothing the troubled waters.

When you, as a paralyzed parent, are confronted with other people's emotions, the trauma app responds: *If bad things happen when people express emotions, and my child is expressing emotions, I am in danger, so those emotions need to be shut down.* In practice, your response is to fawn, or placate—to do whatever it takes to shut down the child's emotions and restore calmness. Your go-to strategy might be giving in or distracting them. Even if you're yelling at your kids to stop yelling, you are people-pleasing, because you're trying to shut down their emotions.

Paralyzed parents often confuse "placating" with "soothing." Placating is people-pleasing, while soothing means empathizing with the child's emotions in real time and is one aspect of how we teach them to calm themselves down.

Soothing is a healthy strategy for *co-regulation*: the way a parent shares their own calm with their child by providing support, guidance, and emotional sturdiness. Co-regulation is a collaborative process where the child and adult work together to regulate the child's emotions. If a child experiences enough co-regulation, they learn how to self-regulate. A mother who is soothing a crying baby will instinctively rock the baby while talking to them, and as she's talking to her baby, she's talking to herself. As she co-regulates, she can self-regulate. Not only does the baby's nervous system start to calm down, but the mom's does as well. Both heartbeats start to slow, to beat in a similar rhythm. This is the basis of *attunement*. Attunement is a building block of attachment—it's when two people's nervous systems are in sync. Research using functional near-infrared spectroscopy (fNIRS), a type of technology that can measure brain-wave activity in real time, shows that when a parent is truly attuned to their child, their brain waves sync up.[2] Attunement is soothing and healing for both the child and the parent. Each feels seen and accepted by the other.

Yet when you are placating, you're doing the opposite. You're not in sync with your child; you're trying to shut down your child's emotions. When you are placating instead of soothing, you are also inadvertently teaching your children to fear big emotions, because you are confirming their own fear.

Now, you might be thinking, *Dr. K, you're saying that I people-please and placate, but what am I supposed to do instead? Isn't it my job to help my kids with their emotions? Don't I have to make sure my home is emotionally safe?*

Sure. But let's understand a fundamental truth—emotions can sometimes be intense, uncomfortable, and inconvenient, but they're never unsafe. In fact, emotions have one purpose: they are a signal system. They exist to teach us something important about the world. Emotions are our body's way of conveying a message to us, sometimes before our conscious brain has figured out what's going on. Sometimes, they do that by making us feel physically uncomfortable sensations. For example, we might feel a sense of fear and heightened awareness and then notice that there's a threatening person standing too close to us. Our sensory system and body perceived danger and sent us a message via the emotional system to take an action. In their most basic form,

- the function of fear is to keep you alive;
- the function of joy is to tell you that an experience was positive and good for you, so you should do it again;
- the function of love is to enhance connection;
- the function of sadness is to identify loss;
- the function of guilt is to let you know you did something wrong and need to repair it;
- the function of anger is to identify a problem or a boundary;
- the function of disgust is to keep you away from toxicity; and
- the function of envy and jealousy is to show you what you want or value.

Often, the emotion signal system comes along with some discomfort, and we learn to shut down our emotions in an effort to block out that discomfort. No one loves how panic, anger, or sadness feels inside their body, and our brains often mistake "discomfort" with "danger." But none of those sensations are dangerous. However, if no one taught us this fundamental concept, it makes sense that we'd be afraid of our emotional responses.

Here's a truth all parents have to accept—little humans will sometimes be upset. They will sometimes be mad at you; they will sometimes say they hate you or that you're the meanest parent in the world. They will sometimes have meltdowns, and that doesn't mean you've done anything wrong. They are allowed to have big, uncomfortable, messy emotions. Intellectually, you may know this. But check within: Does your trauma app get it? Or is your trauma app set up so that "Big emotions equal danger. Shut down at all costs, no matter what"?

When we ignore our own emotions and try to stuff them down, they grow and intensify. That's how a mild annoyance becomes anger and ultimately becomes rage. If we had handled the situation at the "mild annoyance" level, we never would have gotten to rage.

And once we realize that we can tolerate the discomfort of other people's and our own emotions and act in accordance with our values, we can help our kids learn to deal with *their* emotions as well.

Tiny Meditation

The Sky and the Weather

One solution to shut down paralysis is to understand that emotions are not threatening. Emotions are like the weather: they are here now, but they will always pass. Even if they are uncomfortable, you're going to be fine.

The following is an ACT exercise inspired by Steven Hayes.[3] If you're not alarmed by your emotions, the trauma app can't take over. The trauma app can take over only when you panic, which sets all its permissions to "on" and allows it to take control.

Read the following aloud whenever you feel overwhelmed by your own big emotions or the big emotions around you:

> I am the sky. My emotions are the weather. My emotions will come and go, but I, the container of the emotions, am not actually changed by them. Weather passes across the sky. Weather can be dramatic! It can be stormy. It can be very sunny. It can thunder! The weather changes, but the sky remains the same. The sky holds the weather, but it is not the weather, and it is not changed by the weather. As scary as it seems, a storm could be terrifying, but it's just a storm that will pass. Emotions are not scary because emotions pass across my mind and body, but they don't change my mind and body. A storm is terrifying. Good weather is beautiful and glorious, but the sky remains

the same. I am not the weather. I am not my big emotions. I'm the sky. I hold them, but I am not changed by them.

How Children Respond to Paralyzed Parents Triggered by Big Emotions

Because the paralyzed parent is afraid of big emotions—that's why they are trying to constantly calm everyone down—they can unintentionally teach their children to fear their own big emotions. The unintended consequence of paralyzed parenting is that the children are often emotionally dysregulated and have a hard time dealing with their own, often out-of-control emotions. The children don't know how to respond to the unpredictability of their parent; they then become afraid of their own emotions and can cry or act out even more. Sometimes, emotionally dysregulated children appear angry, disruptive, or mean. Can you see the dysregulation under the "angry, disruptive, mean" presentation and have compassion now that you understand the underlying cause?

Children are looking to their parents to help co-regulate their emotional responses, but when they can't count on their parents to do so, they never develop a sense of proportionality. They can never match the scale of the emotional response to the situation in an appropriate manner.

Or because the paralyzed parent is so on edge—always scanning for big emotions, always trying to head off or anticipate trouble—they have little time for conscious decision-making and, in effect, are always "winging it" when it comes to parenting. When paralyzed parents complain to me about their children, they often say: "I hear myself saying, 'This is your first warning. This is your last warning. This is your last, last, last, last warning.'" The problem here is that children of a paralyzed parent realize that they are in fact running the household, because their parent lacks *sturdiness*. Dr. Becky Kennedy refers to this as "sturdy leadership" in her book *Good Inside*.[4] Instead of being a firm support to rely on, where no means no and yes means yes, the parent's no is flimsy and easily dismissed. Their parent becomes just as overwhelmed by big emotions as they do.

A child is looking for their parent to signal safety and competence, to be the lighthouse in the safe harbor. When a child is overcome by terror—or fury—they want a parent who says, "It's okay. You're feeling mad right now. Let's handle that together." They don't want a parent who frantically attempts to placate them, because that just signals that they were right and their emotions really are terrifying.

Sometimes, children inadvertently take advantage of that situation, subconsciously threatening big emotions in an attempt to get their way. These are children who don't accept a no or have a meltdown whenever they're thwarted. They have learned *if my parents are afraid of my big emotions and I want my way, I can threaten to unleash those big emotions, and then I get what I want.* While this feels good in the moment, it can also feel very scary, because success means that their big emotions really are too much to handle.

I know that no parent wants their child to be outwardly aggressive but inwardly insecure, dysregulated, or overwhelmed. And I know that parents want to build relationships with their children in a way that's aligned with their values. If this description fits your behavior, don't fear: I know exactly how to get paralyzed parents unstuck and manage their trauma app permissions.

Maria Was Paralyzed

Maria came into my office in tears. She told me,

> Dr. K, yesterday was especially bad. My first grader pushed my toddler, and I start to yell at him that "we don't push in this family." I'm supposed to teach him not to hit, right? Then the toddler is screaming because she is hurt, so I go to pick her up and comfort her, but by then, my first grader ran outside, yelling that he hates me, and I didn't get to deal with what happened. My whole body was tense, and I was scared that if I ran after him, I would grab him too hard or even slap him. Meanwhile, my eleven-year-old daughter was whining that she wants to watch this violent movie that her friend saw, and I am not sure I'm comfortable with her watching it, and I haven't had a chance to think it over or to discuss it with my husband. I snap at her to stop whining, but I really wasn't angry at her; I was just overwhelmed because my toddler is inconsolable and the first grader is MIA. Now she's insulted and she's grumping around and making snarky comments. I told her that I'm sorry

> I yelled at her, but I wouldn't have to yell if she wasn't so rude. Then I said she can watch the movie, to make it up to her. I'm also trying to make dinner. The house is a wreck. I can't even figure out what to do first. My heart is pounding, and I can't take much more of this. My husband hates coming home to chaos, so I'm trying to clean up while tuning out my daughter's really loud and violent movie, my internal shame and guilt that I'm letting her watch it. Am I the worst mother in the world? Don't they all see how I'm trying to make them all happy? So what did I do? I promised that I would bake my son his favorite cookies to lure him inside and calm down, and I scolded my daughter for her snarky behavior, but then I apologized and brought her a snack when she burst into tears. But first, I made myself a sandwich and took an hour to watch the latest Real Housewives episode, because this day had turned so awful that I deserved some "me" time.

Can you see Maria's paralysis? Can you see how Maria was attempting to shut down all the emotions in the room while also trying to soothe the toddler, clean up for her husband, and negotiate with her middle school child? Can you see where Maria's trauma app took over? Instead of focusing on one situation at a time—simply soothing the toddler for now—she tried to manage the emotions of everyone else.

Maria was triggered when her first grader was misbehaving and then again when her older daughter was being rude. Like other paralyzed parents, she was afraid of challenging behavior because she was afraid of the big emotion that must be coming. So instead of parenting, the paralyzed parent will fall back to placating. Do you see how she was placating both the first grader and the eleven-year-old?

When there is an argument, paralyzed parents will also placate afterward, as in, "I'm sorry I yelled at you, but if you wouldn't get so loud, rude, and disrespectful, I wouldn't need to yell at you." This response is placating because the parent is trying to get the child to forgive them. But think about what this teaches—it tells children that they're responsible for adult emotions and adult behaviors.

"I'm sorry I yelled at you" is a valid and thoughtful response from any parent. It signals that as parents, we know that sometimes, all humans have big emotions, and sometimes, those big emotions lead us to make the wrong choice. We are effectively saying to our children, "As an adult who makes choices, I'm going to take responsibility for making the wrong one."

Is It My Job to Make My Kid Happy?

Paralyzed parents often believe that their behavior is normal and that their job in life is to make everyone feel comfortable. I very often hear paralyzed parents identify themselves as "empaths." While it may be true that they understand very well how other people feel, they aren't going about addressing their feelings in a productive way. In fact, one frequent result is that the paralyzed parent inserts themselves into all kinds of places they're not supposed to be in.

When children are fighting, paralyzed parents often attempt to intervene, because their trauma app is on high alert: "Conflict equals danger. Must stop conflict!" Here's the thing: it's not your job to stop your children from fighting! It's your job to teach your children how to have a *productive* fight. Psychologist Adam Grant says in his Ted Talk that a productive fight is not "you vs. me." It's "you and me, vs. the problem."[5] If Maria's daughter is upset about her parent's rules for appropriate movies, the problem that can be productively resolved is which movies are acceptable, and how we can make that determination. The problem might be "My friends tease me when I don't get to watch the movies they do." But the problem isn't Maria. The problem isn't "Mom," and the problem isn't "the "daughter." The problem is the problem.

When a child is in a grumpy, shutdown, or discontented mood, the paralyzed parent rushes in to "cheer them up," "snap them out of it," or even "talk it through." It's not a parent's job to "snap them out of it" when children are working through tough emotions. It's their job to signal availability for when the child is ready to talk. Maybe the child just needs some processing time before asking for adult intervention.

News flash: it is not the job of a parent to make a child happy. The job of a parent is to teach a child how to handle their emotions so that they are safe and how to have a safe and productive conflict. If your four-year-old is bopping your two-year-old over the head with a toy truck, you need to intervene. But your job is not to set life up in such a way that they never fight. Children need to learn how to share resources, compromise, or pick a different activity.

The next phrase, "if you wouldn't get so loud, rude, and disrespectful, I wouldn't need to yell at you," is a totally different conversation that has nothing to do with the "I'm sorry I yelled at you" conversation. This is not a conversation about boundaries and about the child's choices: it is people-pleasing. It's perfectly acceptable to say to a child, "You are allowed to be mad and you are allowed to do a lot of things with your mad, but you're not allowed to attack me with your mad." It's perfectly okay to give a child healthy alternatives for what they can do when they're mad, but that conversation has nothing to do with the "I'm sorry I yelled at you" one.

The Fix for Handling Big Emotions

Normalizing Emotions and Mastering Co-Regulation

I told Maria that she could get herself out of paralysis when she was ready to acknowledge the first problem, which was her own lack of

Exercise: I Can Tolerate Discomfort (Big Emotions) in Service of a Goal

Here's an exercise I use with my patients to prove that emotional discomfort isn't dangerous or intolerable. Get yourself a treat and an ice cube and set a timer for five minutes.

Hold the ice cube tightly in the palm of one hand. You are going to hold onto it for five minutes. If you can do so, you can have the treat when you are done.

First, ask yourself what your hand would say to your brain if it could talk. It might say, "This is uncomfortable! Let go! I'm cold!"

Now, think about what your brain would say back, knowing that there is a reward for holding onto the ice cube. Would your brain say, "It's just a little uncomfortable. I really want the treat! I can do this. Five minutes isn't so long. It's worth it!"

Were you surprised to see those five minutes pass relatively quickly? Congratulations—as you savor your treat, bask in your newfound knowledge that you can, indeed, tolerate discomfort in service of a goal. That means you can tolerate the discomfort of your emotions without having to shut them down. You can ask them what they've come to tell you instead.

self-regulation. She was so used to shutting emotions down by placating the most dysregulated person in the room, numbing with food, or distracting herself using reality TV (or a combination of the latter two!). I explained that what she thought of as self-care was really anesthetizing herself, avoiding the issues, and keeping her in paralysis.

I started having Maria journal about her emotions: her fear when her first grader hit her toddler, her anger at the unfair criticism by her daughter and unrealistic expectations by her husband, her disgust at cleaning up her house that was, by all accounts, truly filthy. Then we went through each emotion to see what it was trying to teach her. She began to see that it's okay to be afraid when children's behavior turns dangerous. Yes, children are lovable, but we're allowed to be disgusted by the trail of dirt they leave behind. That mess doesn't mean we love them less. And yes, it's okay to be angry when someone treats you unfairly. In other words, she was experiencing completely normal emotions as reactions to stressful situations.

Once Maria could separate three things—the emotion, the bodily sensations associated with the emotion, and the "action urge" the emotion gave her—I was able to explain that feeling an emotion doesn't mean we have to necessarily act on it immediately. Just because Maria was angry at her daughter and feeling incredibly guilty for yelling at her doesn't mean that she had to resolve the situation immediately. She could wait, process the situation, and decide what would be the wisest course of action that aligns with her parenting values. I explained to Maria that sometimes, emotions are uncomfortable. No one likes the feeling of their heart pounding in fear, their stomach churning in panic, or their muscles tensing in anger. Those sensations aren't dangerous; they are just unpleasant. And they might lead us to want to resolve the situation, thinking that "closing the tab" on them will resolve the discomfort. The truth is, discomfort is not an emergency; it's okay to be uncomfortable, to "leave the tab open," and to resolve the situation when you have self-regulated.

Then, using the Welcome Big Emotions In exercise below, Maria learned how to welcome each emotion in, ask for its message, and then make a decision about what to do with that information.

As Drs. Daniel Siegel and Tina Payne Bryson write in *The Whole-Brain Child*, "To name it is to tame it."[6] Previously, Maria had distracted herself from her emotions, worrying that if she paid too much attention to them, she might explode or be extremely uncomfortable. But now, Maria could say, "Anger identifies a problem. What my daughter said is a problem. I get to decide how to handle that problem. I don't have to placate her or yell at her. First, I can soothe my body, and then when I'm feeling more comfortable, I can decide what to do about it."

Once Maria learned how to be with her emotions, and once she learned that discomfort isn't dangerous, she saw that emotions were not the enemy. She could allow herself to self-soothe by deep breathing and doing The Sky and the Weather meditation. Once she learned that even uncomfortable emotions will pass and that they can be tolerated without consequences, she could let her emotions in. The sooner she accepts the message her emotions are sending, the sooner they'll pass.

Then I explained how Maria could learn to navigate her children's big emotions. The truth is, all children are going to have big emotions. She can be uncomfortable in the direction of running away from them. She could be uncomfortable in the direction of placating them. Or she could be uncomfortable in the direction of co-regulating with them. All three are going to feel uncomfortable in the moment, but only the third will change the pattern and shut off her trauma app.

Co-regulation begins by attuning to the child's emotional state, responding to their upset with empathy, normalizing what they are feeling, and modeling healthy coping mechanisms. I told her that she could have first calmed the toddler down. She could have said, "You are so sad. You got pushed, and now you have a boo-boo. Can you say *sad*? Can you point to where your body hurts? Let's put some ice on your boo-boo." Once the toddler was fully calm, she could turn her attention to the first grader and begin that co-regulation process. She could have also turned to her daughter and said, "I know you want to talk to me. Now isn't a good time. I'm going to ask you to wait until I'm available. I get that waiting is hard." While she couldn't co-regulate with the daughter, she could teach the daughter the lesson that not all emotions are an emergency.

Can you imagine how Maria's inner child would react to this co-regulation and normalization?

Four Steps to Self-Regulation

1. Name it to tame it: As the authors of *The Whole-Brain Child* suggest, simply name the emotion. This automatically lowers its intensity.
2. Contain it: Use self-soothe strategies to make your body feel better—deep breathing, progressive muscle relaxation, cold water drinking, exercise, or ice plunges. The instructions for each of these can be found in chapter 12.
3. Rate it to abate it: Ask yourself, On a scale from one to ten, how intense is this feeling?
4. Appreciate it: Thank the emotion for providing information. Use that information. Inform the "emotion messenger" that it has done its job and you're turning your attention to other things now.

Remember Maria's daughter and the movie she wanted to watch? Maria could have said something like, "I get that you're mad that I won't let you watch the movie. You think it's unfair and that other mothers are more lenient. I hear you. And this rule stands. We can find other movies for you to watch that aren't as problematic. Or you can just walk around being mad. Or we can find another solution. But for this movie, my no is final."

And what I'm hoping Maria will say to herself is, "And just like you're allowed to be angry, I'm allowed to not be afraid of your anger. I'm not trying to banish your anger. It's possible that I'm going to be uncomfortable with your anger, but I would rather be uncomfortable in the direction of my values. I value protecting my children from violent content that they can't unsee, and I value teaching the essential boundary of no. I also value demonstrating to my daughter that I'm not afraid of her anger, because anger isn't scary."

If Maria can have that conversation with her daughter, she'll undo her freeze/fawn response. The more she does it, the weaker her response becomes. As you become more comfortable with your own emotions, and less scared of them, you'll also be less scared to use your agency in the direction of your parenting values.

Exercise: Welcome Big Emotions In

To undo the trauma app's people-pleasing and fawning, the key is to let emotions come in without overvaluing them. Each uncomfortable emotion is like an unwanted visitor. Instead of barring the door, we need to invite those visitors in, for they come bearing gifts of wisdom. The following exercise is inspired by ACT:

Imagine you're a teenager throwing a party and your annoying little brother wants to come. He races into the room and starts making weird noises in front of your friends. You're so embarrassed that you pick him up by the scruff of his neck and throw him out of the party. The minute you walk away, he starts to come right back in.

This time you stand in front of the door, which works for a while, but he's persistent, and you're not having a chance to enjoy your own party. You want to give him permission to come in, but you don't want to pay attention to him. So you let him wander while you talk to your friends, but you make the decision that you won't give him much attention. After a little while, he loses interest and leaves of his own accord.

Your little brother is your big emotions. Think about this strategy when you are getting wound up by them:

- Welcome the big emotion in. Remember, emotions are persistent messengers. They're going to knock on the door, knock on the window, crawl in through the basement, and come in through the chimney until they get your attention. Or you could just open the door the first time, acknowledge them, and see if you can accept them.
- Recognize that emotions aren't behaviors. What's the worst thing that could happen if you let this emotion in? You might think, *I will be so sad that I'll never recover and I'll just collapse into a pool of tears. If I let anger in, I might get so mad, I'll yell at everyone. If I let fear in, I will be cowering in the corner and I'll be completely immobilized.* But as you've learned, that's not how emotions work. Emotions last for only a very short period of time. Emotions and behaviors are different. Just because fear is here doesn't mean you have to do what it says. You can take the message and then make your own decision about how to act.
- Think about what the emotion is trying to tell you. Try to decipher the message and then plan for what to do with that information that

aligns with your parenting values. Even though emotions provide information, you get to decide what you are going to do with that information.

Sometimes, parenting is going to be stressful. Sometimes, you will be mad at your own kid. Sometimes, your kid is going to be mad at you. That's okay. When your child is angry, they're allowed to be angry. You don't have to take away their anger, but you can help them deal with their anger.

Trigger #2

Confronting a Lack of Discernment

Sometimes, paralysis comes from having been raised by overly controlling, highly authoritarian parents. Overly controlling parents are often well intentioned. They may adhere to strict beliefs found in high-demand cultures or religions. In these families, no one is actively trying to be abusive; they simply believe that they're transmitting their culture accurately, this belief informs their parenting, and there is only one "correct" way to parent or behave. They believe they are passing down wisdom, but in reality, they are not leaving any room for children to learn by experimentation, to make mistakes, or to develop discernment by trying things out. You're either "good" or "bad" in these families, with no shades of gray or opportunities to explore.

Other parents are not as well intentioned. Covert abuse falls under the category of the *s-ACEs*, the *secret* adverse child experiences we discussed in chapter 1. This type of trauma can develop invisibly and cumulatively. Very often, paralyzed parents come from families where one parent was a narcissist, a person who has a weak sense of self and needs to make sure everybody sees them as perfect, and whose emotional needs and their dysregulation was so big that there was no room for anyone else. My analogy for a narcissist is the Wizard of Oz, who says, "Pay no attention to the man behind the curtain"[7]: you must believe the image I'm portraying and ignore the reality of the person I truly am.

We used to believe that narcissists were people who couldn't admit that they make mistakes, but that definition turns out not to be true. Narcissistic behavior is actually a deliberate attempt to make someone else doubt their own perception of the world, strategically yet subtly undermining others. This behavior is referred to as *gaslighting*, which comes from *Gaslight*, a play from the 1940s where the heroine was made to believe that she was crazy. Narcissistic people utilize a very specific type of gaslighting that's not meant to make you deny all reality but just make you deny your own discernment or judgment.

Let's say your narcissistic stepmother asks you to pick up a few things at the grocery store. As you walk out the door, she says, "Make sure to buy Coke." When you come back with the Coke, your stepmother berates you: "Didn't you notice that Pepsi was on sale? How could you be so careless with money?" The next time you go to the supermarket, your stepmother asks for McIntosh apples. When you get to the store, you notice that Cortland apples are cheaper. This time, you buy the cheaper apples, only to be told, "What did you do? Cortland apples are bitter." Sometimes, these incidents are accompanied by statements about laziness, selfishness, self-absorption, or the need to admit that you're making these mistakes on purpose, to annoy the narcissistic family member. What happens to your sense of discernment in that type of situation? Do you see how this creates a sense of permanent self-doubt?

The victim of gaslighting is always put in an unwinnable situation. If you start arguing to hold your space as "right," you risk being told that you're making a big deal over nothing. If you don't stand your ground, you might be accused of being stupid/selfish/lazy. Eventually, you may default to people-pleasing in an attempt to agree with everything the narcissist says. You start to believe that you don't know anything, yet you still need to keep everybody happy.

The narcissistic parent is hard to spot when you're growing up, because we all inherently believe that our parents are good. If you were raised in the Emerald City, it would have been very hard to see that the Wizard of Oz was anything but wise and powerful. But until a paralyzed parent can understand how narcissism and gaslighting robbed them of discernment, they're going to have a hard time learning it.

When someone raised in these types of families becomes a parent, they truly doubt their own judgment. If you are constantly told that your decision is the wrong one, you begin to doubt your ability to make any decisions, especially when it comes to situations that are emotionally fraught. This is particularly true in families where the word *should* is paired with the word *feel*. "You should feel grateful to me that I punished you, because I'm punishing the wickedness out of you." "You shouldn't feel angry at your brother. Boys are like that; they sometimes get wild." "You should feel forgiving toward Daddy; he only hurt you when he was drinking, and he wouldn't have hurt you if you would have gone to bed on time and not been around when he came home."

A child in these scenarios develops *learned helplessness*. Learned helplessness means that you have learned that no matter what you do, you can't affect the outcome of a situation. Judith Herman, one of the seminal voices on trauma and recovery, believes that learned helplessness is a surface-level concept that doesn't take into account the absolute sense of desperation of being a child and trying to manage a situation that's way too big.[8] When a child is taught to doubt their own perception of events, when a child is put in charge of an adult's emotions, as in, "You shouldn't have made Dad mad; that's why he hit you," that child is coping with something that's too big and too intense for their growing nervous system, and they're coping with it all alone.

I have a maxim in post-traumatic parenting: adulting is hard if you never child-ed. One of the biggest tasks of "childing" is learning how to be a human, learning how to navigate the world and figure things out, learning by experimentation, and developing discernment. When that happens, we develop *agency*, the sense that we know how the world works, we know how to navigate it, and we know how to be effective. Agency is the opposite of learned helplessness.

Parenting is all about agency—we have to exercise agency on behalf of our children, use our judgment and experience when theirs isn't developed yet. We are supposed to know so much more about the world than they do. When you lack a sense of agency, it's really hard to parent.

The Overt/Covert Double Whammy

It's surprisingly common to have an overtly abusive person married to a covertly abusive person or to have an overtly abusive parent who is also narcissistic. This is the paralyzed person's double whammy, because you are left with the job of soothing the troubled waters of other people's big emotions without a sense of discernment. Your trauma app will respond to both these triggers with either or both the freeze and fawn response in an effort to keep everyone's emotions small. The problem is, if you're not feeling a sense of safety and security yourself, you can't share your calm with your child. As Stephen Porges writes, "Only when we are in a calm physiological state can we convey cues of safety to another."[9]

Maria once told me her life's story:

> When I was a little girl, I had to tiptoe around the house. It felt like my father was always angry, and I was scared at the way he would shout at all of us and hit us. Now I know that he was probably drunk a lot of the time, but as a kid, I just was scared of him. And what was actually worse was the fact that his girlfriend had it in for me. She would lie on the couch all day and make us cater to her every whim. She was always telling me how lazy, stupid, and selfish I was. No matter what I did, it was the wrong thing. If I cleaned up the toys, I was making too much noise or doing it all wrong. If I didn't clean up, I was lazy and selfish. If her sons left their toy cars out, I would get yelled at for leaving my junk around, even though I was not playing with the G.I. Joes and Matchbox cars—I was more of a princess, rainbows, and unicorns girl. But if I defended myself, I was accused of lying. And heaven help us all if we woke Dad up—he'd just hit whoever was around. I learned to pay a lot of attention to her and her cues and keep everyone calm. I always felt like I was dumb, lazy, selfish, and spacey. I still do.

Can you see how Maria was affected by both overt and covert traumas? She was raised in a home where her dad's big emotions were very dangerous, so she learned to be attentive to them. She learned how to placate but never learned how to deal with her own big emotions! Her narcissistic stepmom also stole her sense of discernment. By constantly berating Maria, making her feel like whatever choice she made was the wrong one, she led Maria to create a strong sense of learned helplessness. This kind of "heads I win; tails you lose" childhood blocks a child's ability to learn discernment.

The Fix to Build Discernment

For paralyzed parents, the second key to shutting off the trauma app is to first acknowledge that their judgment was tampered with through

Journaling Exercise: Write Your Own Eulogy to Clarify Your Values

In this ACT exercise, which will help you clarify your values, start with the following prompt: How do you want your child to remember your parenting when you're dead?

Fill in the following from your child's perspective. What we're getting to are your parenting values. You're starting to tap into your discernment.

- My mom/dad always ________________________________.
- My mom/dad never ________________________________.
- My mom/dad was really good at _______________________.
- My mom/dad always made me feel ____________________.

If you have a partner or spouse, write your parenting eulogies together:

- What do you want your child to remember of your parenting?

gaslighting and then understand their ability to create discernment: for them to make decisions for their family that aligns with and clarifies their values.

When you can decide what your parenting values are, they're very easy to prioritize. For instance, once you know that you value being emotionally present more than you value a clean home, then you know what action to prioritize when your kids come home from school. If you value a home that's very neat because you think that's important for health, then you're going to make sure your kids hang up their backpacks and coats.

Which value is more important? That's a trick question: my values shouldn't be more important than yours. No one gets to tell you what your values should be. You get to think through your values and decide what they are.

Sportscaster Exercise for Discernment

You now know some of your parenting values from the eulogy exercise. The next step is to keep these values front of mind. At first, you might have to "fake it until you make it." It might take a while for you to take ownership of these values and shut down the trauma app's response. My strategy is to use an algorithm to fight an algorithm.

It's not really surprising to me that so many of my patients complain that gentle parenting seems robotic. The truth is, when you are breaking cycles, any change is at first going to be robotic. But once you get comfortable with it, you can personalize it and make it your own. This exercise is a series of affirmations that will help you create a new algorithm.

First, think of a sportscaster who is commentating on a game, narrating to the audience what's happening on the field. The sportscaster not only relays what they're seeing but also adds in the "color" based on their knowledge of the game. Over the loudspeaker, you hear the sportscaster moaning that the team is going in the wrong direction.

You are the coach. You get to create the next play on the field, and when the sportscaster sees it, their comments will change based on your new strategy. Next, they relay what they see, everyone watching the game is aware of your strategy, and they enjoy watching the team score.

Now, think of the sportscaster as your observing self. It's the part of you that sees the whole picture and gets to tell the complete, authentic story. The sportscaster is constantly stating your affirmations. Whenever the trauma app starts to freeze or fawn, your observing self can say, "Listen, let's remember that in an emotionally healthy home, children are allowed to be upset. As long as I'm acting in accordance with my values, this is okay. I can tolerate the discomfort of their upset."

For instance, if Maria's eleven-year-old starts arguing with her six-year-old, she can update the sportscaster that there isn't a crisis but that the children are experimenting with conflict and learning how to have a good fight. The sportscaster has to keep repeating the right lines because they now know the strategy: "In this home, we teach kids *how* to have a good fight," "Conflict can be healthy," or "My kids are allowed to figure it out on their own."

When Maria's husband is almost home and the trauma app starts warning her to run around cleaning up, Maria can remind herself, "My value is *people over property*: my children are more important than having a neat home." She and her husband can also remind each other that this is a shared value that they have come up with together. They can even write it on their welcome mat!

As your inner child observes your new capacity to tolerate discomfort, to relate to emotions as messengers, to self-regulate and co-regulate, it begins to heal. It will trust you to be the adult in the room, to handle emotionally fraught situations with wisdom, and it doesn't need to keep activating the trauma app as much. As your inner child sees that you are acting in accordance with your parenting values, it begins to trust your adult discernment. As you co-regulate, you can share your calm with both your kids and your inner child.

CHAPTER 8

The Survivor Parent

I GOT THE following DM on Instagram, and it really encapsulates what survivor mode can look like: "I'd love to do post-traumatic parenting, but my life is one unending chaos right now. I'm in a custody battle with my coercive and controlling ex-husband, a financial and legal mess, and my kids are really suffering and acting out. I hang up with the lawyer, only to pick up the phone with the school because my son got in a fight—again. I love everything you post, and it all sounds plausible, but I just can't. My bandwidth is gone, and I don't know when it's going to come back."

My heart went out to this mom. The truth is, she's not yet a PTP. Her trauma is ongoing—she hasn't reached the level of "post." She's still in what I call survivor mode and what would clinically be called "acute stress disorder." Acute stress disorder is what happens *before* PTSD kicks in. Remember, your trauma is not the incident that happened but the impact of what happened. It's analogous to when a boxer gets punched really hard in the ring. In the moment, they might not be in much pain, because the swelling hasn't set in. Yet they know the bruise is coming. Acute stress disorder is what sets in immediately after you're punched and you are "dazed and confused." This mom is still in the boxing ring.

A survivor parent looks very different than all the other parenting type defaults, so they are easy to pick out. Have you ever seen a YouTube video where a child faints on a rollercoaster and goes completely limp? That's what a survivor's psychological functioning looks like. When there's no escape, our psyche goes into freeze mode. The survivor can't do much of anything at a very high level, except react to basic needs or emergencies. Compared to the disengaged parent, they are much more overwhelmed, reaching a level of freeze and exhaustion. So instead of running around and not accomplishing anything, they are just collapsed on the couch or in bed.

Because they are not post-traumatic, their trauma app has not even turned on. There is no superpower to tap into. Part of this freeze mode is that the trauma app is using up psychological resources trying to program itself into existence: it's scrambling to create itself to start the process of returning to a sense of safety.

Often, a survivor parent has experienced a recent trauma as an adult—divorce, death of a loved one, natural disaster, school shooting, etc. The survivor default can also develop in a parent who had an extremely dangerous, extremely chaotic environment growing up. Tina Payne Bryson, PhD, writes in *The Bottom Line for Baby* that children can't count on their parents to be their safe harbor if they are also the storm that rocks their world.[1] In this type of chaos, a child becomes stuck in survival mode, and that feeling can last for a lifetime. Or a parent can become retriggered when their child becomes the age when their own trauma happened and be plunged back into survival mode.

Here's the thing about trauma: it happens in the future, not the past. We think of trauma as "a difficult memory of a past event." But really, it's the persistent sense of threat or danger when a trigger—something that reminds us of the trauma—occurs in the present. There are people who were victimized as children, entered survival mode, had their trauma app turned on, and processed some aspect of the trauma. Their process may have been more or less healthy, but they created an operating system for handling it. Then, when the PTPs' children reached the age that their original trauma occurred, they suddenly are catapulted back into survival mode. Sometimes the trigger is, "This age is a very dangerous time" or "That age is so heartbreakingly young."

In some instances, our brains aren't capable of understanding the magnitude of our trauma, and it isn't until we reach a certain developmental stage that our brains catch up, begin to be traumatized, and trigger survival mode. A child who loses a parent at two years old, before they can understand the idea of "permanence," might first become traumatized years later, when they are eight. *Matrescence* is the developmental stage in which a woman becomes a mother. For some post-traumatic women, becoming a mother will suddenly retrigger their trauma—either because they lost a mother and now can fully comprehend the magnitude of that loss or because they feel the powerful tug of attachment and love and suddenly comprehend just how much love they never got, how love is supposed to feel. For *patrescence*, the retriggering when a man becomes a father can be similar. That's when the bruise begins to form. That's when we either get catapulted into survivor mode or, ironically, start to become "post-traumatic" so we can finally heal.

In my practice and in the social media community, it seems like survivor parents are more likely to deal with physical health complaints compared to other PTPs. They report recurring severe headaches, autoimmune diseases, or chronic fatigue. These health issues may be a result of being in an intense stress state, known as chronic adrenal overdrive, and flooding the body with the stress hormone, cortisol. And these symptoms are sometimes the body's way of keeping us immobilized, on the couch, because we simply can't function anymore. This syndrome is real—I don't want to be one of those people who gaslights PTPs, because there are enough of those on TikTok! I have several autoimmune diseases, and I also have a black belt, which is especially useful when people want to tell me my joint pain or asthma is "all in my head." A headache is "all in my head" in the sense that this is where the symptoms lie, but it's not because I'm making it up. As I said before, the body doesn't only keep the score, but it also calls the shots!

Eventually, the survivor parent will either jolt out of or ease out of their shutdown and then transform into the PTSD state. That's when they will dip their toes into one of the other parenting types. This transition is actually a good sign, because it shows that they are progressing back into life. When a survivor parent starts to go into a disengaged default, instead of lying on the couch, they will scroll on their phone, which is actually more active. They're doing more; they're moving forward. When a parent tells me that they went from feeling completely out of it and just reacting to crises to wasting time watching reality TV or arguing with their ex-spouse's new partner, it's actually good news! That means they're moving out of the survivor default and into one of the other PTP defaults. It's actually a sign of progress.

Everything You Need to Know About Polyvagal Theory

In order to understand survival mode, let's go back to *polyvagal theory*. Dr. Stephen Porges created polyvagal theory to explain how our sense of safety or threat can impact our biology and our behavior. Polyvagal theory has many implications for parenting.

The word *vagal* comes from the Latin word for "wander," which aptly describes the vagus nerve, which wanders throughout your body. If you experience a "freeze" response in the aftermath of trauma, as in acute stress disorder, the vagus nerve shuts down the transfer of information. This creates a sudden loss of energy or motivation, decreased heart rate and blood pressure, shallow breathing, and a sense of emotional detachment or apathy.

A healthy, stress-free state is called the *ventral vagal state*. The sympathetic nervous system is regulated. We feel safe, at peace, and ready to connect with others. Some refer to this as feeling "safe and social," and it is the state we'd like to be parenting from.

When an emergency happens, like when a toddler takes a nasty fall, we go into *sympathetic mobilization*. Our hearts begin to race. Our breathing becomes rapid. We have a sudden surge of adrenaline. We feel anxious. This is our "fight-or-flight" state. The world suddenly feels dangerous. In short bursts, this isn't a bad state to parent from. We need our sympathetic mobilization to keep our little humans alive. In a normal situation, as soon as the threat is handled, we go back to our ventral vagal state.

Our bodies were never meant to live in a chronic freeze state, but when we do, survivor mode can occur. When we're in a chronically threatening environment, like living with an abusive parent or spouse, we go into a *dorsal vagal state*. This is the "freeze" state of survivor mode. We have low energy, shallow breathing, and can feel foggy and alone. This state is meant to help us conserve energy so that when it's possible, we can go back into the sympathetic mobilization state and escape.

Imagine taking a leisurely walk in the woods. You are in a ventral vagal state, enjoying the smell of the pine trees and the sound of birds chirping. Now, imagine you see a bear peeking behind one of those trees and it's baring its teeth and growling. Your body automatically goes into sympathetic mobilization—fight or flight. You beat a hasty retreat to your car. Phew, you're safe! You drive home, slam the door, and flip all the locks, only to turn around and realize that . . . the bear is in your house and it's going to live there forever. That's the dorsal vagal state. If you've spent your whole life living with a bear—otherwise known as a dysfunctional mom or dad, a chronic and disabling illness, or political unrest—the dorsal vagal may be where your nervous system hangs out.

Polyvagal theory is often described as a ladder, where the ventral vagal state is the top, and we have to climb up until we can get back to "ventral vagal." You may also hear this described as the *autonomic nervous system ladder*. Healthy people can easily move between states, up and down the ladder. Stephen Porges uses the term *neuroception* to describe the process that our autonomic nervous system uses to scan our environment for cues of safety and danger. When our neuroception recognizes a situation as safe, we can automatically be in a ventral vagal state. When our neuroception sees a situation as threatening, it moves us down the autonomic ladder. It's very hard to be a good parent when we're not in the ventral vagal state, and many of us need to be taught how to get there. That's what part III of this book is for. The AIM model can help you learn to restore safety so that you can parent.

Lourdes Is a Survivor

When I met Lourdes for the first time, she wasn't sitting in my waiting room mindlessly scrolling her phone. She was sitting still, staring into the distance. I wasn't surprised by her demeanor, because I've met many survivor parents before. They are often referred to me by their children's school when something doesn't happen for the child that is supposed to be automatic, like the paperwork from yearly physicals. Lourdes was referred to me by her sons' principal at their new school, because she had never handed in their vaccination records, and the boys couldn't come back to school without them. This was her final warning.

Lourdes has two sons: Andy, who is seven, and Josh, who is eleven. Although she is technically married, it is a high-conflict relationship, and her husband no longer resides at home. She told me that she spends much of the day dozing, lying down on the couch to rest. She jolts into activity only when there's "a real emergency." Even meeting her children's basic needs, like making dinner, took too much energy. Lourdes told me, "My boys know how to make their own meals. . . ." before her voice trailed off. When I asked her what they typically made for dinner, she told me that she had signed up for a program in her town where restaurants deliver their excess food to families in need, so her kids just eat whatever gets dropped off. Some nights, supper might be wonton soup, but it could also be donuts, because it all depends on what is in the box. She really didn't know.

Next, I asked Lourdes to tell me her story. She recounted that her mother had a terrifying mental illness, and growing up, she never knew which version of her mother she was coming home to. Sometimes her mother was extremely calm, but on other days, she would be shrieking that there were demons in the house. As a little girl, Lourdes knew she couldn't see what her mother saw, but at night, she had trouble sleeping, worrying that there was a chance that her mother was right. She couldn't go to her mother for comfort because her mother scared her. By the time she was a teenager, she was removed from the home and put into foster care with a much safer family.

I commiserated with Lourdes and shared that what she had been through must have been terrifying. And while she was lucky in some ways to get away from her mother, she never learned any coping skills beyond numb detachment and apathy. In the time away from her mother, she was able to regroup and feel safe enough to move forward with her life, eventually marrying and having children.

Lourdes said,

> Yes, Dr. K, but that's when my problems began again. My marriage was overwhelming. There was always a lot of fighting and stress, and I had absolutely no one to turn to for support. When my husband yells—and he yells a lot—I just numb out. I can't even think. My foster family had been great, but they were kind of done with me once my kids were born. Or maybe I'm embarrassed about reaching out to them; they warned me not to marry my husband. When it became clear to me that my boys weren't safe at home, I knew I had to leave and go out on my own. My husband has completely washed his hands of the kids. So we moved into a new apartment two months ago, and I'm still terrified. I'm scared that I have my mother's crazy genes. I'm scared that I don't know what to do with the boys when they get home from school, so I just do nothing. I'm just too tired all the time. I love my boys—I do. They're good kids and they deserve better. But I have nothing. I used up all my energy moving out. Now it's all gone.
>
> Andy, my younger son, is super active, and he gets angry easily. Every time he gets wild, or has a meltdown, I start to worry—is he crazy like my mom? Does he have anger issues like his dad? It sounds terrible, but just being around Andy sometimes is exhausting and makes me panic. I feel like I'm a terrible mom. Do I only love my kids when they behave? Am I toxic? Josh is like a little dad—he takes great care of Andy, but I worry that the whole thing is stressing him out.

Lourdes's story showed me that she had been in a state of extreme collapse. The good news was that she was aware that her parenting wasn't helping her children, which meant that she was starting to thaw out of survival mode. It was clear that she wanted a better life for her kids. The fact that she walked through my door tells me that she's starting to mobilize again.

She knows that her behavior isn't like her mother's, because she is not terrifying to her children, but she also knows that she isn't present. She was resilient enough to follow through and see me, and that's often the first step toward breaking the cycle of shutdown.

I didn't have to teach Lourdes how to feed her boys, because I knew that there's no mother in the world who doesn't know that kids need to be fed. She needed to feel safe. I explained to Lourdes, "Look, you have taken the baby steps to the right path. The school has done you a favor, because their insistence on getting you help has forced you to snap out of your frozen state, at least temporarily. Let's work together on getting you to feel safe again in your new home so that you can actively take care of your children."

Lourdes told me that she actually felt safest with Andy's teacher. "She's an angel. She gets what I'm going through. She's the one who convinced me to come see you. I just trust her. She sees the good in Andy. She tells me that underneath all of the stress, she sees that I'm a good mom, and she has faith in me. She was raised by a dad who was violent, and she knows how hard it is for a woman to leave. When I'm around her, I start to feel like I can do this."

I knew that I could help Lourdes, but I also knew that I couldn't do it alone. For survivor parents, we have to pay attention to biochemistry. Lourdes needed to see a psychiatrist who could prescribe antidepressant medications that would provide her brain with the calm it wasn't producing on its own. We also needed to put together a circle of support—people like Andy's teacher—who could help her get through this. In other words, we needed to intervene from the inside out and from the outside in. Then, we could begin to do the work together to reconnect her and her sons.

Transitioning Out of Survivor

One thing is for sure: no one stays in survivor mode forever. What will likely happen next is that you will find yourself reacting to your children

When the Shock Ends

Sometimes when a danger or threat is over, a survivor parent will seemingly revive all by themselves. It's like the families we see on the news after a natural disaster who say, "We will rebuild." Once they realize that the threat has passed, they can move forward.

I often see this scenario play out after the death of a spouse or a divorce. The surviving parent experiences a time of shock, numbness, and emotional detachment, but it doesn't last forever. Eventually it passes, and the new reality becomes the new normal.

It's like when your leg falls asleep. At first, you feel nothing. As you shake it and the blood returns to it, you feel "pins and needles," maybe even extremely painful cramps. That pain is a sign of life coming back.

The new normal does become normal—with time and with some processing. That doesn't mean that you won't feel the pins and needles of life. Abrupt changes can be painful, but with time, your sense of safety can be restored. As sad as it sounds, getting into the "post-traumatic" state is a good thing, because it does mean that the traumatic events are over.

using one of the other PTP defaults. This is good news, because it means that you are progressing up the autonomic ladder. Read through those chapters now to get a handle on what may be in store for you.

Now, it's time to start dreaming of a future again. Start thinking, *How do I want to parent? What will my life be like when I'm able to be proactive, rather than reactive with my parenting? Is there something I can picture myself doing with my kids—like baking or taking a nature walk—that feels exciting? What can I do to make that vision a reality?*

Lourdes told me that she always pictured herself spending more relaxed time with her kids. It was something her foster mom did, and it always felt so safe and cozy. "We'd make popcorn, and we'd all sit around playing games, like Candyland or Trouble. Sometimes, she'd take out the projector and we'd watch movies on a bedsheet, and we'd pretend to be those characters for days and days. It was fun."

I asked Lourdes what was stopping her from having a family game night now. She looked at me like I was crazy. "Dr. K, I don't cook dinner for them. I don't clean the house. They're supposed to have doctor visits and all that stuff, and I haven't done it. And you want me to have a family game night?"

Journaling Exercise: Restoring Your Sense of Safety

For Lourdes, the next step was to restore her sense of safety. I had her work on the following journaling exercise and bring notes to her next session.

Write down what or who makes you feel extremely safe. It doesn't matter what the answer is: there is no judgment! Even if it seems illogical on the surface, write it down and then seek it out. It may be going back to see your childhood home or school or seeing a relative that always made you feel safe. For Lourdes, it might be remembering her foster family or even reaching out to them. Or do something that connects you to a time and experience of safety, like listening to specific music or eating certain foods that are pleasurable. It may take a while to find what brings you a sense of peace, and that's okay. You may need to journal every day until you realize that you don't need this exercise any longer.

Ask a friend to check in with you. Survivors generally need to experience safety in the context of a relationship. For some, that may mean mental health counseling. Or it could mean leaning on a friendship or a romantic relationship. This is called "co-regulation," and it's a precursor to the "self-regulation" we need for parenting. In the other parenting default types, I've listed many self-regulation techniques that you can try. And you'll learn more about it in part III.

When my father died, my mother's best friend, Janice, called every single day at the same time, right after my mother would have her morning coffee. Janice somehow knew to time her morning call to the instant my mother swallowed her last sip of coffee. And she called my mother every single day for years. I'm sure that this little ritual helped my mother out of her survival mode because she always felt safe with Janice.

If you are reading this and you can't journal yet, repeat this motto to yourself: This is survival mode. It will pass.

I replied, "I know it's hard to believe, but family game night is actually a parenting skill you can learn. It's going to be good for your kids and it's good for you. It will make cooking dinner eventually become possible. Once you break out of survivor mode, you can focus on all the other parts of parenting that haven't been possible. You'll be able to put any energy you have into that one shining dream—the family game night. It's going to be your path out of survival mode so that you can parent from your values."

Lourdes left my office feeling hopeful. I knew that it was another sign her survivor mode was losing its grip. Will she transition to another post-traumatic parenting type? Likely. But I know Lourdes and I have a long road to travel, and we've taken that first important step.

Now that you've learned how your trauma app was controlling you and you've started to work with its permissions, over time you'll notice that, like Lourdes, it loses its power over you. In the next section, you'll learn how to reclaim your psychological resources so that you can parent consistently with your values.

Part III

From Cycle Breaking to Cycle Making

CHAPTER 9

Becoming the Parent You Want to Be

THE BOND BETWEEN a parent and child is supposed to be deep and formative. As parents, our job is to gently, responsively, and consistently respond to our children's physical and psychological needs. If this happens predictably throughout their lifespan, they will develop a sense of security, which is foundational to their overall psychological health. These are the goals of good parenting. In this section, we'll focus on parenting as a verb—what to actually do with your children, to parent in accordance with your values.

If you're thinking, *Dr. K, this sounds great! I'm totally on board. But how do I actually create this kind of bond when I have no idea what it should look like?* you're not alone. I remember reading all sorts of parenting books when I was a new mother and feeling like they were guiding me to the fifth floor of a department store but I was still in the basement—and couldn't find the exit. They offered great suggestions for how to relate to our children, yet the lessons were beyond my capacity to carry out. No matter how clearly it was explained, romanticized, or rhapsodized about, good parenting just felt more out of reach for me.

Can you relate? Is that your experience when reading parenting books? If so, let's find the elevator out of the basement together. We start by understanding *attachment theory*. Earlier in the book, we talked about attachment in terms of your trauma. We need to provide attachment to our children as well. It's basically our job as parents.

Psychologists Tina Payne Bryson and Daniel Siegel break attachment into what they call "the four S's": safe, seen, soothed, and secure.[1] If you can provide the four S's, your child will come to understand that the world and relationships are safe, predictable, and worth investing effort in and that they can develop resilience to handle minor setbacks.

These same four S's can be further sorted into two simple categories. When we are told that we can make our child feel "safe," "soothed," and "secure," we're basically being asked to find our calm, expand our calm outward, and then share that sense of calm (which is called co-regulation). When we are told that we can make our child feel "seen," that's about sharing our joy. The hallmark of good attachment is mutual delight—the parent delights in the child, who reciprocally delights in the parent, and they both delight in the relationship.

Yet the two emotional capacities that trauma steals from us are calm and joy. If you have PTSD, you don't have calm and you don't have joy. Sit with that for a minute. We've already discussed how PTSD leaves you hypervigilant, removes your illusion of safety, impacts your ability to self-regulate, and blocks your connection to your emotional life.

You can't share your calm if you don't have any.

You can't share your joy if you don't have any.

Realizing that attachment boils down to the same capacities that you've lost due to your trauma can feel overwhelming. Overwhelming feels traumatic. But I know you can do this. Now that you understand how your trauma app has been influencing your behaviors and informing the type of parent that you have been, it's time to turn down the volume on the trauma app and become the parent you want to be. Now that you understand just how badly trauma can block you, you can finally fix it.

The good news is that it's easier than you think. We do this by following my three-step AIM model—acceptance, integration, and meaning/mission. I use the AIM model with my patients every day. This process is the only way I know that can affect real, lasting change. It aggregates the best practices from many forms of trauma therapy into a simple set of steps we can use right now, because we have kids who are depending on us right now.

The point of the AIM model is for us to reclaim our calm and our joy so that we can share it. It's about healing ourselves so that we can parent and stop our damage from damaging our kids.

Acceptance

Acceptance means that we see our traumas for what they are: the awful things that have happened to us that we cannot undo and the parts of a normal life that we missed because of them.

In order to achieve acceptance, we need to stop dwelling in *counterfactual thinking*: the "if only" thoughts we conjure about imaginary alternatives to real past events. Have you ever watched a horror movie and had the temptation to yell at the main character, "Don't open that door! Don't split up from your friends. Never ever hunt for the lost pet when the creepy music is playing!" Your present-day knowledge gives you insight into how those characters should have acted. Yet we don't have the power to effect change in something that has already happened—not when we're watching a movie and not in real life. That actor is going to look for Fluffy and meet their predictably gory end.

Counterfactual thinking is the constant review of your trauma in an attempt to convince your past self to make a different decision. "Don't go to that party." "Don't go to sleep without checking the smoke detectors." "Don't get into your dad's friend's car." Your brain is trying to undo something that was already done.

A great deal of research on counterfactual thinking reveals how it may be responsible for the persistent nature of PTSD. Researchers who studied survivors of the 2011 Oslo bombing found that those who reported more counterfactual thinking reported much more PTS symptomatology than those who reported less counterfactual thinking.[2] In another study, survivors of sexual assault, parents of children who were targeted in a terrorist attack, and mass casualty event survivors who engaged in more counterfactual thinking had much higher levels of PTS and were more likely to experience more severe forms of PTSD than those who reported less counterfactual thinking.[3,4]

Other research connects counterfactual thinking with flashbacks.[5] Imagine that you were in a car accident and then for weeks afterward you kept thinking about the moment right before impact. These flashbacks are your trauma app's attempt to undo the past: to turn left instead of right. The part of your brain that is associated with trauma and flashbacks is your limbic system. It can't tell time. Since the trauma app is partially housed in the limbic system, it also can't tell time. Put simply, your trauma app doesn't understand the concept of "the past." It thinks you can still undo the outcome and turn left. This is where the trauma app creates an algorithm, which is the "if, then" rules.

Not everybody has flashbacks. Some of us skip directly to counterfactual, "if only" thinking. *If only I had turned left, I wouldn't have gotten hit.* The trauma app needs to restore your illusion of safety, so it creates a rule aligned with your counterfactual thinking. Maybe it's *I don't drive, I can't trust myself,* or *I'm not competent enough to take care of my kids.*

In order to reprocess that memory so that you can reclaim your psychological resources, you have to accept that the accident happened, which will get you off the dwelling hamster wheel. Dwelling wastes precious mental energy that we should be using on parenting. If we accept that the accident happened, we can use our counterfactual thinking as data: *Thanks for reminding me that the accident was scary. Now I know to be more careful when I drive. I got the memo—I can't change what happened. I can learn to live with it. All the psychological energy that's wasted in trying to undo the past can now be reclaimed and can be put to use toward a more valued purpose, which is whatever you need it for.*

American psychologist and author Marsha Linehan calls this process *radical acceptance*,[6] which refers to emphasizing acceptance of the present moment without trying to change it or deny it. The events that happened aren't going to ever change. We can't wish them away. In DBT, we often say, "It is as it should be." This motto doesn't mean that traumatic events were acceptable. It means that we can acknowledge that they happened, yet we can remain in the present moment rather than try to change the past. We can move forward with the information the event provided.

For instance, I'm still mad that my father continued smoking his pipe and the occasional cigarette after he was told he had heart disease. Sometimes, I feel intense anger when I smell tobacco smoke or see a cigarette ad. Whenever I think about it, my brain is engaging in counterfactual thinking: *If only my father had given up smoking, he wouldn't have had the heart attack and died on me.* In essence, my brain is trying to persuade my father to stop smoking. That's a waste of my psychological resources because there is nothing I can do now to prevent my father's death. The truth is, losing my father at an early age was a terrible loss that shouldn't have happened, but it did. And I can't put any more energy into rewriting the past.

ACT focuses on the idea of *experiential avoidance*. This is when we try very hard not to feel our psychological distress. We try not to feel our anxiety, our anger, or our shame. Instead, we intentionally try to shut down those signals by not paying attention to them. ACT tells us that the only thing we have control of is our attention. We either focus our attention on "away moves"—moving away from pain, distress, discomfort, or emotions we don't want to have—or we can focus on "toward moves," focusing our attention on our values. The *A* of ACT means accepting all our emotions without trying to avoid them. Through acceptance of all our emotions, we can move closer to our values.

Remember that in chapter 3 we talked about IFS and the concept of "parts." IFS includes a concept called *welcoming the exiles in*. Exiles are those parts of self that we wish to disavow. We try to pretend they don't exist and even try to will them out of existence. I can recognize that there's a part of me that's still mad about my father's death. That part is allowed to have a voice, because all my parts are welcome (I am therefore welcoming the unwanted, exiled thought in). I'm allowed to be angry at my father, and I have to also acknowledge that every time I try to judge or silence my anger—every time I have the shaming thought *How can you be mad at a dead person?* or *You're being disrespectful to your father; you're not remembering all the good things about him*—I'm exiling a part. When I do that, I waste a lot of resources that could be used for something more productive.

With acceptance, we can see that our trauma caused us real psychological damage, yet we are not necessarily damaged, nor have we become a bad person. In ACT, possibly in DBT, and certainly in IFS, a person is never considered to be damaged. Instead, we hold damage. There were

Accepting That You Are the Attachment Figure

Most people aren't prepared for the emotional intensity of parenting or just how overwhelming it can be. The same is true for attachment. Like trauma, this realization can be too much, too soon, too big, too fast—something too big for the brain to metabolize.

Now that you know that you are the attachment figure, the responsibility can feel overwhelming, especially if you didn't have a good model growing up. That sensation in and of itself can be traumatic. It's very tempting to start engaging in the counterfactuals about everything you didn't get.

Now is a perfect time to start using acceptance. You can try to accept that your trauma happened. Try to tune out the counterfactuals and focus on learning the skills to be an attachment figure that are outlined in the rest of this book, because you can totally do that.

probably incidents that have occurred with your children that you wish you could have done differently. But dwelling on these perceived failures is counterfactual thinking. Our brain wants us to hit the reset button and go back to their infancy for a parenting do-over. Yet we can focus only on becoming better for the future. In the future, there's always the possibility of repair.

The most important benefit we get from acceptance is that it restores our calm. When we're not trying to avoid uncomfortable emotions or wasting brain space on counterfactuals, we have so many more resources to self-regulate and co-regulate. If I'm calm, I am regulated, and my children are going to be able to access my calm when they need it. For me, I knew I had reached a place of acceptance when I realized that my self-regulation was getting easier (but not easy). Manageable. Possible. That's what acceptance will do for you.

Accepting and Using Your Superpower in Parenting

You can change the way you parent: that's the whole point of this book. Yet it's going to take considerable effort to ditch reflexively relying on your superpower. Your trauma response is a strategy that is hardwired and does have real value. For instance, a people pleaser can't help but notice someone's facial expressions and be able to read their emotions. It's up to you to decide whether taking this skill from automatic to consciously controlled is worth the effort. The truth is, there's literally nothing about yourself that you can't change.

However, acceptance means ignoring the trauma app's frantic alarms so that you can use your superpower and act in accordance with your values. As we discussed in chapter 1, in literally every superhero movie ever, the one skill that makes a hero great can also lead to their downfall. The trick is to use the information without being ruled by it. For instance, if you've always wanted to be the chill, spontaneous parent, but you are a perfectionist parent who needs structure, organization, and routine, you can build unstructured moments into the day. In effect, you can quiet the trauma app and hold onto the superpower.

At first, transitioning your superpower skills during a stressful time might feel uncomfortable, because there are parts of your trauma app that you are actively deselecting. Acceptance means being willing to embrace this discomfort in service of a value. The difficult truth is knowing that there are no magical words that will automatically change your point of view. Acceptance means becoming your own arbiter of reality. You're always going to react to stress with one of the four F's—flight, fight, freeze, fawn—and all four feel uncomfortable. I tell my patients all the time that parenting is often like swimming. We have to accept that water is wet and, most of the time, swimming can be fun. But sometimes, the water is cold. Sometimes, the current is strong. That doesn't mean you don't give it a try, even if at first you don't want to go in. You can't change the water, but you can wear a wetsuit. You can learn to surf and master the currents. And when you do, you will be able to use the water to your advantage. Because the water isn't going anywhere.

The following chart shows some typical parenting superpowers by parenting default types. If you don't see yours here, can you imagine how it would work for you? What is something you're good at—something you've received praise for in other environments, like work or in your social life—that also interferes with your parenting?

Acceptance Means . . .

- Traumatic experiences happened. They can't be undone. We're not going to waste psychological resources on counterfactual thinking.
- Uncomfortable emotions happen. We're not going to shut them off; we're going to learn to tolerate them, and we're going to learn from them. Discomfort isn't danger. Beware of the off buttons that shut off uncomfortable emotions and sensations. Instead of shutting those emotions off, we can accept them, learn to tolerate them, and crucially, learn to learn from them.
- The trauma app is going to resist being powered down, and that will feel scary, but that's okay. We have the courage to do difficult things.
- Acceptance means trauma did change our brains and did give us some superpowers. Yet those skills that kept us alive are now keeping us from living our lives, from being present parents. We get to decide what we want to do with them.

Parenting Type	Your Superpower	How It Negatively Affects Your Parenting	A Better Use of Your Superpower
Entangled	You love deeply and value and maintain relationships.	When you care too diffusely, it's hard to care in a concentrated manner. If you are so busy caring about your ex-spouse's new relationship, you can't put as much psychological energy into your kids.	Decide where to put your loving energy. Put your attention on your current family, instead of past relationships.
Perfectionist	You value data, procedures, and organization because you want to do tasks correctly.	Perfect isn't human. Children need to be parented by authentic humans who are willing to risk messing up. Predictable and manageable ruptures are healthy and build relationships—allow for some of them.	There's a lot to be said for structure, routine, and organization. If you get panicky without them, use them. When your kids feel big emotions, that's okay. Embrace rupture and repair. Embrace the fact that kids are going to have big emotions and that their discomfort isn't dangerous.
Disengaged	You have an emergency brake for your stress response.	Dissociation leaves children feeling unseen and unheard. Dissociation is by definition the opposite of presence.	Use your adaptive dissociation and schedule when you can afford to "tune out" so that you can be present the rest of the time. For example, create a rule that limits your phone use when you are with your kids.
Paralyzed	You are attentive to other people's wants and needs. You notice all the tasks that should get done.	Life is always chaotic because you can't place your attention on one task at a time. You end up focusing on the loudest voice in the room, but that might mean other quieter, more important needs get ignored.	Put your passion where it belongs. Try stacking tasks instead of doing everything all at the same time. Figure out what you value so that you can accept that some things just won't happen and that's okay. Create your own "if-then" rules to combat the trauma app's algorithms.

Parenting Type	Your Superpower	How It Negatively Affects Your Parenting	A Better Use of Your Superpower
Survivor	If you're reading this book, you have enough self-awareness to know that this is where you are at.	Surviving isn't thriving, and parenting is all about thriving.	If you have self-awareness, acknowledging that there is a problem is a great first step. Recruit as much support as you can. This is not the time to develop a "hyperindependence" attitude. Even if you *could* do it yourself, you don't have the luxury of DIYing it while your kids need more from you.

Acceptance Affirmations

As you reach acceptance, you honor yourself without judgment. You honor your superpower for the important information it provides for you. You can honor the emotion that is grabbing you by the throat because it wants to tell you something.

Use any of the following affirmations. Repeat them in the morning with your coffee; tape them to your bathroom mirror. Remind yourself every day in the moment that trauma changes the brain but so does healing.

Tell yourself:

- My trauma really happened; it wasn't okay; there is nothing I can do to change it.
- My trauma changed me, and that's okay.
- I am allowed to be uncomfortable.
- I am entitled to live my life according to my values.
- I own my psychological energy, so I get to decide where to put it.
- For the entangled parent: I can't fix my family of origin, and I am not responsible for any other adult's emotions.
- For the perfectionist parent: I am going to make mistakes, and that's okay. My kids are going to sometimes be upset, and that's okay. My kids are not me—my kids *have* me. They are not alone.
- For the disengaged parent: I am allowed to feel stressed; stress is not an emergency. Discomfort isn't danger.
- For the paralyzed parent: I don't have to fix all the problems in my family simultaneously. I can and should prioritize.
- For the survivor parent: I am in survival mode right now. It will pass.

Exercise: Achieving Acceptance Through Mourning

Counterfactual thinking is tied to anxiety. And very often, underneath anxiety is sadness. One way to undo counterfactual thinking is to intentionally choose a different way to think about your trauma and subsequent anxious thoughts. If you can welcome all your parts, including your sadness, you can also allow yourself to experience a moment of mourning for your sadness.

Have a funeral and let it go. Say goodbye. You're mourning what you would've been had your trauma not happened.

Find pictures of yourself as a young child and see how joyous you were. Acknowledge the loss of your joy. Recognize that it wasn't fair and it wasn't okay. Say aloud the thoughts and feelings you weren't allowed to say or the thoughts you are first admitting to feeling. Mourn what you've lost; mourn who you were. And like any mourning period, it will pass.

Now, try saying the following: "I remember what happened. I'm putting it aside, but I'm going to continue to use my superpower in service of my values. It will make me a better parent."

Integration

Trauma survivors often tell me a version of the same issue: they can't predict or understand their reactions. *I don't know who I am. I'm a chameleon. I'm different in different situations. I don't know what I want. I don't know what I value. I'm good at faking it, but I know that I'm confused.* As one PTP, who learned to people-please from a very young age, told me: "You're telling me to parent with presence, to bring my whole self to parenting. My entire life, I was taught to be selfless. That's what won me praise and social acceptance. That's what kept me alive. How can I bring my whole self to parenting if I'm selfless?"

The reasons that PTPs are confused is that their trauma has shattered their sense of self and their trauma app is running the show. Instead of relying on their "observing self"—the "I" who tells their story—the trauma app's algorithms replace the self with what it sees as the best way to stay out of danger. But as you've learned, the trauma app is often wrong when it comes to parenting. Your job is to update the trauma app so that you can take your trauma coping skills and superpowers and mindfully decide how to learn from and work with them. This process is called *integration*.

Integration builds on acceptance. It allows us to have a conversation with all our parts—our inner children, the parts we tried to exile, the parts that try to take over—but does not let any one of them run the show. Integration continues the work of undoing experiential avoidance so that we can use emotions as one data point, along with our cognitive abilities, good judgment, experience, and newfound courage, to create true wisdom. Put simply, integration means our trauma becomes just one aspect of our lives: it's one extra-strong superpower, yet it doesn't have to do all the heavy lifting in our psyche. We want to hear from all our inner voices, and then we get to make our choices.

In *Trauma and Recovery*, Judith Herman writes about integration in the context of the therapeutic relationship: "The therapist assists the client in learning to notice the ways in which her mind and body have adapted to the trauma, and that the old procedural tendencies of safety through extreme biological reactions or maladaptive coping have receded."[7] We can do this same work on our own. Can you notice how much of your distress, counterproductive behaviors, and even instincts are really a trauma app response? Can you see if those responses really fit, or provide support, for parenting?

Herman's emphasis on integration is consistent with Dr. Daniel Siegel's model of interpersonal neurobiology (IPNB). Siegel's concept of neural integration is referred to as *self-organization* and is basically how you create a sense of self after trauma. For IPNB, integration means linking our disparate parts—our trauma narrative, the trauma app, and its associated survival behaviors—with a new capacity to tolerate uncomfortable emotions, difficult thoughts, and our new self-understanding. While we can't change the kind of childhood we had or the trauma we have dealt with as adults, we can change the kind of childhood our children can have. The mistakes we've already made with our kids won't change, but we can focus on repairing with them and improving ourselves.

The final lesson of integration comes from a famous quotation that is often attributed to Viktor Frankl, Holocaust survivor and author of *Man's Search for Meaning*: "Between stimulus and response, there is a space. In that space is our power to choose our response. In our response lies our growth and our freedom." Hypervigilance, emotional reactivity, and dissociation are all negative, reactionary responses to a stimulus and show that your trauma isn't integrated. They are also frequently trauma symptoms that block your parenting. As you learn to widen the pause between a trigger and your response, you are either using your trauma superpower mindfully or choosing not to use it at all. Integration means that you are exerting your choice how to respond, moving the trauma app from the driver's seat to the back seat.

Integration Means Finally Understanding Your Triggers

Trauma can either intensify or block your emotional responses to your children. Whenever you get triggered and feel panicked, frozen, furious, or terrified, every parenting technique you know flies out the window because your trauma app is calling the shots.

Many PTPs think that their child triggers them, but it's not true: their child reveals their triggers. Children are not responsible for your behaviors. One of the most dangerous things we can say to a child is, "Don't trigger me. It's your fault." Once you make your child the caretaker of your triggers, you've reversed the roles of a parent-child relationship. Suddenly, it's your child's job to tiptoe around you, to create safe spaces for you. It's the parent's job to provide safety and security for the child, not the other way around.

When a parent makes their child the caretaker of their triggers, it creates intense shame in the child and can be the beginning of *emotional incest*. Emotional incest is when an adult relies on a child to provide the adult's attachment needs. This dangerous territory is discussed more fully in Alice Miller's book *The Drama of the Gifted Child*, and it's one way that trauma cycles are perpetuated.

Integration means that you know you have triggers, can see the damage they cause, and have a plan for when they occur. You'll be able to say, "My child's behavior just triggered me. But it's my job to manage my big emotions, and it's not their fault."

When a stress response takes you by surprise or you're disproportionate in your reaction to your kid's behavior, then you aren't integrated. This is particularly relevant to our kids, who keep growing and changing. What may trigger you as a people pleaser with a five-year-old is not going to be what triggers you with an eleven-year-old or with a thirteen-year-old. That's okay—when our kids reveal our triggers, that gives us a new path toward integration.

The following chart shows typical triggers for the different parenting defaults. Think of it as another piece of important data. Ultimately, you get to decide what to do with the data. To my mind, that data can be used as a throughline to your values, so I've created mottos/affirmations you can use to make integrating easier. As you're integrating this motto, you are reclaiming the psychological energy that the trauma app has seized.

You might have a trigger that's super specific to your trauma and not listed here. You can still use the process by coming up with a specific motto for yourself, using these as a model.

Common Triggers That Lead to Personality Hijacks	Associated Parenting Default	Associated Superpower	Interferes with Parenting Because . . .	Motto For Daily Integration
Overly Critical	Disengaged Perfectionist	Finds problems	Child doesn't feel accepted or unconditionally loved.	Children aren't problems; they are people. People can't be solved.
Conflict Avoidant	Paralyzed Entangled	Values relationships	Child doesn't feel secure; the parent is not a sturdy presence.	We can learn to have a good, productive fight.
People-Pleasing	Entangled Perfectionist Paralyzed	Is attentive to social cues	Child feels less important than other relationships; child feels they have to reassure the parent when the parent people-pleases the child. Teenagers will push boundaries by exploiting the parent's reluctance to say no and to people-please.	In order for me to be present with my child, I have to set boundaries with others. I'm the adult. I'm responsible for my reactions. I can apologize/take responsibility, but I don't need my child to reassure me. I am allowed to set boundaries, even if my child is upset.

Common Triggers That Lead to Personality Hijacks	Associated Parenting Default	Associated Superpower	Interferes with Parenting Because . . .	Motto For Daily Integration
Worrier/ Frequently Anxious	Paralyzed Perfectionist Disengaged	Spots danger easily	Child doesn't feel safe and soothed; child becomes fearful and anxious.	My child needs roots to feel secure and wings to explore. I won't clip their wings. I will bravely witness their bravery.
Control Freak	Perfectionist Paralyzed Disengaged	Is decisive	Child develops resentment of their lack of freedom; child doesn't feel accepted.	Good enough is really good enough, for myself and my child.
Reactive/ Easily Angered	Entangled Paralyzed Perfectionist Disengaged Survivor	Finds problems with passion	Child can become a people pleaser and lose out on an authentic relationship; child feels insecure.	When it comes to emotions, I know that I can name it, claim it, and tame it. Anger identifies a problem. I can solve problems without blowing up.
Avoidant/ Reserved	Disengaged Survivor	Observant	Child feels rejected, becomes clingy, or learns to be fearful of social situations.	A relationship is a practice of mutual knowing. I can learn to be vulnerable.
Irrational Fear (of a specific gender, age, or characteristic of a child)	Entangled Paralyzed Perfectionist Disengaged Survivor	Master of the Work-around	Child feels rejected at their core; child has a persistent sense of "not good enough" or unlovable.	I can mindfully create a strategy to manage my fear so my child feels loved and accepted. I will do the work to manage these triggers, even if that work is uncomfortable.

Common Triggers That Lead to Personality Hijacks	Associated Parenting Default	Associated Superpower	Interferes with Parenting Because . . .	Motto For Daily Integration
Ineffectual/ All Over the Place	Paralyzed Survivor	Creative and Divergent Thinking	Child feels unsupported.	Time and project management are skills, and all skills can be learned.
Shut Down	Survivor	Survival	Child feels abandoned and alone.	A state is not a trait. This feeling is temporary. I can reengage by making myself feel safe enough. If I can't do that, I can recruit support.

The minute you are triggered and do not act on your trigger, or act in a different way, is the minute you know that you're beginning to be integrated. Sometimes you realize you're integrated when it's been three years since you had "that" fight with your spouse or months since you had a disproportionate reaction. For example, the last time your friend canceled dinner plans, you were miserable for a week. This time, you were upset for a few minutes and moved on. Or it's been a couple of weeks and you have not been fighting with your eleven-year-old. When you get upset, your reaction is proportionate. Integration can sneak up on us: we don't know the exact moment it happens, but when we do notice it, we should celebrate it.

Make Meaning by Defining Your Parenting Mission

In this last phase of our AIM model, you will be transferring your fully integrated self into actions: putting to work your distinct parenting goals and values and forming a parenting mission statement that can be referred to over time.

Integrating Means Creating Workarounds

So many people live with the illusion that there's some moral value in suffering. There just isn't. If you're not a morning person and it works for your partner to do the morning routine, let's integrate that reality. In the same vein, not every fear has to be overcome. Sometimes, even when you achieve integration, you are still Little Red Riding Hood and you're always going to be afraid of wolves, so you don't get a puppy.

I wasn't a light sleeper before my father suddenly died in the middle of the night, but now I am. I have a feeling that I'm always going to be a light sleeper who has a lot of trouble falling asleep. My work-around for getting to sleep is a very specific ritual I have to do before I go to bed. I need a white noise machine and I need to take a bath. When I'm very triggered, I need to take an ice bath (Yes, really. It's not as bad as it sounds.) and then a hot bath in order to manage my PTSD symptoms and successfully fall asleep. Acceptance for me means not struggling with that reality. Integration means using my work-around mindfully, because sleep is important.

A work-around isn't protecting you, it's in some ways a part of you because you have integrated your true self. You know who you are, and you know what has to happen in order for your life to run smoothly.

You Can Rewrite Your Story

Our sense of self is based on the story we tell ourselves about ourselves. Trauma changes that story and often makes it impossible to understand or learn from. The job of integration is to rewrite and reclaim your own story.

In order to recast your story, you have to bring in an outside observer. In chapter 7, we used the analogy of a sportscaster, which comes from ACT and the sportscaster is our "observing self." In this exercise, think about a narrator who will be telling your story: the third-person omniscient voice. The omniscient narrator is not the voice in our head. In some ways they are smarter than we are, because they have much more information than the character does. And they aren't feeling our emotions. Our job is to update that narrator so that they can help us tell a new story.

First, write your story as if it were a fairy tale, using the omniscient voice of the narrator. Cast your trauma as the villain. The traumatic events could be scary, dangerous, geographical terrain or scary, dangerous, mean monsters. Try tapping into your deep, emotional core. In a fairy tale, the agency is outside of the self: stuff just happens to you. Write down how you felt, how you reacted to your trauma (your triggers), and what you think the moral of your story is. Can you see how this moral matches your trauma app? For instance,

> Dana, the little girl who had nothing and no friends, didn't have clean clothes in middle school when her family was forced to live out of their minivan. She stayed very quiet in school so that no one would notice that she was wearing the same shirt all week. Yet the teacher noticed and shamed her in front of the entire class, saying, "Dana you're so lazy, why can't you put on clean clothes?" Once the other children heard the teacher's comments, they started to bully Dana. Dana was so ashamed. She used to sneak into the bathroom during her lessons to cry.

Now, let's update the narrator with the information about your story that you didn't know at the time. For instance, there are families where daddies didn't get drunk or it wasn't okay when a teacher made fun of a girl's outfit in front of the whole class. Dana's story might change from lazy Dana who always looks sloppy to

> Dana didn't know that teachers aren't supposed to shame their students; they're supposed to be empathetic. Dana didn't know that even if some girls were mean, there were other girls who would value Dana for herself, not for her clothing. Dana was brave, and she kept going to school and trying her best. She kept trying to make friends, because she knew there were some good friends out there for her. Inside Dana was a little voice that said, "You're so unlucky and poor. Things are never going to change. No one wants to be your friend because you're weird. Even your teacher hates you." But Dana bravely ignored that voice. One day, Dana met a new group of girls that really liked her for who she was. They suggested that she talk to the school guidance counselor, who helped her deal with the teacher. Slowly, things got better. Dana is someone who keeps on trying, even when it's hard.

Can you see how Dana turned her story from victim to hero? When we can do the same, and turn a fairy tale into a hero's journey, we reclaim our *agency.* Suddenly, we have the power to make choices, the power to reframe our experiences, and the power to reprocess our trauma narrative into something more useful.

Integration can be a "work in progress." You may have to integrate many traumas, one at a time. You might continue updating the narrator as new stories come to light. But once you write down your new story, it will always be there for you to build on. My story went from a fairy tale about "Robyn, the girl whose mistakes can kill people" to "Robyn, the girl who was willing to try," to "Robyn, the woman who has the courage to take uncomfortable action."

Once we can integrate our story, we can do the same for our children. We can listen to our children when they're sad and then teach them the power of the magic word *yet. Yet* will help reframe the story from "my son who can't catch a football" to "my son who can't catch a football yet" to "my son who keeps practicing, and slowly gets better."

Can you start telling yourself your own story of your life, weaving together the fragments? If you can't rewrite your story, or if you have no understanding of your triggers and your response to them, you may need someone to help you reframe your story. That person can be a therapist, a spouse, a supportive friend, a spiritual mentor, or a coach. But that person is never your child. Your children can't be responsible for your emotional health. Your children can be what motivates you to reinterpret your story, but your children cannot be your observing self. That would create a new cycle of emotional incest.

Integration Affirmations

Use the appropriate mottos from the chart above or try any of these that resonate with you:

- My superpower has both negative and positive traits that are part of my coherent sense of self: I know who I am, I know why I am the way I am, and I know what to do about it.
- I can let uncomfortable emotions in and give them a voice.

- For the entangled parent: I have the right to my boundaries—my anger helps me protect them.
- For the perfectionist parent: I can value doing things well without having to do them perfectly.
- For the disengaged parent: It's safe for me to be present.
- For the paralyzed parent: My children are allowed to experience their emotions without me having to manage them.
- For the survivor parent: My trauma narrative is still happening. I will work toward integration when I can.

Nietzsche was known to say, "He who has a why can endure almost any how,"[8] and Victor Frankl took this lesson to heart. Frankl realized that when we give meaning to our suffering, by discovering how our trauma informs our values, we can recover. Frankl directly lived this philosophy, founding a form of psychotherapy known as *logotherapy* that is still impacting lives. His student Edith Eger, who also survived the Holocaust, wrote two books, *The Gift* and *The Choice,* expanding on this philosophy.

Finding *meaning* doesn't focus on searching for the "why" of our trauma, but it is a way to learn from the trauma, a way to utilize it for resilience, growth, and our values. It's saying, "This terrible thing has taught me a precious and hard-won lesson, and that lesson is valuable."

A friend and I were debating the oft-quoted mantra from DBT—"It is as it should be." Sometimes, that mantra doesn't sit with me. My father should not be dead. I should not have PTSD. My friend should not have lost a child. Yet we have to move forward with our losses, to create a coherent sense of self out of what happened, and to find meaning. For me, *it is as it should be* is the sense that *I* am as I should be. Meaning doesn't imply that we have to be okay with having been abused, and it isn't about determinism. Meaning simply means that this is what I learned from it. This process doesn't mean forgiveness or that you should be thankful for what you endured. And it certainly doesn't mean that what happened to you is okay. Yet my trauma taught me that I can do difficult things, that I can be comfortable with discomfort. It taught me to value relationships and that parenting is essential. It taught me something about PTS and post-traumatic growth and how to help people who have experienced trauma.

Your meaning will be the positive lessons, the deeply held truths and convictions that you take and grow from. Instead of shunting your trauma to the side, trying to become a different person, or trying to forget, you use it to inform your passion. And when you do that, you can decide what you are taking away from your trauma: the wisdom of lessons learned. The trauma app is algorithmic—*if this, do that*. Algorithms are small and are meant to keep you contained. Wisdom is big and deep: it takes in all the information, all the emotions, all the conscious values we want to embody, and it allows us to truly decide what we want to do.

For instance, Molly's house was completely destroyed when a tornado swept through her town. Her family had to start all over again: move to a new city; find a new home, new jobs, new schools; and make new friends. She found surface-level meaning in the practical. In her

The Meaning of Sadness

PTPs often tell me that as their parenting improves, they become conscious of an intense sense of sadness. I'm not surprised, because sadness tells us what we value. The focus of their sadness is actually pointing to the parenting values they want to develop. And when they can transform their sadness into meaning, real change happens.

For instance, my patient Sandy was overcome with sadness when his son, Jacob, turned six. Sandy had a sense that this particular year would be difficult, because he was six the year his parents divorced. But he didn't expect to be so profoundly sad all the time. He told me that there was a lot of neglect in his parent's home and that he always envied his childhood friends who had tight-knit families.

I explained that Sandy's sadness was trying to point him toward meaning, which could be used to find his values. I suggested that he consider the idea that "family closeness is something I value and want." He agreed, and we were able to work on a concrete plan that would foster a deeper closeness with his wife and their children. Soon, his sadness began to lift. It had done its job.

As you work through this chapter, you may feel both sadness and loss for what you didn't have. Use your sadness to inform you. Let it in. It's a messenger—take the message and do something with it.

new home, she took steps to preserve the really important stuff she didn't want to lose again. In fact, Molly now educates others on how to keep track of truly important mementos. Over time, she realized that she found meaning in the idea that even the most important "stuff" is replaceable and that relationships are what's valuable. Molly makes sure to keep up with old friends, to keep relationships going, and to focus on the relationships within her family.

Turning Meaning into Mission

Every person will find their own sense of meaning and then create a mission that is related to that meaning. Mission is what allows us to create the full coherence of our narrative—it's our "why." A mission answers the question, *What did your trauma teach you that you are therefore going to value? What do you want either for your parenting, for your kids, for yourself?*

A mission doesn't have to follow linear thinking, as in, *I was bullied, so therefore my kids are going to stand up to those who are bullied.* It doesn't have to translate exactly. It could be, *I was bullied, and I felt alone. I want my kids to always feel supported.* Can you see the difference? Either works—it's your very own mission, and you get to define it.

Some can pour themselves into a worldwide mission related to their trauma. There are so many wonderful organizations and initiatives started by people who wanted to give others the help they never got. Sharing the concept of post-traumatic parenting and writing the book I needed when I became a mother is part of my mission.

A mission can try to fill the gap of the experience you didn't have. Let's say that growing up, you felt deprived because all your friends got to participate in extracurriculars and there was no money in your family. You might start out with the mission *My kids will get to take piano lessons.* But what if they don't want to take piano lessons? Then it's time to go deeper, to find the function of what you're trying to accomplish. *Not getting to take piano lessons made me feel like my world was small and I couldn't follow my passions.* So perhaps, your mission could be redefined as *If my kids want to explore something, they can, and I'm going to support that interest. I want my kids to feel a sense of abundance. I want them to feel safe.*

I also have micromissions—small practices and truths that I want to emphasize in my family, with my kids, in my relationships, and in my work. For instance, when I think about the importance of sleep, my mission is that even when I don't want to take the time to do my work-around ritual, I am going to because I can't show up as the present parent that I value being if I don't get enough sleep. You may have a micromission that defines the way you want to parent that was different from how you were parented.

Create a Parenting Mission Statement

A mission statement helps parents use their superpowers to home in on what they wish their parenting looked like: the kind of parent they want to be and the kind of parent they do not want to be. In essence, the mission statement connects their trauma with their values.

The mission statement is a great way to accept that values are inherently hierarchical, and saying yes to one value often means saying no to another. Your trauma app may want you to value everything that can lead to better parenting. This is especially true if you've been raised by a critical or narcissistic parent or if you spend a lot of time on social media. But the truth is, if I value my kids being creative, I can't value my house being perfectly neat. I can value my kids being in a lot of after-school activities, but that means I can't value family dinners every night. You can do one or two values reasonably well. And you're allowed to make the mindful choice that works for you and your family.

Many PTPs struggle with making choices like these because of our intolerance of shame and vulnerability. If you value the emotional cleanliness of your home over physical cleanliness, someone might judge the shabbiness of your home decor aloud, and you will feel stressed and bad about yourself. Yet once you have a mission statement, you are in a better position to heal from your internal shaming voices because you're doubling down on your choice: *My house is not the tidiest house in the world, and that's okay because making tidiness a priority is not consistent with my values.* Here, you are actively living up to the expectation of your mission statement, thereby fulfilling the mission, which releases your shame.

A mission statement is a thoughtful way to show your kids that they can give you feedback and tell you how you are doing in relation to the family mission. This doesn't mean that they get full responsibility for the execution of the mission—it just means they get a vote. If part of my mission statement is "In this family, we value one another," my kids have

Exercise: Draft a Mission Statement

A mission statement starts by asking your integrated self this one simple question: What's the overall sensation I want my child to associate with growing up in my home? Perhaps it's feeling safe, heard, seen, valued, protected, loved, competent, or capable. This sensation might be how your trauma directly transforms into your mission. In acceptance, when you learned that your trauma app's people-pleasing strategy made you an exceptional empath, how can you relate that skill to the sensation you want for your mission statement?

Write down those sensation words in your journal.

My sensation words are *valued* and *capable* because my superpower is prioritizing relationships (valued) and getting stuff done (capable).

Now, can you think of a statement that supports your thematic sensation words as well as your superpower? For instance, I want my children to grow up feeling capable and valued, so my mission statement reflects those sensations: *I am raising capable future adults, who are both independent humans living in a reality of their own and interconnected beings who support and value one another.* It reflects my superpower because it shows that I value both competence and humanity, without emphasizing one at the expense of the other.

Write down your statement in your journal, keeping in mind that your trauma wasn't mine, so your mission may not be the same as mine. Drill down on what you mean by discussing it with your partner, a friend, a therapist, a spiritual adviser, or anyone else you respect. Once you've done the preliminary work, it's also fascinating to discuss with your children.

the freedom to tell me about times they don't feel valued. Your child might point out when your behavior isn't consistent with your values. I've definitely heard feedback about my phone use during family time, which doesn't make my children feel as valued as they would like. I need that feedback to keep me honest and true to my mission.

Policies Support a Mission Statement

Policies are the operational definition of the mission statement that can then be broken down into very specific rules or procedures. For instance, Google's mission statement is "Don't Be Evil." But without a policy, I have no idea what that means as a user of their software. Their policy of not allowing government agencies to access my computer is one way that explains what their mission statement means in real life.

Some of my policies that support my mission statement are that *in this family we value each other, and in this family we communicate respectfully.* I can use these policies when I'm teaching my kids skills or when their behavior crosses the line that is in opposition to my family mission statement. Using these policies makes me a better parent.

What are policies that support your mission statement? Write two or three down in your journal.

Procedures Are Policy Rules

Procedures ensure that policies can be honored: they create an operational definition for the policy and the mission statement. Procedures solidify the meanings of every word in the mission statement.

Procedures offer a great shorthand for intervening when children are struggling with the giant task of becoming humans. If children are calling each other mean names, rather than intervening directly with some form of heavy-handed consequence, we can remind them of the procedure: *We follow steps for a productive disagreement in this family. How can we have a productive disagreement about this situation you're fighting over?* This puts the onus of the mission on the entire family and gives children an opportunity to think things through—How do I communicate my frustration with my brother in a respectful manner? What would be the best words to use?

Some of the procedures I've chosen to support my policies and mission statement include the following: *We communicate respectfully. During dinner, we focus on the humans that are in the room with us, which means no screens. We follow steps for a productive disagreement. We are all citizens of this home, which means we all chip in to keep this home functioning.*

What are procedures you can put in place that support your policies and mission statement? Write two or three down in your journal.

Putting It All Together

Sandy values relationships over possessions, and his superpower is noticing that relationships are more important than anything else. He created the following:

- Mission statement: I'm raising a family who feels a sense of closeness and connection.
- Policy: In this family, we prioritize together time.
- Procedure: "Together time" specifically refers to "family dinner," a weekly "family game night," and "no phones after 6:00 p.m. for both the kids and the parents."

Using the same model, can you try to use your superpower to influence all three aspects of the mission statement?

- Mission statement: ____________________________
- Policy: ____________________________________
- Procedure: _______________________________

The AIM Model and Mr. Rogers

Did you know Fred Rogers, the beloved Mr. Rogers of our childhoods, was bullied, fat-shamed, and invalidated as a child? It was precisely this experience that led him to create *Mister Rogers' Neighborhood*. He hacked his trauma into his mission: to get into the mind and the heart of a child.

Fred Rogers's life is the perfect illustration of AIM. First, he *accepted* his uncomfortable emotions. He learned to embrace them and use them to build wisdom. There's no emotion that's so terrible that we need to numb ourselves out of it.

Next, he *integrated*. He accepted that these experiences happened; he didn't deny the experience. Fred Rogers had to work hard to integrate, and he built us a road map. Initially, he tried to transform himself. Like many bullied kids, he first internalized a sense of himself as deficient, in need of fixing. He wrote away for bodybuilding courses, yet eventually learned that he was okay just as he was. He did discover a lifelong love for swimming during his bodybuilding phase, but he also learned to accept himself.

He never forgot being bullied, and he used those emotions to create a mission: he wanted a world in which emotions are talked about and normalized. He embodied his mission statement by treating children to a kinder, safer place—his neighborhood, which was a world where children could access a vocabulary for the challenges they are going through, the experiences they want to share, and their emotions.

Rather than seeing yourself as damaged, can you accept, integrate, and find meaning in your trauma? Whatever your mission is, whether it is a macromission like Mr. Rogers's or a micromission that affects only your family, you have the unique insight to make it possible. It is the ultimate alchemy of transforming your trauma into your superpower. You can stop worrying that your damage will damage your children. You are giving them the unique gift that is you. And with that, you can begin to find joy.

Joy is different than happiness or pleasure. Joy is the sensation we get when we're flourishing, when we're living our life in accordance with our values. Joy feels pleasant and happy, but it's deeper than that. Joy is meant to be fleeting and momentary. The AIM model restored my joy, and I know it can do the same for you.

I remember the sense of joy I had the first time I handled a parenting situation from a fully integrated place. We were having a family meeting, and one of my children brought up a problem—she was being bullied, and she wanted support, ideas, and practical help from her siblings. My trauma app tried to shrill an alarm: *She's being bullied! Danger! Solve it! You were bullied and bullies are way too dangerous.* Yet integrated me was able to shut off that alarm, and I watched with pride as we all came up with solutions to the problem. I realized in that moment that I'm good at parenting. I have created a family that values one another and is capable of handling challenges. My children know how to talk about their problems. They turn to one another for support. They come to me with their dilemmas, because they trust I'll be there for them. I had created the family dynamic I always wanted.

CHAPTER 10

R2 Parenting

Being Both Responsive and Responsible

PARENTS HAVE ENDLESS to-do lists: bathe the baby, buy more diapers, buy school supplies, bake twenty-four pink cupcakes for the class party, wash the soccer uniform, make doctor and dentist appointments, the thousands of breakfasts, lunches and dinners that need to be made and cleaned up after, and finally getting everyone to bed every day. PTPs also have a giant list of internalized *to-don'ts*: don't yell, don't get mad, don't make the kid feel insecure, don't mess them up, don't get into power struggles, don't make them feel unloved, don't make my kids responsible for my triggers. Basically, don't traumatize them. It's really hard for anyone to navigate the to-dos, and it's even harder to navigate the to-don'ts.

If you have a natural capacity to react appropriately to parenting dilemmas, toddler meltdowns, or to your middle school child's push-back when you set a limit, it's likely that you had good parenting role models in your home. The technical term for this skill is *discernment*. You intrinsically understand that there will sometimes be challenges, that your child will sometimes experience distress or frustration, and that you might sometimes make mistakes, and that's okay. But for many PTPs, any challenge has the capacity to overwhelm and create more to-don'ts.

Can PTPs meet our children's needs even if we didn't have these same skills modeled for us? Absolutely! The key for us will be to adopt the best parenting practices and discard ideas that don't serve us or our kids. In this way, we can whittle down the to-don't list so that we can more easily get through the to-dos.

If you experienced "good-enough" attachment with your own parents, you probably have developed an "internal working model" of how to securely move through the world. If there's a dilemma, like any of the daily parenting situations that typically come up, you can trust yourself to figure it out. Yet when you're experiencing a lot of self-doubt, your internal working model isn't as strong, and that's called being *insecure.* A parent who doesn't have that internal working model is already feeling shaky before the day even starts.

Evaluating your own attachment can feel depressing. If your internal working model is a lemon and there's no way to get the updated version, or even a refund, don't worry: there is a lesser-known concept in attachment research called *earned security.* You can repair attachment in adulthood by providing good attachment to your children, increasing your earned security. As we've said before, in parenting, we are parented.

Understanding New Trends

Responsive Parenting

Parents today are embracing a gentler, more compassionate parenting approach that's a pendulum shift away from the more authoritarian way I was, and you may have been, raised. The truth is, certain strategies that even the most well-intentioned parents used were actually not ideal. For instance, I am not a big believer in time-outs. I believe in controlling a child's environment rather than trying to control the child. I don't believe in blaming or shaming children for developmentally appropriate errors. And I don't ever promote harsh punishment, like spanking or the silent treatment.

You may have come across terms like *gentle parenting, conscious parenting, low-demand parenting, responsive parenting,* or even *natural parenting.* All these practices are basically the same, and the goal is to foster a new sense of responsiveness between parent and child by taking attachment theory and child development research into consideration. These parenting styles prioritize connection over correction, seeing a child as a Little Human figuring the world out, rather than as a blank slate to mold and train into proper behavior. It's a style that I find appealing and, for the most part, effective. The basic philosophy behind these parenting strategies is that parents should be tuned into their child's emotions and individualize their approach to meet the child's developmentally appropriate needs. For instance, if your toddler is crying because they are overtired, you need to have a strategy for calming their upset that works for a toddler, not a teenager. You need a strategy that works for "overtired," not any of the other toddler stressors, like separation.

Responsive parenting starts with two major foundational concepts: empathy/attunement and mindfulness/presence. We help our kids learn self-regulation by teaching them about their emotions, *attuning* with them to help them celebrate their joys and deal with their discomforts. Attunement is being deeply aware of and responsive to a child's emotional and psychological needs. It means recognizing and validating a child's feelings, being present and engaged, and understanding their perspective. When my child is dysregulated, I don't "punish" or "shame" them, I help them co-regulate by using the exercises you'll find in chapter 12. Once they've learned to co-regulate, I relate to their emotions and come up with effective strategies so that they can manage these same challenging emotions in the future. A mindful presence is the foundation of an attachment relationship.

Responsive parenting means communicating respectfully and reciprocally with children rather than using the more authoritarian response of "You'll do it because I said so." It means truly listening when a child has a question, comment, concern, or feedback. It means taking the temperature of the relationship every so often, asking ourselves, How am I actively providing the four S's—making my kids feel safe, secure, seen, and soothed? How am I balancing my daily decisions with the crucially important role of being the attachment figure?

When we are at the crossroads of a parenting decision, we can ask ourselves one question: Is my decision/reaction going to help or harm my overall relationship with my child? A responsive parent always prioritizes the relationship rather than the "behavior." My child being "disobedient" in a store isn't the measure of my parenting; it's simply

Measuring the Success of Responsive Parenting

- Are my strategies informed by child development?
- Am I co-regulating with my child?
- Am I helping my child understand their emotions and develop self-regulation?
- Am I communicating respectfully and reciprocally with my child?
- Are my child and I experiencing moments of attunement?
- Am I paying attention to the attachment relationship?

a data point of a skill I need to help them learn. If my child is having a meltdown, that's not a temper tantrum that needs to be "trained out of them,"; it's a developmentally appropriate response to overwhelming stress. If I help my child gradually learn to cope with stress, eventually, meltdowns will stop on their own. Simply put: responsive equals permission to care.

Why PTPs Struggle with Responsive Parenting

Some PTPs find responsive parenting to be triggering. Here's why: many gentle parenting proponents on social media are judgmental, using harsh and stark terms for parents who don't live up to their ideals. One of my personal favorite assertions is the suggestion that anyone who uses a sticker chart is abusing their child. I've been asked to comment on social media posts that assert opinions like day care ruins attachment, children shouldn't leave their parents until kindergarten (or ever—we should all apparently move to a farm and homeschool), not babywearing will traumatize your child, co-sleeping is the only way to make children feel supported, and so on. There's a strong undercurrent of parent—particularly mother—blaming in the online gentle parenting spaces. I've seen parents ask a genuine question like, "I'm trying not to punish my son, but what should I do when he beats up his little sister?" be met with responses along the lines of "If you're getting frustrated with your child, the problem is you. Why did you even bother having children?"

These judgmental stances feed into our shame and guilt, which ironically makes us less emotionally available to be responsive. And if you're post-traumatic, you experience parent guilt on steroids because you already have all kinds of self-doubt, and your trauma app is constantly screaming that you're going to mess up your kids. As I've already said, it's difficult to be attachment-focused if your internal working model is defective. When you're self-blaming about how other parents seem to be able to keep their cool and be so responsive and gentle all the time, you now know it's not you; it's your trauma.

Perfect parenting is a myth. You are not always the problem. I don't think Taylor Swift has a PhD in psychology, but she clearly gets trauma (see the figure on the following page).

It's also not surprising that a lot of PTPs who are trying to be responsive end up erring on the side of being overly permissive. Instead of trying to engage in "low-demand, high responsive" parenting, they're

trying for "no-demand, only responsive" parenting. This is both unrealistic and ultimately disabling for children. Sometimes we have to set limits, enforce a boundary, and ensure safety, and sometimes these limits will create distress. That's okay.

I don't think the actual responsive parenting experts really meant "if your child is experiencing distress, this means you're a bad parent." I think they'd more readily endorse "if your child is experiencing distress, empathize with the distress." Yet it's very easy to turn empathy into "I'll fix it." If my child is truly distressed about having to wear shoes, and I'm empathizing—"I see you're so frustrated about wearing shoes. Shoes can sometimes feel yucky. You're so sad."—it feels like the next logical step would be to remove the shoes. After all, you theoretically can lug a forty-pound toddler in your arms because they won't wear shoes. But this isn't responsive—it's permissive.

Understanding Responsible Parenting

When a parent is following an authoritarian style, they are requiring certain behaviors or outcomes from a child in a coercively controlling fashion. This style isn't intended to be hurtful or malicious: these parents typically believe they are being "responsible" parents who teach their children the skills they need to navigate the world. While the goal of responsive parenting is to maintain the parent-child relationship, the goal of authoritarian parenting is controlling behavior. But we're not raising behaviors; we're raising little humans.

PTPs don't want to be that authoritarian, "my way or the highway" parent. We don't want our kids to be coerced, especially if we felt coerced in our own lives. And we don't want our kids to feel that our love for them is contingent upon a particular behavior or mastery of a skill.

We also don't want our kids to feel alone with their emotions. When parenting is too strict, children can shut down or dissociate. Your inner child may remember what this feels like and will avoid it at all costs. The result is a permissive parenting style where anything goes in order to avoid being strict.

Sometimes, we end up unconsciously reinforcing our children's fear because we are afraid to make demands. The technical term for this is *reification*. When a child is afraid of something and they look to us for guidance, if we're afraid of the same thing, we might reinforce it. For instance, let's say you are dealing with a toddler with a sleep issue. Most toddlers are sleep avoidant: I've met very few kids who will gladly tell their parents, "I'm tired. I'd really like to stop screen time and go to bed now." If you are having difficulty getting your child to sleep and you have your own phobias about sleep, you're going to transfer that fear in your child.

What Does Diana Baumrind Say?

The gold standard of parenting research was done by Diana Baumrind, PhD, in the 1980s, when she came up with the idea of parenting "styles." If you've heard of *permissive* or *authoritarian parenting*, those are her terms. Her research has been shown to apply to many cultures, with some consideration for nuance.

In her research, Baumrind writes, "Parenting is a balance between responsiveness and demandingness,"[1] and I completely agree. When parents are highly responsive, without being demanding at all, we call them "permissive." Permissive looks a lot like letting kids do whatever they want and is a fallback strategy for my paralyzed and survivor parenting types.

The other end of the spectrum is a parent who is entirely demanding. Those parents are called "authoritarian." Authoritarian parenting is the old school, disciplinarian-style parenting—my way or the highway, "spare the rod and spoil the child" parenting. There's very little warmth or reciprocity, and it is a fallback strategy for my perfectionist and entangled parenting types.

This is going to sound like splitting hairs, but I think there's a misconception regarding the term *demandingness*. When Baumrind said that good parenting means balancing responsiveness and demandingness, she meant that a parent needs to help children deal with the natural demands, or realities, of living in a world that isn't always easy to navigate. It's not about a parent "demanding" that a child must go to bed on time. We don't have to be the strict, coercive, authoritarian parent who demands respect, obedience, compliance, or perfect behavior. But we do have to help our kids navigate a world that has many real demands. Libraries are spaces that demand quiet, bodies demand rest and nutrition and attention, school demands focus and concentration, lines demand waiting, and social situations demand an understanding of basic etiquette—it's our job to help our kids learn to navigate those demands.

Baumrind recommends a parenting style that is balanced between both, where parents are both responsive and warm, as well as demanding certain behaviors from their children. She calls this "authoritative" parenting. My R2 Parenting style is a type of authoritative parenting that is attainable for PTPs and also takes more recent research on child development, attunement, attachment, and interpersonal neurobiology into account.

Introducing R2 Parenting

I believe that we can be responsive to our children's emotional needs, to parent more gently than the way we were parented, and at the same time, be responsible and teach our children self-regulation competencies, social skills, and empathy, without being authoritarian in our approach.

By combining the best of these two approaches, I've come up with a practice that I call R2 Parenting: responsive and responsible. The outcome is closer to Baumrind's idea of *authoritative parenting*, which when implemented correctly, is nurturing and supportive while also providing clear expectations, setting firm limits and boundaries, and focusing on accountability. R2 parents have the flexibility to teach children skills in a gentle and noncoercive fashion: to manage tasks, responsibilities, and obligations; deal with frustration; and think about other humans and their rights. Authoritative, R2 Parenting suggests that when a child's behavior is not welcome, it's our job to teach them what to do instead. In other words, when a child says, "Just one more level of the video game" but the clock shows that it's bedtime, an R2 parent can state the expectation without the child feeling shamed or blamed. R2 Parenting equals permission to parent.

Aliza Pressman, PhD, states this essential duality well: "All emotions are welcome, all behaviors are not."[2] All emotions are welcome—that's responsive parenting. All behaviors are not—that's responsible parenting. R2 takes this idea a step further, because while we always lead with responsiveness, I also want you to replace the child's behaviors you don't want with skills you want your child to have. And I want your child to feel like they are part of developing the solution.

R2 Parenting is skills oriented. If my kid has a problem with virtually anything—meltdowns at the dinner table, inability to take no for an answer, school refusal, difficulty making or maintaining friendships, chronic lateness, constant low-level anger—I believe there is likely an underlying skill they don't have. I either need to teach the skill or, if this child's brain is not yet ready to learn the skill, I need to control the environment, not the child. I need a *scaffold*, or to break down the skill into smaller, more manageable steps until the child is ready to learn that skill and use it independently.

In R2 Parenting, we always address our children with responsiveness, starting with the foundational principle that children are little humans who need our attachment, compassion, and curiosity and that our relationship with them is primary. Then we can go to the pragmatic, responsible side of the equation—How can I teach my child skills and competencies so that we can get through the quandary that is right in front of us? Which strategies make sense to me? Do those strategies line up with responsiveness, or is there a way to make them more responsive?

Here's an example of R2 Parenting from my client Anita. Ten-year-old Patricia was being cruel to her seven-year-old sister, Sophie. Patricia yelled at her, shoved her, and called her a brat. Every time Sophie tried to object, Patricia would snap, "Brat! Brat! I don't want to talk to a brat!" Anita couldn't stand the tension in the house for another minute, so she put her R2 Parenting into action. She asked Patricia to step away and took a deep breath so that she could mentally prepare herself.

Instead of yelling at Patricia, who was clearly the instigator, the R2 way first focuses attention on Sophie, making sure she's okay.

Anita hugged Sophie until she stopped crying and soothed her—she was responsive to her daughter's feelings in the moment. Anita said, "Sophie, sounds like the past few minutes have been challenging. Let's get to the bottom of this together."

Then, Anita moved on to Patricia, who was stewing angrily on the couch. Even though Patricia's actions upset her, Anita knew that every parenting interaction starts with a responsive approach. Anita also knew that if Patricia acted out, there was likely a reason. What competency does Patricia need help with? What doesn't she get about the family value of communicating with respect? Which emotions are blocking her?

As Anita sat next to her daughter and co-regulated with Patricia, her responsiveness restored a sense of calm. She expressed empathy by saying how she understood how Patricia could feel frustrated with her little sister and that it's okay to feel angry. She said, "You know, your anger is identifying a problem. Since people cannot be problems, Sophie is not the problem. What's really going on?"

Patricia blurted, "Sophie's always ruining my stuff!"

Anita said, "I get it. No one likes it when their stuff is ruined. That's really frustrating."

Patricia nodded, and they took a moment to breathe.

Anita went on: "What do we have to do to keep your stuff safe? What's a better way to solve the problem than yelling at her and calling her names?"

Patricia said, "I could put stuff in my room, but she still comes in whenever she wants and touches everything."

Anita turned the interaction into a problem-solving conversation and used her curiosity to transition from a responsive to a more responsible approach. "What do you think we should do to separate Sophie from your stuff? Should we put a lock on your closet, put up a high shelf in your room where she can't reach, or remind her of the rule that she can't come into your room without your permission?"

Patricia liked the idea of putting a lock on her closet door, and she agreed to make sure to put her most precious belongings in the closet. She asked her mom to remind Sophie of the family expectation of respecting other people's possessions. Anita said, "I'm happy to do all of that. Do you think that you followed our family value of communicating with respect?"

Patricia said, "Probably not. But it's still Sophie's fault that I got upset."

Anita said, "I totally get that you felt provoked, but there's a smarter way to handle your big emotions. You could have asked for help, you could have taken a breather, or you could have explained to Sophie what she did wrong without making her cry. So next time Sophie frustrates you, what do you hope you'll do?"

Patricia said, "I'll ask you for help."

Anita said, "Great. Now you've got to figure out how to restore peace between you and your sister."

Patricia said, "Fine. She's still annoying, but I'll tell her she's not a brat."

Anita said, "I think you need to do a little better than that in order to make her feel better. I'm going to find Sophie so we can all talk about the new procedures together."

This scenario may seem like a labor-intensive solution to a simple fight between siblings. But think about how many social and emotional competencies Anita was teaching along the way. She modeled co-regulation. She focused on the person who needed the most help first. She was teaching emotional fluency—helping the girls understand that anger is an emotion that provides important data about problems we need to solve. She also helped them engage in dialogue and emotional intelligence skills they'll need for life. Finally, there was no blaming or shaming, yet everyone learned important lessons. No punishment was needed!

Adopting R2 Parenting Is a Skill

When you first try R2 Parenting, your trauma app is likely to push back. Your trauma app is going to warn you of the impending danger of your child experiencing discomfort as you teach them a skill. But your trauma app is operating from inadequate and outdated information: while it was true that you experienced challenges and didn't have a resource for help, your child is in an entirely different situation. Your child might experience some of those same challenges that you did, but they have you to help them navigate. They aren't you—they *have* you and your guidance, and your support, and your willingness to listen, be there, and most of all, parent.

If you've experienced coercive control, if your child's distress is too triggering to witness, or if you doubt your own ability to parent, you might err on the side of too much responsiveness. If you personalize your kids' behaviors, you might err on the side of authoritarian parenting. Balance is the key. When I think of balance, I think of a seesaw. No parent is ever going to be able to keep a seesaw perfectly level. The trick is to use both approaches, and if we are tipping too much to one side, we can balance out by leaning more toward the other.

R2 Parenting Goals

It used to be that children's behavior was the hallmark of "good parenting." If children were obedient or polite, the parents would hear about what a good job they were doing. In R2 Parenting, it's not behavior but the relationship. If the relationship is strong enough to be resilient, you know you're doing a good job.

What are the cues your kid is going to give you to tell you that you're doing a good job? When your child knows that the relationship between both of you is front and center and the child sees you as a solution, not a problem, you have reached the right balance between responsive and responsible. You will become the person they go to with their problems, and you don't have that sense that you're walking on eggshells in addressing their concerns. You know what's going on in your child's life and the relationship feels reciprocal. They see you as someone who provides the four S's: they feel seen, safe, secure, and soothed by you. The child feels your love and you feel like you have someone who loves you. When your kids come to you with their problems, you might think, Oh my gosh, what am I doing wrong? The truth is, you're doing everything right.

Mentalization is the process by which a relationship becomes an inner voice and an inner voice becomes a capacity. Let's say your child's best friend rejects them. Your child's first thought is, *I'm going to go to my mom or dad. They're going to know what to do.* When they come and tell you, you validate how sad and rejected they feel. You tell them what an incredible person they are and all the good things you know about them. This feedback becomes their inner voice. Over time, that inner voice becomes a capacity for resilience, to try again, even after something was painful. That might mean the capacity to start life again in adulthood, after much more devastating losses.

One of my most cherished memories is when my son went off to college. He saw how sad I was, and he created a cover for the Daniel Tiger song "Grown-Ups Come Back," except he changed the words to "Children Come Back." It was a full circle moment—I used to sing him that song to prepare him for kindergarten, when he was reluctant to go inside, and now he was singing it to comfort me. We had created a relationship that we both wanted to nourish. To me, that's the ultimate sign of good parenting.

Children do come back when they have a wonderful relationship with you. The fact that my adult children love to spend time with our family, include my husband and myself in their lives, and still are close to me tells me that I did do it right, that when I resisted using "good behavior" as a measure of good parenting and instead focused on the relationship, I'd made the right choice.

R2 Journal Prompts

- What are your specific "parenting pain points"? Examples might be the morning routine, bedtime, homework, siblings fighting, children losing possessions, screen time, meltdowns.
- What skill or capacity do you need to teach your child so that they can handle these situations more effectively?
- What is the main challenge for your child that blocks them from developing or using this skill?

Temperament and R2 Parenting

Every child is born with their own temperament, which is our biologically based, hardwired, predictable stress response. For example, how strongly you react to new situations or stress comes from your temperament. Some kids are chill; some are loud. Some kids are cautious; some kids are friendly. None of these reactions are related to you or your parenting. You may feel responsible for your child's temperament, but in truth, it says nothing about you as a parent, with or without trauma. Your child is who they are.

If your child has a very different temperament from yours, parenting can be difficult because your expectations of their behavior will be challenged. Someone with naturally low energy and activity levels is going to have a hard time with a very active child. Sometimes, your child's temperament is exactly like yours, which can also be challenging. A reactive parent and a reactive child might end up getting very loud and then feel bad about it. How you react to your child's temperament is much more important than their temperament itself. Your child is going to be different from you in both predictable and unpredictable ways. And that's not only okay, but it's also to be expected. Accepting who your child is, and how they react to the world, is also part of the AIM model's acceptance concept. Sometimes, we engage in counterfactual thinking about temperament—*if only my child didn't inherit my shyness, if only my child was more like me and less like my ex . . .* However, we can use our acceptance capacities in parenting to remember *my child is exactly who they should be.*

R2 Parenting takes a child's temperament into account and uses it as a data point so that you can develop strategies that work for them. A clear line connects temperament and behavior. So while there is no such thing as a good or bad temperament—it's just one way to understand children—child temperament plus life experience becomes their adult personality.

In temperament research, we talk about "goodness of fit" and "poorness of fit." Every temperament profile will do well in some situations and be challenged by others. As parents, we basically have three choices: we can find and promote the good fit situations for our kids, avoid the bad fit situations that aren't really important, or we can teach self-regulation so that they can handle themselves in other, unavoidable poor fit situations. It's not your job to change your kid's temperament. It's your job to find that good fit between the parent you want to be and can be and your child's temperament.

This is exactly where R2 Parenting comes into play. If your trauma superpower is a poor fit for your child's temperament, it's on you to figure out a work-around so that you can be responsive to them without triggering you. For example, my trauma app doesn't do well with extremely loud noises, and I have children who are naturally exuberant. I found earbuds that can block out the loudest frequencies of sound so I can interact with a naturally loud child without going into freeze mode. When my children were older and capable of learning new skills and this type of exuberance was becoming a problem in spaces where quiet was expected, I used my responsible parenting skills and created a game to teach them the concept of controlling their voice to match the environment.

Temperaments to Look For

Can you see any of the following temperament qualities in your child, no matter their age? If you can identify where your kid lands, it's easier to predict what challenges they're going to have. You'll also be able to see their temperament as their superpower so that you can teach skills that acknowledge what their brain is hardwired to do and is naturally good at. For example, if your kid is cautious and shy, you can focus their attention on why that new girl in class is not a threat—she enjoys the art corner just like you do, so you probably have things in common. The following temperament profiles were first introduced in *Your Child's Unique Temperament: Insights into Children's Temperament* by Dr. Sandee McClowry, who was my mentor and dissertation chair.[3] If you'd like to learn more about your child's temperament or have your school use temperament-based teaching approaches based on *INSIGHTS*, check out her website (https://insightsintervention.com/what-is-insights/).

- Reactivity: If they're startled, do they scream and have a hard time being soothed, or are they more mellow?
- Cautiousness: Are they happy to meet new people and enter new situations, or are they avoidant, more cautious, and slow to warm up to people or situations?
- Task persistence: Can your child complete a task? For babies or toddlers, see what happens when you interrupt their play. In older kids, see how they feel about completing tasks. Does it stress them out to stop in the middle? Does it stress them out to have to persist until they're finished?
- Activity: Some kids need to be constantly moving and find stillness stressful. Others are the opposite.
- Rhythmic: This refers to the strength of biological rhythms, like circadian clocks and appetites. Some children need to be highly scheduled and thrive on predictability. Others can be more flexible.
- Effortful control: This aspect of temperament is usually relevant when children are school-age. This is how good the child is at self-control or how impulsive they are.

Co-Regulation to Self-Regulation with R2 Parenting

Each temperament has situations for which they are a good fit and situations for which they are a poor fit. Just because someone's temperament is a poor fit to a certain situation does not mean that they have to change everything about themselves or the situation. However, it's our job as parents to teach them how to handle themselves in situations when there is a poor fit.

Poor fit situations are particularly challenging when your temperament and your child's are at odds. If both you and your child are reactive, it means that your child is easily upset and difficult to calm and you are easily upset and take a while to self-regulate. Your job is to figure out the self-regulation capacities your kid doesn't naturally have and how to help your child through those challenging situations. The good part of knowing this is that you can problem-solve in advance: if you know that a certain environment or activity is going to be challenging, you can figure out how to set the situation up for as much success as possible.

Sometimes, making accommodations can be very necessary for resolving a parenting situation. For instance, one of my kids had a hard time holding a pencil correctly, so I bought her a pencil grip: this is a reasonable accommodation. The goal for accommodations is always to act like rubber bands, not pretzels. *Pretzeling* means making convoluted accommodations so that your child doesn't have to do something that they are not good at, not a good fit for, or find upsetting.

Pretzel accommodations can get ridiculous. For instance, I once met a parent who told me that his son, Ryan, "has a phobia of loud noises" and therefore can't handle fire drills at school. In an effort to keep his son calm, he asked the principal to excuse his son from fire drills. Perhaps in the very beginning of the school year, this type of "pretzel" accommodation is helpful, allowing a phobic child to enter an environment they feel threatened by. But pretzeling can be disabling. Eventually, a child needs to learn how to handle a challenge. Fire drills in particular are simply not optional!

It's okay to start with pretzeling, especially when a new skill or capacity is overwhelming and this feeling is likely to interfere with the child's ability to learn the new skill. But pretzeling should always be a first step. Then we can slowly raise the expectations so that the child learns the skill they need to handle a challenge. This strategy is called *rubber banding*, because you are gently "stretching" the child so they can learn the skill.

Remember, rubber bands can snap if they're pulled too quickly or with too much force. It's important to very gently stretch a child into learning a new skill by gradually increasing their exposure to the skill, teaching new steps, rehearsing, and focusing on self-regulation along the way. The stretch should be gentle and playful. In the next chapter, we're going to learn how to gamify rubber band exercises.

When Ryan and his dad came to see me, I started rubber banding with an explanation as to why loud noises can set off a panic response. I then taught Ryan how to do deep breathing and relaxation exercises so that when he does feel panicky, he can bring his heart rate and breathing back under conscious control and manage the panic response. At the next session, I played the sound of a fire drill, getting gradually louder and louder, and showed Ryan how to breathe and self-regulate through the noise. Eventually, with the permission of the fire department, we set up an actual fire drill, which this boy was able to handle with ease. Not only did he learn a valuable skill, but I also pointed out how brave and courageous he was by facing a fear head-on. The fire chief even sent him a letter of commendation and a medal of bravery, telling him that by learning to handle this phobia, he is making himself, his classmates,

For Neurodiverse Children

R2 Parenting can look a little different for families with neurodiverse (ADHD to the autism spectrum) or psychodiverse (anxiety disorders to OCD and/or mood disorders) kids. These children may need a greater degree of responsiveness vs. responsible feedback because their psychological capacities might need to be more slowly scaffolded. You may have to act as a mediator for their struggles so that they can operate in a world where other people don't even realize that there are struggles.

It's also harder to give yourself to a child if they are not capable of taking the love you're trying to give in the way you're giving it. That can be frustrating and lead to self-doubt for the parent. It may be more difficult to look at the relationship as a marker for good parenting—some neurodiverse kids may not provide indicators of a strong relationship. Instead, look to your own behavior as a marker for good parenting. If you met your child where they are, connecting in a way that they feel most comfortable with (even if the world wouldn't see it that way), and if you are your child's best advocate and staunchest support, then know this: you're a good parent.

If your trauma is that you are neuroatypical, then you already figured out how to live in the world. You might not know what works, but you definitely know what doesn't work, and you can be an advocate for your child.

and even the firefighters of the town safer. Yes, there was also a reward for participating in the exercise, but the greatest reward was the sense of satisfaction Ryan got from facing his fear head-on, from stretching the rubber band gently until the unthinkable became the achievable. I recently ran into Ryan's dad, who told me his son now wants to grow up to be an EMT and work at a firehouse!

The Capacities of Healthy Parents

There are some fundamental truths about parenting that PTPs may intellectually be aware of but don't quite believe. Some of these ideas may be completely startling to you; I know some of them startled me. These are the implicit assumptions about parenting that many people who had a healthy, normative childhood just know. They might not know the specific terminology, but they implicitly understand how these concepts work.

It's okay if these ideas are new to you. Once you read them, see if you can remind yourself of them every so often. These are the building blocks of R2 Parenting: skills you need to learn.

Truth #1

When It Comes to Resolving Conflicts, the Focus Is Not the Rupture but the Repair

As I explained in chapter 5, a breakdown or disruption in any relationship is referred to as a *rupture*. This could include misunderstandings, conflicts, emotional outbursts, or behaviors that cause feelings of hurt or neglect. *Repair* is how we fix the rupture.

There will always be times when you and your child are not seeing the world the same way or can't be in the same place. If you, like me, can't co-sleep because of PTSD and your child sleeps in a crib and maybe you sleep through their crying once or twice, that's a mild rupture. The repair is being attentive and loving during night feedings or when the toddler wakes up in the morning.

While ruptures can be uncomfortable, they are not typically devastating to the relationship. In fact, when we pay close and mindful attention to repair, the relationship gets stronger. Yet many PTPs interact with their children in ways that avoid conflict, because they believe that all ruptures are terrible. If babywearing, co-sleeping, child-led weaning, homeschooling, or elimination communication works for you, go for it. But if you are using these practices only because you're deathly afraid that if you don't, you'll irreparably damage your child's attachment, please know that the attachment system is not fragile: it can handle the bottle instead of the breast, an adult-only date night, or standard-issue toilet training. I use the acronym REPAIR (ruptures eventually provide adaptations in relationships) in my parenting classes. It's the rupture that allows the relationship to grow, change, evolve, and adapt.

Can you see how you may be sidestepping conflicts in your home? If you've never experienced true repair, it's easy to understand why you could be conflict avoidant. However, sidestepping conflict has ramifications and leads to overly permissive parenting. When parents try to cocoon their child from distress, separation, or any level of frustration, not only are they avoiding ruptures, but they are also avoiding the benefits of repair.

Whenever there's a rupture, R2 parents focus on what they can do to repair that rupture. They ask, What can we—myself and my child—learn to ensure a better experience in the future? When there's a rupture because the child lashes out, do I make myself available for repair, or do I feel the need to "punish disrespect out of them"? Do I remember that the relationship is the most important asset we have as parents?

We don't need to look for opportunities to rupture the relationship, because life will do that for us. Luckily, there is a "right way" to get to repair. Here's how:

- Step One: Prepare yourself mentally to begin the process of repair. This means turning off your trauma app's permissions. Mindfully tell your trauma app that its alarms are not helpful right now. Then press "mute." (I literally visualize doing this.)
- Step Two: When you're ready to engage with the person you ruptured with, begin by acknowledging that the situation was challenging or difficult. Acknowledge what went wrong ("Wow, that was hard getting out the door this morning"). Acknowledge how you think they may have felt ("You must have felt really tired and scared when

I yelled"). Validate any feelings they express ("You weren't only scared; you were also mad. I get that").

- Step Three: Acknowledge what you did wrong ("Even if it was a frustrating morning, I shouldn't have yelled at you to 'hurry up'"). Do not dramatize the situation with "How could I have yelled? I'm the worst parent ever." You don't need to apologize in a way that gets your child to absolve you of your behavior; it's not your child's job to make you feel better about yourself. I was raised to believe that parents don't apologize to children because it interferes with the hierarchy of respect. Others on social media claim that apologizing to kids makes kids feel insecure. I don't see it. To me, when kids know that their parents could mess up, they see them as humans they can model themselves on. If my parent can mess up and then repair, so can I! In addition, when children see that their parents respect the relationship enough to repair it, they feel valued.
- Step Four: Problem-solve for the future. Offer suggestions and ask for input. This might sound like, How should we handle it the next time I need you to get your shoes on, if we're very late? Is there a special code word we can agree on so that you know it's time to put on your shoes?

Exercise: Repair Strengthens Relationships

Take a clean piece of paper and draw two circles to represent you and your child. Then, draw the most efficient way to connect the two of you. Now, crumple the paper into a tiny ball. As you crumple the paper, think of all the ruptures you had with your kids. The time when they were fussing and you reacted with frustration instead of kindness. The time you said those words you truly regret.

Now, open the paper, smooth it flat, and trace all the wrinkles.

People think the best relationship is a smooth, conflict-free one. But now that we've wrinkled the relationship, can you see that there are so many paths between you and your child? Every single rupture creates a new path toward each other, forming a stronger relationship.

Truth #2

We Have Time to Parent

When it comes to teaching our children how to be their best selves, we have plenty of time. Our trauma app creates a false sense of urgency to resolve the problem, fix the child, and make the stress go away. The truth is, your child's temperament is pretty set, and they are going to behave according to it in the same way forever. If five-year-old Michael is way too active and impulsive and struggling with learning to read, your trauma app wants you to "drill and kill" those phonics flashcards and "fix" him. But if we're curious, responsive, and open, we can see that learning to read is a process that takes time. Forcing a distractible child who is active to sit and drill phonics is likely to be counterproductive. Instead, can you make learning to read more fun? Can you give him frequent breaks and gamified ways to help him practice? In this way, you're being responsive and responsible: you're noticing the child's temperament and creating learning opportunities that are consistent with it while also helping him get better at reading.

Truth #3

There Is a Difference Between Punishments, Consequences, and Rewards

It's easy to confuse punishments and consequences. A punishment is intentional infliction of pain to deter the repetition of certain behaviors. If I'm trying to teach my child time management, punishing them by taking away their phone will not teach them that "time moves more quickly than I realize." Instead, they will learn that "Mom is going to be mad and I will lose my phone, so I better get my sneakers on."

I'm not a big believer in punishments. I don't believe in silent treatments or "punishments" that have nothing to do with the situation at hand (withholding dessert for bad grades, for example). Instead of looking at a challenging behavior as a moment to teach a skill, punishments tend to shut the situation down. While they may "work," they erode a child's sense of trust in the parent. Punishments can inspire stress and fear, and I know that I don't learn well when I'm scared. Do you? I'm certainly not a fan of harsh punishments: the research is clear that spanking does not work,[4] and it is associated with many negative outcomes in adulthood.[5]

A consequence is a policy and a procedure that is put in place so that a behavior doesn't happen again and, hopefully, you learn a skill to replace the behavior. A consequence can evoke distress, but that's not the point of the consequence. If my children are getting overstimulated on the trampoline and playing in a way that could be dangerous, I might say that trampoline time is over because I'm seeing a behavior where someone could get hurt. I'm not angry, shaming, or blaming. I'm simply stating the boundary. Will children learn from experience that fun trampoline time can end when we get overstimulated and roughhouse a bit too roughly? Sure. But they're learning from the safety rule, not from my upset. The consequence of playing unsafely on the trampoline means we don't get as much fun time on it, so it's not a wise choice for them. Consequences are clearly intended to help children manage their emotions, learn to handle stressful situations more effectively, or keep everyone safe. A consequence might be something like, "We spent a very long time leaving the playground and now we don't have time to stop off in the water-sprinkler area like we usually do. So we have to go home."

Many people associate rewards with punishments and consequences. While there is some truth to the notion that "behavior that is rewarded is repeated," I don't think every single parenting decision should be shaped by a system of rewards and consequences. Yet many parents use the word *reward* when they mean *bribe*. A bribe is the promise of a treat for delivering a desired behavior. *If you get on the bus right now, I will give you extra ice cream at dessert* is a bribe. A reward comes after a behavior and exists to reinforce that behavior. A family movie on Sunday night is a reward that follows a week of Chrissy making the bus on time.

Setting expectations so that they are not just about the reward or the consequence is one of the major objectives of R2 Parenting. When Taylor receives a new Lego set for brushing his teeth every day for a month, make sure to explain that this isn't just a regular set of Lego: "Taylor, this is a really special reward. Every time you play with it, I want you to think about how hard you worked. I want you to remember what it felt like to remember to brush your teeth. I want you to remember how proud you feel right now. Every time you look at it, think, I'm someone who can do the right thing, even when I don't really want to."

Rewards create a linear connection to "future me." One of the competencies I model for my kids is constantly thanking "past me" or talking about "future me." For example, if I prepare my breakfast, my to-go mug, my car keys, and my work bag the night before, the next morning I'll make a point of saying, "Thank you, Past Me, for making sure this morning would be hassle free." When my children bring home a project or grade they're proud of, after rejoicing with them and asking them about it, I remind them to thank their past self for doing the hard work that earned the grade as we enjoy the payoff. As they start their homework, they might say, "Future Me, you're going to be very happy when you feel great about the science project you're going to hand in."

Here's an example of the right way to use a reward: the sticker chart. Responsive parenting sees sticker charts as unduly coercive because there is a lack of consent on the part of the child. I get it—many PTPs revert to their to-don'ts list—and if there was coercion or overcontrol in their childhood, they don't want to repeat it. (Hello, entangled, paralyzed, and perfectionist parents! I see you.) But throwing the baby out with the bathwater is a trauma response. The truth is that a sticker chart, managed in a responsive and responsible fashion, can absolutely teach a child skills. More importantly, it can help a child reinforce a sense of accomplishment. You're not buying a specific behavior. The goal is to instill a capacity and help the child learn to tolerate discomfort in service of a goal. You're drawing a direct, linear connect to "future me."

When you set up a sticker chart reward, think of the acronym CHART:

- **C**onsent: The child has bought into the idea that there is an important skill they need to learn and a reward they would like.
- **H**ope: The child is able to see that "future me" will be happy that a skill is mastered.
- **A**bility: Take your child's developmental level and psycho/neurodiversities into account. We don't allow our trauma app to say, "When I was your age, I walked to school, through the snow, uphill both ways." Is this particular child capable of learning this capacity or skill? If not, what foundational skills do I need to teach first?
- **R**easonable reward: Match the reward with the skill. A family trip to Disneyland following five days of good oral hygiene seems unreasonable because the stakes are too high. The child runs a risk of being shamed and blamed by the entire family. However, a new Lego toy or book seems more reasonable.

- Trackable: Choose a tracking method that isn't onerous for the child or the family. We never ever want to lie to kids, and setting up a reward system that isn't reliably trackable is akin to lying, because we're not transparently doing what we said we're going to do.

Truth #4

All Parents Make Mistakes

Being a parent is a scary responsibility. We may feel flawed and damaged by our damage. The thought that we're going to make mistakes seems intolerable. And there are so many mistakes to make. You're going to encourage a child to try something that backfires, choose the wrong school, or trust the wrong advice. You're going to miss the signs of an infection or tell them that you are "sure" that they can win, only to have them shot down. You're definitely going to be wrong.

There are going to be ruptures. And you can repair. You and your child are in the journey of life together. Sometimes, you're going to take a wrong turn, but usually, you'll course-correct.

Truth #5

It's Never You vs. Me. It's Always You and Me vs. the Problem

When we're trying to help our children navigate the demands the world sets, we're always on our children's team. We're their ally, their staunchest advocate, their coach, and their cheerleader. Yes, sometimes, it feels like we're at odds with them—hello, morning routine, homework assignment, bedtime, and every trip to the dentist.

Whenever parents talk to me about "power struggles" with their children, I sense the influence of a trauma app. R2 Parenting avoids the power struggle altogether by ensuring that it's not the parent who is demanding the behavior, skill, or capacity. For example, the parent is not the one who is demanding that a child wear shoes, but the simple existence of germs, gravity, and heat are.

You and your child together can figure out how to handle the fact that "I don't want to wear shoes." Frame the demands of life not as "you vs. me" in the sense of "You must put on your shoes now because I said so." It's you and me together vs. the problem, as in, "How can we keep your feet safe when you go outside? Are your shoes uncomfortable? Do you want to wear a different pair? Do you want to pick out your socks?"

Truth #6

You're Going to Feel Guilty Even When You're Doing Everything Right

The feelings that are associated with parenting are intense, but that doesn't mean that you're doing something wrong. For instance, a mother might feel a strong sense of guilt when she leaves her son with his father and the child protests, "Only Mommy!" Normally, when we feel guilt, it's a sign that we did something wrong. With parenting, however, there's a lot of unjustified guilt. When we're post-traumatic, the unjustified guilt can be an internal signal, not that you did something wrong but that you did something right: you created a strong attachment relationship. When there's a strong attachment relationship, children engage in "protest behavior" when you leave them. When you see this behavior, it means you did a good job!

I remember preparing one of my children for routine surgery, making sure I was doing everything "right" in terms of preparing her: gamifying the experience by playing hospital, introducing a *Doc McStuffins* picture book and playset, and reading picture books about kids in the hospital (of course, I did my due diligence about the surgeon and the necessity of the surgery as well). I was right there, soothing her and keeping her calm, dressing her in the hospital gown, and I was able to stay with her until the anesthesiologist put her to sleep. And as they wheeled her away, I felt an intense wave of irrational guilt. As a PTP who has some complicated history with hospitals, my guilt was a sign that my trauma app was starting up. All of a sudden, the situation felt out of control and unsafe, so my trauma app tried to put the responsibility of the surgical outcome on me, even though I knew that it wasn't mine to bear. Short of running into the operating room and grabbing the scalpel from the surgeon, I wasn't going to be able to influence the outcome of her surgery. Hence, the trauma app guilt.

Guilt isn't a reliable signal when we're PTPs, so when we feel it, we need to ask ourselves, Am I acting like a typical parent? Are the other parents around me making the same decision? Did I betray my values?

Or you can ask a trusted adviser to help you make sense of your guilt. Maybe that's a parenting partner, a therapist, a fellow PTP, or another parent. Guilt is not a signal we should turn off entirely, but it's one to treat with caution. For instance, a toddler crying at drop-off for the first week of school is normal; if the distress seems excessive, you might want to get another opinion.

Truth #7

Curiosity Is a Parenting Superpower

Healthy parents use curiosity to teach skills, in an effort to find the underlying reason behind a particular behavior. Instead of focusing on "How could my child embarrass me like she did? She's so . . .," you can use curiosity and think, *What was driving my child's behavior?*

Yet trauma shuts down our ability to access curiosity or transforms it into a shaming/blaming voice, yelling at us to either "fix" our child's behavior or blaming us for being incompetent as parents. Whenever we hear that internal shaming voice, we have to literally say out loud, "Thank you, shame, for trying to be helpful. But please step aside and allow me to access my curiosity so that I can solve this problem."

Truth #8

Discomfort Is Not Dangerous

Our kids will sometimes be uncomfortable, and that's okay. In fact, it's what's supposed to happen. Just like exposure to some germs strengthens our immune system and mildly overusing muscles makes them stronger, our kids need to experience adversity in order to thrive. What's important is that they're not alone with their distress and that their distress doesn't rise into the "intolerable and alone with it" levels. As Jonathan Haidt has said in interviews about his book *The Anxious Generation*, bruises are an important part of growing up, but scars are not.[6]

As PTPs, we don't want our children to be traumatized, and we want to shield them from adversity. It makes sense, but it's a risky strategy because it creates a sense of fragility rather than resilience, which is really what parents want to teach their kids.

CHAPTER 11

Post-Traumatic Parenting Hacks

PTPs CAN USE TWO different kinds of parenting hacks: those that make parenting more manageable and those that help children learn the important lessons of being human. I remember a mom in one of my parenting classes saying, "I'd love to parent, but my kids need to be fed, my boss thinks I need to show up occasionally or he won't give me my paycheck, and the orthodontist's office should put me on payroll, I'm on the phone with them so often and I live in a chair in their waiting room." I can completely relate. Parenting in accordance with our values takes a lot of mindful, focused presence, and for PTPs, that energy is hard to tap into. Yet I've found that when I simplified or routinized some of my other household responsibilities, the real art of parenting no longer felt like a chore. These hacks are the way to fully enjoying spending time with your children.

Parenting Hacks for Parents

Hack #1

Reducing the Load of Parenting

First, let's free ourselves up to create more time for parenting so that we can be the attachment figure we believe in being. Before we can talk about adding anything to a parent's long list of tasks, let's talk about how to remove/systematize what's already on our plate.

Systematizing means coming up with hacks to make the day-to-day processes easier and less stressful. For instance, while I value cooking for my family, I don't always have the bandwidth for it. So, I created a hack that systemizes meal prep: I cook in large batches and maximize my freezer. I always double recipes so that I'm freezing one supper for the future. It's one cleanup for twice the meals. I also block out time in August, which is traditionally a quiet time in my practice, to cook huge batches of food I'll need for the year and freeze them. A "good August" for me means that by the end of the summer, I've made lots of staple meals—meatballs, lasagnas, soups, and casseroles—and they're all in the freezer, so I can pull them out as needed.

There are many ways to figure out what your daily hassles are and decide which ones can be systematized and made easier. In my post-traumatic parenting classes, parents have shared hacks like buying two pairs of identical sneakers for each kid so they don't have that dreaded "Where are the sneakers?" rush every morning. I'll never forget when one dad discovered that his child's Catholic school uniform had a time-saving duplicate online—he found a shirt that looked identical to the uniform, but it didn't need ironing!

What household tasks can you streamline, eliminate, outsource, or delegate? Can you think of ways to get everyone in the family more fairly involved?

The Mental Load of Parenting and Gendered Expectations

Once, one of my children's day camps didn't have an information box to fill in "father" as the emergency contact. The form read "Emergency contact—mother's cell" and automatically populated it with my cell number, which could not be altered. I called the camp's secretary and explained that I can't be my son's emergency contact, as my cell phone is frequently on silent mode when I'm with patients. I needed to add my husband's information.

The secretary sniffed, "What kind of mother doesn't want to be the first person to know if her child is injured?"

Thankfully, I teach people how to deal with being bullied and have gotten a handle on my people-pleasing trauma app. I just laughed and responded, "A mother who wants to make sure that you actually reach a parent in case of emergency, because she'd like her child to survive."

If you've been carrying too much of the load of "home manager," check out *Fair Play* by Eve Rodsky. She does a good job of delineating how moms became the "default parent," how to talk about redistributing responsibilities with your spouse, and how to deal with the inevitable shame that comes with bucking societal expectations around what moms "should" do. There are wonderful worksheets to help you learn how to rebalance the family load.

Hack #2

Learn the Pomodoro Technique

The Pomodoro Technique is a time management method I love. It was created by Francesco Cirillo in the 1980s as a study method: the premise is that limiting your focused time actually helps you to focus better so that you avoid procrastination.

I use this method for any task that I need to complete but that I'm not necessarily excited to do. Mostly, those are the tasks that make me feel incompetent and are also a bit boring (Hello, bills!), that just aren't intrinsically enjoyable for me (Hello, home organizing!), and for anything that makes me panic (Hello, blogging on a deadline!).

The Pomodoro Technique involves the following steps:

- Step One: Set a timer for twenty-five minutes.
- Step Two: Work on the task without stopping until the timer goes off. You will practice absolute presence. You will not look at your phone. Seriously. Shut that thing off.
- Step Three: Take a short break, such as five to ten minutes, to walk around, get a snack, relax, or do something mindless and fun (this is when it's okay to scroll social media or play that game on your phone).
- Repeat steps 2 and 3 for four rounds.
- If the task is still not finished, take a longer break, such as fifteen to thirty minutes, to rest and rejuvenate.
- Go back to the task and repeat with shorter breaks until you are finished.

Hack #3

Review and Refine Your Parenting Values

You and your partner may have different post-traumatic parenting defaults, different triggers, and different parenting values. My client Jayme related this anecdote: "I didn't realize how different Steve and I were when it came to parenting until our daughter Evyn was a few months old. That's when Steve started saying things like, 'If you pick up the baby every time she cries, you'll spoil her.' Comments like that trigger me because I remember what it felt like to be abandoned and neglected by my alcoholic mom. Steve was raised in a much more 'normal' family than me, and I wanted to trust his judgment. Yet I just knew deep down, his advice felt wrong to me."

I explained to Jayme my hack for parents who may not be on the same page is to set clear guidelines, using the family values/mission statement exercise in chapter 9. She agreed that it was a good idea to sit down with Steve and create a mission statement and values, but she wasn't looking forward to the inevitable conflict that would occur. She believed that they were very far apart on more than a couple of parenting issues.

I know that for many PTPs, conflict is a trigger. No one wants to "ruin" a perfectly good, conflict-free evening debating parenting styles. But it is so much easier to handle those parenting style conflicts when you've already come up with an operating principle for how to handle them. I explained to Jayme that when she was ready to hash out her thoughts, it was important to concretize the consensus with an actual operating principle. Jayme learned to say, "We both agree that a baby's needs should be met, and Dr. K already taught us that babies can't strategize, so it's impossible to spoil a baby. When Evyn cries, we will check to make sure she isn't hungry, has her diaper changed, and is comfortable."

The more "if-then" rules you can create within your mission statement and values, the more consistent responses you will generate and the safer you and your children will feel. Here are a few examples:

- If there's a snow day, then our screen time rules will be relaxed, since I'll be working from home while supervising kids.
- If one parent feels more strongly about a value than the other parent (for example, completing a chore or taking a certain class), then it's that parent's job to ensure it happens.
- If one of the children is having a meltdown, then we pause what we're doing to co-regulate, even if that means changing our schedule.
- If we (parents) notice something is becoming a problem—conflict at mealtimes, homework routine, sibling fighting—then we will have a family meeting and figure out an operating principle that we can all follow.

Hack #4

The POD System

In an effort to do everything right, many PTPs overvalue "consistency" and "the rules" (Hello, perfectionists!). When you're parenting with a partner, or even when you have a dedicated caregiver like Grandma or a babysitter, I'm a big believer in the parent on duty (POD) system. In a POD system, whoever is "on duty" is in charge and their rules apply. Maybe your spouse is a bigger believer in "no screen time until after dinner and homework," but you are more in the camp of "screen time is okay as dinner is being prepped." Children can absolutely switch from following one parent's rules to another's as long as we remind them what the expectations are.

It is important, however, to make sure that children know that all their caregivers are aware of all the rules. We don't need to keep secrets or play one parent off the other, as in, "Don't tell Mom I let you eat dessert first!" For instance, it's totally fair to say, "When Grandma is taking care of you, I'm okay with her rule that you can eat dinner in front of the TV, but when I'm around, we eat dinner together at the table, as a family."

Hack #5

Self-Care Is Child Care

A lot of PTPs have a hard time with the idea of self-care. Some of that may be because we've been taught that caring for and attending to the self is "selfish" (hello, people pleasers and entangled parents), because self-care means momentarily disregarding the to-do list tasks that give us little hits of dopamine and tell us that we're excellent "human doings" because we have some doubts about our worth as "human beings" (hello, disengaged, paralyzed and perfectionist parents), because we've never seen it modeled, or because we've seen it actively mocked (hello, all parenting types). For some of us, the fact that self-care time is often time carved out of other overwhelming obligations makes it feels unattainable.

Many PTPs don't understand the difference between self-maintenance, self-care, and anesthesia. If you go to the gym, eat nourishing food that gives your body energy and maintains your health, go to bed on time, or meditate, you might think you have a great self-care plan. But all these strategies are self-maintenance: you are giving your body and brain the tools it needs to function. On the other end of the spectrum is anesthesia. Ever hear of scrolling through YouTube watching silly cat videos? Wine, shopping, and a few rounds of that ridiculously addictive game on your phone are not self-care. They're a way of escaping.

Self-care is about engaging in activities that restore your sense of self. It's a night out with friends or coffee with some neighbors. The gym can be self-care if the class you're taking is joyful rather than a prescription to reduce osteoporosis risk. Maybe it's going to a paint night or going out of your way to experience something new.

When you engage in self-care, your kids will sometimes protest. You'll be headed out the door to book club and your two-year-old will proclaim, "Only you can put me to sleep!" and that inner voice of guilt will start. *Maybe I'm damaging them. Look how sad they are. Do I really need to go to my book club? I can skip it.* But as we said in the last chapter, your children will sometimes be distressed, and that, in and of itself, is not enough to tell you that you've made the wrong decision. In fact, by going to that book club with your friends, you're restoring your sense of self so that you come to parenting tomorrow from a place of joy. You're making yourself a parent for your child by restoring yourself. In this way, self-care *is* child care.

Parenting Hacks for Children

There are some parenting practices that are so important that every parent must master them. In this set of hacks, we're going to concretize the real "secrets of parenting" that people with healthy internal working models inherently use, and what we know from child psychology research is critical to healthy development.

Each of these parenting hacks are shortcuts to teaching any skill by capitalizing on the way a child's brain naturally learns—through play, joy, connection, and delight. These hacks follow the R2 Parenting advice of teaching skills in a gentle and responsive way.

Imagine that you never had a "power struggle" again, because you've taught your child how to delay gratification, how to manage their time responsibly, or to handle pretty much any problem, using a skill that you taught in a connected, *attuned* way. As we discussed in the last

Making a Decision Is Step One of Good Parenting

Some PTPs get very hung up on the details of parenting, which doesn't always serve us. I love Emily Oster's books and her ParentData project because she looks at the concerns that keep parents up at night and helps us understand what's a valid fear and what's just hype. She helps us understand how to make sense of all the information we're bombarded with.

In her book *The Family Firm*, Emily Oster covers the idea that it's not so important what we decide but that we decide and how we decide. For example, she shows that it's less important what you read to kids, because the critical parenting skill is that you take the time to read with them. Later in the chapter, I include a list of games/toys/books that you can use to teach specific skills, but the goal isn't "play only the games Dr. K suggests." If you already have a game that teaches the same skill, go for it: the goal is teaching the skill, not buying a specific game.

chapter, attunement is when you and your child are in sync: it is a joyous, merging experience that healthy parents instinctively develop with their children in infancy. Attunement primes children for learning, because they are wired to learn from their parents. A child's brain development depends on receiving directed attention, and attunement is what starts them on this path, especially when we use language to narrate experiences. For instance, when a baby reaches for a toy and a parent says with joy and music in their voice, "Yes, that's your rattle," the baby is more willing to explore because they have connected a parent's attention to them with positive sensations.

We can create attunement experiences at all stages of life. By doing so, we're supercharging our parenting: we're capitalizing on the brain's innate function to teach skills that can be complex to learn.

Parenting Hacks for Babies

Babies need the four S's of attachment—we want babies to feel safe (fed, dressed, dry, attended to), seen (noticed, resonated with, feeling "felt"), soothed (knowing that when in distress, someone will come and comfort them), and secure (there's a familiar and predictable grown-up present, so they can relax). Here's all you need to know about parenting babies: attend to their biological rhythms—feed, change, bathe—and provide a predictable, safe environment. You don't have to "optimize" their babyhood. Do what works and doesn't trigger you. Is bottle best? Is breast best? Fed is best. Is room-sharing best? Is a crib in their own room best? A good night's sleep for parents and baby is best. Is Baby Einstein best? Is another developmental toy best? A baby that is played with and attended to is best.

Remember, attachment isn't all that fragile—there are a lot of ways for a baby to experience the four S's, and if they miss out on one of those four S's once in a while, it's fine. If you're generally attentive and responsive when the baby is crying, that one time you slept through their diaper blowout in the middle of the night might result in a diaper rash, but it won't harm attachment. Attachment is about the overall relationship, not any one specific incident (unless that one specific incident is horrifically abusive or traumatic).

The infant brain likes predictability and consistency, because it uses patterns to make sense of the world around it. Babies prefer the familiar, so make sure they have a lovey (doll, stuffed toy, or blanket) that smells like you, their primary attachment figure. You can create this by putting a blanket next to your skin and walking around with it for a while, until it smells like you.

Babies also need a predictable sleep environment, one with the same level of light and the same sounds in the room and as consistent a bedtime routine as possible. Babies' brains are hungry for language, so sing and talk to your baby as often as you can. This idea is consistent with the Resources for Infant Educarers (RIE) parenting philosophy, founded by child and infant specialist Magda Gerber. While it may sound funny to narrate a diaper change to a baby, in actuality, even if they don't understand the specific words, they are paying attention to our intonations. For instance, when we spread cold diaper rash cream on their most sensitive bits and say, "I know this will feel cold. That's okay; it's going to feel better in a minute," your baby responds more to the tone in your voice and the musicality of it than the actual words. Eventually, our chatter helps a baby make sense of the world. And yes, it's okay to use baby talk. The parent brain was designed to speak in a higher pitched, more engaging tone to a baby, because that's what attracts their attention and feels good to them. Disengaged parents have an especially hard time talking to their babies, because they are used to dissociating and going inward. Narrating life for a baby can help treat dissociation, because it demonstrates to us how often we're in our heads instead of being present.

Babies enjoy the "serve and return" nature of interactions. When your baby smiles at you, smile back. Soon, your baby will be making a bid for your attention by cooing, pointing, or gurgling. These are all opportunities to engage with positive, reinforcing words.

Babies do not need to learn to self-regulate in order to be soothed. Babies need to learn to accept soothing from an attachment figure. Singing, rocking, or using "motherese" all help a baby feel soothed. I'm a fan of babywearing because babies love to be as close to an attachment figure as they can and it frees your hands up to go about your other tasks, as long as your baby is calm. This is the only time a human is capable of multitasking—you absolutely can fold laundry and make a baby feel loved at the same exact time.

For the times you do have to be away, you can record your voice reading a story or singing your usual bedtime songs for another caregiver to play at bedtime. It can really help a baby link their ordinary routine to a time of disruption.

Parenting Hacks for Toddlers and Preschoolers

Toddlers are busy figuring out autonomy. They're discovering that they are a separate creature from you and can do things by themselves. This doesn't mean that toddlers are done with the four S's of attachment. They still need to feel safe, be seen, be soothed, and have a secure base so that they can venture forth and discover.

Parenting decisions for toddlers fall into two categories: how you are going to teach them self-regulation (which involves allowing them to express their autonomy) and how you can continue to teach them skills to enrich their world (which involves them seeing you as a resource for mediating the world for them).

When it comes to self-regulation, too often, our trauma app gets turned on when our toddlers' idea of autonomy begins to look like a power struggle. But as I've said before, there is no such thing as a power struggle. The toddler is just trying to figure out autonomy. In order to manage the behavior, you can give your toddler a choice: "You have to wear shoes, so you can pick which ones to wear." What's more, I'm not a fan of time-outs. I'm a fan of time-ins. When a toddler is having a meltdown and they're miserable, telling them to go to their room or sit in a corner and isolating them isn't really teaching them anything. A time-in allows you to sit together on the floor or have your child on your lap. Soothe them in order to stop the meltdown. As you calm down together, you can figure out what to do next. Your toddler will learn that grown-ups are sturdy enough to handle their big emotions and will help them weather their storm.

Resistant behaviors like going to sleep, picky eating, and separation are all normal toddler behaviors. *If I like Mommy and Mommy and I have fun, why would I want to go to day care and leave Mommy?* Here is where reading together comes in. Reading is a way to borrow other people's experience to help us learn. Stories can also give them exposure to solving a resistant behavior problem that they're having and that other children have faced. If your child doesn't want to go to preschool, there are many books where the main character overcomes this same problem. There's *Maisy Goes to Preschool*, *Llama Llama Misses Mama*, *Miss Bindergarten Gets Ready for Kindergarten*, *The Pigeon HAS to Go to School*, and *D.W.'s Guide to Preschool*, to name just a very few out of many. When you read your child those books and weave their own experience into the story as you go, you'll be surprised how quickly kids get the point. Once, my three-year-old son said to me, "I was like the llama, I was 'shy-ing' today. I wanted you to come get me." I was able to reply, "And just like in the story, Mommy came." You can use this hack for dealing with picky eating, getting your child to sleep, seeing the doctor, or any other resistant behavior.

Reading a book to a toddler or preschooler also allows you to engage their interest about the world. Try introducing your children to experiences that aren't theirs: picture books that have families that don't look like your family or stories about completely different cultures.

Toddlers really like to hear the same story over and over because they connect to its predictable nature. You can also look for books that promote a sense of coziness, including picture books with baby animals and their parents. Authors like Amy Krouse Rosenthal, Audrey Penn, and Amy Hest create sensations of coziness well.

When it comes to teaching skills, toddlers need outdoor play to explore and use their big muscles exuberantly, with supervision but not smothering. If you live in an area where outdoor play isn't practical, there are many home installations you can create—I've seen foam pits, balance beams, climbing walls, rope swings, and crash pads, all designed for small spaces, so that kids can play exuberantly yet safely.

Toddlers also need imaginary play, because role-playing helps them develop their imagination skills, which are the building blocks of the executive functioning they'll need for school. Imaginary play with toddlers is often about the toddler bossing you around. This allows the toddler to play with the concepts of autonomy and control and allows the toddler to feel a sense of agency. The nice thing is the toddler's imagination does all the heavy lifting; all you have to do is follow the toddler's lead. Whether you are playing house, grocery store, or restaurant, your child will tell you exactly the behavior they expect from you and what you should be doing to interact with them.

Toddlers enjoy a sense of wonder and discovery. The world is new and exciting. This is when taking a nature walk and playing the game I spy can be fun because it focuses on mutual discovery. You can say, "I spy with my little eye something that is YELLOW," and then the toddler can point and show you what they find. You're teaching the beginning of empathy, seeing the world through another's perspective.

Books that provide a sense of wonder, like Ezra Jack Keats's *The Snowy Day* or Nina Laden's *Peek-A-Who* (which is a fun lift-the-flap book), are great for helping toddlers engage with this sense of discovery. In general, toddlers do well with interactive books—scratch and sniff, multisensory, or lift-the-flap books that allow them to discover what's going on.

Another hack for play that teaches skills is to allow your preschooler to help you with household chores. Yes, work can be play! It's a missed opportunity when parents don't allow kids to do household tasks alongside them, with tools that are appropriate for them. Preschoolers actually want to help from a place of happiness and interest. Try to quiet your trauma app's hangups of worrying that you will "parentify" your child. Instead, provide child-sized tools (I find Montessori websites helpful with sourcing these) and remember the goal is not to have a clean and swept floor. The goal is to allow your child to experiment with sweeping and to feel helpful. Nothing beats the look on a child's face when the whole family is praising a stew and the child knows that they helped make it. This also can resolve picky eating—it's fun to taste foods we had a hand in creating.

Yet for some PTPs, any type of play is an issue (Hello, disengaged!). If you find play intolerable, go back to the instructions for the Pomodoro Technique. You don't have to play endlessly, even if they're distressed. Set a timer and play for twenty minutes with your full presence. When the time's up, you can excuse yourself for a few minutes and then decide if you want to go back in.

Special Days

When my children enter elementary school, I set up a policy called "special days." A special day is a day (or two) when my child and I go on a one-on-one adventure. It might be to a museum we both find interesting, an entertainment center, or a crafts place. It might be a trip to another city or even an overnight stay if the attraction we're visiting is far and has an early start time. I love going anywhere I can take a train, because we can bring a box lunch picnic to eat on the way and really focus on bonding and talking rather than focusing on the road. The idea is a shared adventure, just the two of us, that we can anticipate and plan for and reminisce about. It's been so valuable and enjoyable that this year my daughter, oldest grandchild, and I are going on a special day! My daughter remembers them so fondly, she wants to continue the tradition with her own children.

The purpose of a "special day" is to show my child that this relationship is something I value and that I'm interested in their interests. It also has the side benefit of reducing "school reluctance." My policy for each child is the same: there is one special day a year that's free, and another one or two can be earned. This policy gives us all something to plan and look forward to.

When toddlers and preschoolers start to develop a sense of humor that has to do with novelty and surprise, like knock-knock jokes, or they find the unexpected answer to their question hysterically funny, it means that they have pattern recognition down pat. This is the stage for silly picture books, like the books by Mo Willems, husband-and-wife team Anna Kang and Christopher Weyant, Sandra Boynton, or Ryan T. Higgins. When they enjoy these books, you know that they're ready for the next stage of development: elementary school.

Parenting Hacks for the Elementary School Years

Elementary school–age kids recognize that the world is so much bigger than their own house and their family. They're starting to feel the sense of comparison, learning how they are different—and the same—as their peers. Psychologists like me talk about these competencies as a "hidden curriculum"—the social skills and norms that children are meant to simply absorb from interacting in the classroom and on the playground. Kids may wonder, *Do I know how to fix a conflict with someone else? Will someone hurt my feelings?* This is when children start feeling socially awkward, wondering why some of their peers are better at reading, playing sports, or making friends.

Think about the family and your home as a social learning laboratory, starting with implementing a family meal where there is interactive conversation. We know that creating a ritual around family meals is important, because the majority of cultures in the world connect together over food. It's not an accident that sharing a meal is a time for enhancing bonds.

Shared meals are also a wonderful time to increase children's exposure to other cultures, their foods and rituals. My children often request recipes we find in books—our current favorite dinner was inspired by a book one of my children was reading. You can also buy recipe books themed around experiences, such as the Disney World cookbook, the Harry Potter cookbook, the US history cookbook. This allows kids to have some agency around cooking, having meals, and collaborating with a parent and extends these areas of interest to the entire family.

If you are a PTP who is triggered by "family meals" or "forced participation in anything family," it's worth figuring out a way to create family meals that doesn't trigger you. You can create your own version and a new nuclear family tradition around sharing a meal. Maybe it's breakfast instead of dinner. Maybe it's a snack time. Maybe it's Taco Tuesdays or Breakfast for Dinner Fridays. Family meals do not have to be replicated every night or at dinner specifically. There are no formal rules that have to apply: Emily Post doesn't have to be at your table. The point is for everyone to enjoy a meal together, to enhance attunement by talking and sharing an interest that you can discuss and explore together. In a single conversation.

There are several companies that manufacture "conversation starter" games. Do an online search for "family conversation cards" or "campfire questions" for resources. These make the heavy lifting of dinner-table conversation easier.

Elementary school age is a great time to gamify skills. One hack is to establish a set time to play games and use that time for playing together without any agenda. Mostly, you're playing together and having fun, yet every so often, sprinkle a lesson into the gameplay. You don't want to use this hack too frequently, because it will be recognized as an opportunity to lecture. For example, if I want to teach the concept of strategic thinking, I play Connect Four and teach the importance of capturing the middle row, so that the player has so many more options to win. Then, create an analogy that brings the game lesson into an "in real life" situation. For instance, "Remember when we played Candy Land and you were sent back to the Peppermint Forest even though you wanted to get to the Candy Castle. We have to stay goal directed to get to the Candy Castle. Your science project is like the Candy Castle. What do you have to do to get there?"

Parents often make the mistake of trying to teach self-regulation skills in moments of stress. When the school bus is honking outside and you just can't find that elusive left sneaker, it's not the time to start lecturing your child about why it's important to put things where they belong and lay out their clothes the night before. A stressed brain is the opposite of a learning brain. Instead, when we're playing a game, we're primed to learn. If "organizing possessions" is a problem, play a time management or resource management game later that same day.

Whenever your child is struggling, think: What is the skill or capacity they need to handle this well? What game, toy, or craft utilizes this skill? For example, Monopoly (or Monopoly Junior for younger kids) is a resource management game. If the child is organizing their money by denomination, that's instinctive strategic reasoning. Point out to the child how they're already doing something smart and strategic. Then, you can extend that lesson into the morning routine and talk about ways to organize their stuff so it's easier to find what's needed. This is also a good time to ask the child for feedback. Maybe they need a dedicated space to put their shoes, more than one pair, or some other system that makes it easier? By following this game hack, you have successfully moved away from "parent lecturing" into "collaborative problem-solving."

On my website (drrobynkoslowitz.com) and YouTube channel (search "Dr. Robyn Koslowitz" or "post-traumatic parenting"), I have dozens of videos featuring specific games, toys, and ideas for teaching children pretty much any skill. Sometimes, the perfect game to teach a skill does not come in a box. For example, I created an ice cube challenge for tolerating frustration in service of a goal. I ask kids to hold an ice cube tightly in one fist. I set up a time limit—maybe it's three, five, or ten minutes. If they can hold on to the ice cube for that amount of time, they get a treat. Then we talk about how we can be comfortable being uncomfortable and how that applies to a challenge in their lives.

Elementary school age is also the time when children begin to express their fears. The antidote to fear is exposure. Marty Franklin,

PhD, who focuses on obsessive compulsive behaviors, once said in a training I attended, "Do the thing you're afraid of. The more you do it, the easier it gets." When it comes to overcoming childhood fears, our job as parents is to create fun, gamified, and friendly ways to make exposure easy. For instance, if your child is afraid of dogs, you can expose them to dogs by reading about them together. You can teach your child the safest ways to be around dogs and eventually take a trip to a dog park and start petting smaller, less threatening dogs. So many games, books, and toys can be used as an exposure to something that initially feels scary. If your child is generally anxious, books about other kids with worries, like *Wemberly Worried* by Kevin Henkes, *Jabari Jumps* by Gaia Cornwell, *Sophie's Squash* by Pat Zietlow Miller, and *The Gruffalo* by Julia Donaldson are great ways to talk about worries and how to manage them.

In general, there are some lovely children's books that are a bit more "educational" when it comes to emotions. Hallee Adelman's *Way Past* series features relatable kids feeling "way past" mad, sad, or mean. Julia Cook does a wonderful job of teaching social skills in her numerous picture books about everything from executive dysfunction to stealing to being a poor sport. If you're stuck, ask a children's librarian. I promise, there's a picture book about a situation that's pretty similar to the ones your child is dealing with.

I also love to have toys with emotion faces. Moodles has a face that can be flipped to reveal several emotions. Lego recently started manufacturing Duplo figures with different emotions/facial expressions that are endlessly reconfigurable, and there are so many others. Children can come home from school and clue you in to their emotions by choosing the face on the toy that most accurately reflects their mood at the moment. You can also take them through the different emotion "faces" and ask if they felt each one that day.

Although we like to think that our children know in their hearts that we are always there for them, that feeling actually needs to be firmly established. Psychologists like me talk about this feeling as *mentalization*—the process by which an experience becomes a memory and then repeated memories become a capacity. When we repeatedly show our love for our kids, our belief in them, and our sense of connection to them, this love transfers into their own inner voice. Elementary school age is a perfect time to plant the seeds of mentalization. The book *The Paper Dolls* by Julia Donaldson shows how the action of making

Kids and Age-Appropriate Chores

I believe in assigning children chores and actively including children in many of the tasks of running a home that most people assume belong to adults. Starting when they're toddlers, I've let my kids help chop veggies or sweep, continuing in elementary school by allowing them to set the table (and have free rein on décor and placements). As they get older, they have cooked side dishes independently (building up to cooking an entire meal) and have helped care for their younger siblings.

The function of a chore is to teach citizenship in a family, as opposed to getting a task completed. There are also side benefits—they can see when hard work does pay off and tune into the good feeling we get from doing worthwhile work and feeling satisfaction in a job well done.

Chores allow children to develop their unique family identity. If your child enjoys baking, it makes their identity richer and fuller to be the "baker" in the family. This is particularly true for teens, because you want them to have a sense of being part of more than just their world of peers. Also, teenagers like to have a sense of agency, and their label that is associated with their preferred chore makes them feel good about themselves.

paper dolls jumps into a little girl's memory, and then she later passes on the memory by making similar dolls for her own daughter. *The Invisible String* by Patrice Karst, *A Kissing Hand for Chester Raccoon* by Audrey Penn, and *I Love You, Stinky Face* by Lisa McCourt can all be helpful in teaching children to mentalize their connections to us and to install our voice as one of their inner voices. You can also create mentalization opportunities with an item, like a lovie, a teddy bear key chain, or a locket with a picture of you. Whenever your child needs a boost of reassurance or is missing you/feeling lonely, they can squeeze the key chain or locket, think about you, and feel your love and a sense of your presence.

Parenting Hacks for the Middle School Years

When I teach social and emotional curricula in middle schools, I always tell the students that they are learning the science of "you": the more you understand about how humans function in groups and how to handle interpersonal interactions, the better equipped you are to handle all of life. If your child's school doesn't offer social and emotional learning, there are wonderful resources online. Check out the Yale Child Study Center, the Child Mind Institute, Collaborative for Academic, Social, and Emotional Learning (CASEL.org), and PBS Kids (pbskids.org) and search for social and emotional learning. I have many social and emotional learning resources on my YouTube channel and website as well. One way or another, your children must learn the "hidden curriculum" of social skills. If they aren't learning it on their own, it's up to you to teach them. Even if they are picking some of it up, it's important to reinforce those skills.

The middle school years are when peer groups start to become super important. Our role is to help our kids navigate those demands and support the normal trials and tribulations that friendships bring. The goal is to create a relationship where you as the parent are the person who always believes in them and has their back.

The connection you have to your child's education continues in middle school. Stay informed on what they're reading, listening to, and exposed to in and out of the classroom. I started using this hack as a child therapist, because when a child uses a metaphor from a book or TV show, I want to be able to understand what they're talking about. Then I repurposed this strategy for my own parenting, because I see how valuable it is to always have shared points of reference with my kids. Yes, you might have to watch a lot of hours of MrBeast or some other YouTube prankster. You might have to watch a whole bunch of Nickelodeon, TikTok videos, and the preteen movies they're currently obsessed with. Then, you can discuss what they are being exposed to from a place of curiosity. You want to know what's in their head so that you can have a shared dialogue and a shared understanding of what they're thinking about and what they're going through.

I have a strong belief that kids should not be exposed to social media until they are twenty-one, which doesn't make me the most popular mom. The truth is, studies have shown that the teenage brain is not capable of handling those pressures. If your kid is on any form of social media, even just as an observer, you need to be on that account as well. For me, social media poses an issue of informed consent. Parents are in a better position to weigh the risks and benefits than their children, who are literally not capable of accurately weighing risks and benefits until they're anywhere from eighteen to twenty-one. If your kid is desperate to follow along with what their peers are seeing, you can watch together so that you know what's going on and they're not completely left out from their friends.

Middle school is also the time when kids start figuring out their comfort zones and sticking with them. Comfort zones are great as long as you know how to break out of them. You can help your child learn to take healthy risks by introducing them to new activities and new skills. I like to encourage a balance between activities my kids are already good at, pushing on the boundaries of their comfort zone, and activities that aren't in their wheelhouse. For instance, I have a strong value of having my children taking at least a basic self-defense course, which is probably rooted in treating many children who have been abused. For some of my children, who like me, have more of a "sedentary" comfort zone (they'd rather be reading), taking a self-defense class also had the added benefit of forcing them out of their comfort zone and into learning a completely new skill.

Middle school is often a time when the social dynamics of the school day spill into the home environment. One easy hack I use is to create a transition time from school back to home so that my kids can demarcate their experience. First, we make our bodies feel better by having a snack, using the bathroom, and getting a drink of water. Next, we talk about our day, specifically the highs and the lows, and then we actively put our school day aside and focus on our family's evening. This strategy helps my kids realize that their day wasn't all good or all bad and that they can make new choices about their evening.

In order to help them navigate their day-to-day experience, I also like to talk to middle schoolers about the concept of collecting *feedback.* If a teacher says, "You were being disrespectful," a child doesn't have to take it as a shaming statement of "You are bad." Take it as data—this teacher finds this type of interaction disrespectful. They're giving the child information for how to interact with them, and that can be useful information. They may be explaining that the recipe for interacting with this teacher requires different word choices or a different tone of voice. For instance, I remember the first time I presented a professional development day. The evaluations stated that the teachers loved the content of what I was teaching, that I was fast-paced and stimulating, but that I talked way too fast and there was way too much content in the training. On the way there, I was panicking because I thought I had included too little information! Getting this feedback, while mildly uncomfortable, gave me insight into my presentation style and how I had to adjust it. It's the same with feedback from middle school friends—it may be painful to hear that your friends are perceiving you as a sore loser, bossy, or too quiet, but it can be helpful data for learning new social skills.

Every so often, the school will be wrong: they'll perceive disrespect where none was intended or choose the wrong child as the guilty party in a fight. This can happen a lot with neurodiverse kids. I've intervened in many a situation where a more physically imposing student hit a less physically intimidating child, but the "victim" was actually goading and harassing the "bully" before they were attacked. If this happens to your child, you will be their best advocate by dealing with your own emotions and triggers before mindfully and effectively intervening.

I like to teach children the concept of effective, efficient, and relevant communication. This is relevant for any conflict, but it is particularly important for the school environment. When I'm trying to resolve any conflict, I want to be effective—to say what works. I want to be efficient—putting exactly the amount of energy into the interaction to get my point across (yelling is likely too much energy; passively going along with something unfair is too little energy). Relevant means discussing only the information that pertains to the situation at hand.

Getting Kids Off Their Screens

Jonathan Haidt's book *The Anxious Generation* makes a very good point all parents should hear: we oversupervise kids in the natural world and undersupervise them in the digital world. Especially during the middle school years, parents need to know what kids are doing online, who is communicating with them, and how much time they're spending in the digital world. Algorithms are hungry monsters that really can alter our thinking very quickly. I have seen for myself how quickly social media can change my mood when someone says something mean about me on the internet. And I'm an adult with good boundaries.

Even if you're like me, and you want to keep your kids off social media, there are many ways they can still experience harm in the technological world. Don't ever feel like "I've set these safeguards, so my kids are fine." Periodically check in and make sure.

I always want the child to try those interventions first. If they don't work and I keep hearing complaints, that's when I will approach the teacher with curiosity, trying to understand what's going on. Maybe there's a skill my child needs to learn. Or maybe there is something bigger going on, something that is an "adult-level" problem, like bullying, a learning disability, or systemic unfairness. If it's an adult-level problem, I am going to intervene directly.

Parenting Hacks for the High School Years

I've heard it said that we're supposed to give our children roots (a stable base they can return to) and wings (the ability to be independent). When it comes to teenagers, wings are much scarier to supply, because their actions can have real, irreversible consequences. At this age, it's our job to take that giant step back and let them step forward.

The high school years are all about separation and individuation. Just like toddlers are supposed to experiment with autonomy, teenagers are supposed to experiment with breaking free, and that might mean breaking some rules. They will absolutely be rejecting some of your values outright as they try to form their own. Many PTPs see separation and individuation as dangerous because they feel rejected or they are afraid that their child's failures are too consequential. Yet not letting our children fail is one of the biggest mistakes parents can make.

This is the stage in life where engaging their critical thinking and curiosity is most valuable. That's why I put a lot of effort into reading what they're reading, watching what they're watching, listening to what they're listening to, and making their home as inviting a place for their friends as it can be. I want to be an observer of the parts of their world I don't belong in so that I can help them reflect on their world. I also love to create family game nights, mostly because it creates shared experiences outside of the usual routine.

One important hack is a big mindset shift: you need to consciously move your brain from seeing your teenager as past child and instead view them as future adult. Whenever you feel the urge to swoop in and save the day, just pretend that instead of fifteen, your child is thirty-five. Then, ask yourself if what you were planning on doing would be viewed as acceptable. So if my fifteen-year-old daughter made the choice not to study for her science test and now wants me to write an excuse note, would I be writing a similar note to her boss when she is thirty-five? This decision tree doesn't mean that you no longer have to teach your teenager skills. In fact, you may have to scaffold them into new social skills, like advocating for themselves or learning how to say no to their peers.

Another way to give teenagers autonomy is by making it their responsibility to acquire some of their wants. For instance, if they want a sweatshirt that costs more than you would be willing to pay, let them know how much you would contribute and let them work out how to get the funds to cover the rest. This hack is not a no, and it's not a

Teen Pushback and the PTP

Adolescence is the time when the brain literally rewires into what will eventually become an adult configuration. During this time, the emotional centers of an adolescent's brain are strong, yet the executive functioning parts aren't fully operational. The result: the teen brain has a strong motor but weak brakes. This mismatch presents as strong emotions.

At the same time, the brain's rewiring is helping them shift between "past child" and "future adult." The most efficient way to make this shift is often with a pushback against your house rules, values, or ways of being. The pushback allows them to try on new identities. Yet it also comes with stress: the challenges and the emotional intensity that is normal for adolescents. Their behavior doesn't mean that teenagers are ill-intentioned; it's simply their developmental task.

This stress can create self-doubt in all parents (as in, What did I do wrong that my son is always so angry? etc.) and especially in PTPs. Teenagers will take advantage of parental insecurity and inconsistency to push the boundaries of what you find acceptable, and we have plenty of insecurities. Sometimes teenagers can spot our trauma app operating and take advantage of it in an effort to get what they want.

If we recognize that pushback behavior is normal, we can stop personalizing it, blaming ourselves, and feeling the need to "put them back in their box." It's not pleasant to hear that you're ruining their life, that you're so embarrassing, and that you just don't get them, but it's also reassuring that your child feels safe enough to go through this process without trying to shield you from their emotions. Hearing you've ruined their life generally means you haven't. They need to see you as out of touch and embarrassing, because that's how they will figure out which parts of you they secretly want to emulate and which parts don't resonate. The key is to remain a stable, loving presence and be available for repair when they want to engage in that process.

compromise. You are treating your teenager like the future adult they will become.

You can also create invisible supports for your high school kids. Let's say you have a kid who enters a new school and is finding it hard to break into a social group. An invisible support would be working with the teacher to create a group project so that your child could be included. The kid doesn't even have to know that you and the teacher had this conversation. However, it's a fine line: more active social engineering than that is disabling.

Journaling Activity

Who Is the Perfect Parent?

All these parenting hacks are going to make a difference in your parenting, but as you can imagine, they don't represent everything that healthy parents already know. These journaling prompts will point you toward the intangible qualities you may feel are still missing:

- Is there a character from fiction, or a real person in your own life, that you've watched and felt, "Wow, that's the kind of parent I want to be." Who is that parent?
- What is it about watching them interact that makes you think, "Wow, I wish I could do that."
- Which of the four S's of attachment is that person good at providing? Whatever you have identified is likely to be what was missing for you.
- What did that person do to make it clear that they had this skill?
- Which skill that you learned from this book would you need to implement in order to get you closer to your goal?

Hopefully, the advice in this chapter will make parenting easier. Even if "good parenting goals" seem overwhelming, breaking them down into smaller, attainable lessons will lighten your mental load. You can do this; just follow the steps in this chapter.

CHAPTER 12

Bringing Our Whole Selves to Parenting

YOU ARE THE best parent your child can have. Their brain and attachment system are primed to want you, not some perfect Mary Poppins figure, not some Instagram influencer, and not some idealized, unrealistic version of you. They don't want to be parented by a script or an algorithm. They just want you.

You may feel damaged by your damage, too depleted to parent, or simply overwhelmed, but to your child, you're simply their parent. The fact that you're reading this book and you're putting in the work means that you're already doing far better than you think you are. You're ready to parent with your full presence, bringing the most authentic version of you.

Part of bringing your whole self to parenting is coming to terms with your trauma app. As you've learned, your trauma app funnels you directly into your parenting defaults, and they can feel inescapable. As you become comfortable with yourself, you'll also become more skillful at recognizing your triggers, how you respond to them, and how you can better respond to your child. You've also learned that you can shut off your trauma app just by saying, "Thanks for the data; I'll take it from here."

At first, you might find that it's a big sacrifice to let go of your trauma app, because while it kept you from bringing your whole self to parenting, it worked. Your trauma app kept you alive, and anything that effective is really difficult to give up. But parenting is about thriving, not surviving. When I was caring for small children while working and going to grad school, my trauma app would tell me, "Stress detected—enable dissociation mode." This default worked because it allowed me to get through my day without yelling, which to me was the worst type of parenting. Purposefully letting go of my trauma app felt terrifying because I didn't know what else to do when I was around my children.

Breaking out of the algorithm was hard. I had to be willing to occasionally yell because when I let go of dissociation, I didn't have another stress management tool yet. Ultimately, I realized my lack of presence was harming my children more than a momentary lapse into yelling. I also learned that yelling wasn't the end of my relationship with my children: there was always the possibility of repair, even when I made a mistake. I had to be willing to learn on the job, and this one realization meant that I had to be okay with occasionally messing up and being willing to repair, which is actually the best kind of modeling for kids.

Now, when I get activated, instead of letting my trauma app take control, I've increased my repertoire. I've learned several self-regulation strategies to bring my emotions under control. When I feel tempted to dissociate, I can instead take a mindful break, even for a few minutes, and then reengage. Or I can be physically active and work through my emotions. When I feel tempted to rely on a perfect parenting default instead of what my instincts are telling me to do, I can acknowledge the instinct and then act with intention. I've found that these skills not only lower my emotional response, but they can also help my child lower their own, calm down, and move forward.

When you're trying to actively remove the trauma app's permissions, remind yourself, "My trauma app is about surviving. Parenting is about thriving." Yes, it may feel terrifying. But it can be done. And as you do it, you're healing your inner child while parenting your real-world child.

Throughout this book, I've given you many tips to help you achieve self-regulation in the broader context of daily life. There will also be times when you need a quick fix to get you into a calmer state. However, keep in mind that self-regulation doesn't mean that you have to fake being calm all the time. Self-regulation means purposefully working on making the body feel better to make our brains smarter in the moment. A child will notice when their parent takes a moment, a breath, or a mindful drink of water in an effort to self-regulate. When they see us working on ourselves, they learn that emotions aren't an enemy, that stress isn't a permanent state, and that they can self-regulate in an age-appropriate manner too. Most importantly, they realize that we're the adults in the room and that we know how to keep everyone safe.

The knowledge that we can always self-regulate allows us to bring our whole self to parenting. We're not afraid of our big emotions, because we know that we can self-regulate whenever we need to. We don't have to fake calm or allow our trauma app to take over. We're here for our children in all our authentic imperfection. We don't have to be perfect—we just have to be as present as possible.

Body Up Techniques for Self-Regulation

Most treatment modalities for trauma recovery suggest that the best way to achieve self-regulation is often a physical "body up" approach. When I'm having any of the PTSD physical symptoms listed in chapter 1, I know that I need to purposefully self-regulate. Once my body feels better, my brain can be more in control. I can trick my body into feeling better so that I can function and parent in the moment. Then, if I need to, I can always come back and unpack the emotion or event that triggered me.

In the following exercises, the goal is a biology hack. You will calm down your stress response and PTS symptoms—created by the production of the chemicals adrenaline and cortisol—by flooding your brain and body with naturally occurring chemicals like serotonin, endorphins, oxytocin, and dopamine. DBT suggests a set of strategies known as TIPP: temperature, intense exercise, paced breathing, progressive muscle relaxation.[1] I've expanded on those in the list below, adding suggestions from my own trial and error:

- Cold water plunges: Cooling down your body can decrease your heart rate, which is usually faster when we are emotionally overwhelmed. Splash your face with cold water or take a cold shower. I find a cold face plunge works best for me. To do this, hold your breath and submerge your face into a bowl of ice water for about thirty seconds or hold a cold pack (or Ziploc bag filled with ice) on your eyes and cheeks.
- Warming techniques: Warming up the body increases your heart rate, which is usually lower when you feel depressed, sad, or shame. Take a hot bath or shower or get cozy under a weighted blanket. Drinking warm, decaffeinated beverages, like herbal tea, can be both calming and soothing.

- Try intense exercise: Raising your heart rate and then mindfully allowing it to slow, can flood your body with "feel good" endorphins, burn off excess energy and jitteriness, and lower an unwanted stress response by using up some of the excess adrenaline and cortisol your body needs to get rid of. You can pair this technique with parenting by going for a walk or dancing with your children so that you can lower the stress response together.
- Paced breathing: Breathe in through your nose for a count of four. Hold your breath for a count of four. Blow out your breath through your mouth for as long as you possibly can. Repeat until you feel calmer and your breathing is back to normal. This works especially well if you are hyperventilating or having a panic attack.
- Progressive muscle relaxation: This discrete exercise is a form of progressive muscle relaxation that you can do at any time of day. Sit in a firm chair. Push your entire body weight down in your chair as hard as you can (as if you're trying to push the chair through the floor). Then, pull up in your chair as though you're trying to pull the chair up through your body. Loosen your muscles and dangle your body in your chair, as though you are boneless, like a rag doll. Repeat ten times in a row.
- Co-regulation: I often find that co-regulation with my kids can be so much more effective than self-regulation. Using any of these practices with my child reminds me that they are the reason why I need to feel calmer. Sometimes, I create a game with these strategies. For instance, when I do paced breathing with my children, I call it ABC breathing. We breathe in for four, hold for four, and then blow out while mentally reciting the alphabet, and see just how far we can get before taking another breath. I also make sure to provide developmentally appropriate information about my emotional state. When we normalize and communicate about our own stresses, our kids learn that emotions are just data rather than something to be feared. All I typically need to say is, "I'm feeling some big emotions right now, so I'm going to take a break. Who wants to join me?" It's

excellent modeling for children, and as our inner child witnesses this, it begins to heal as well.

- Joke books/laughter therapy: Sometimes, it just feels good to laugh, because you quickly release a lot of tension. Whenever I'm sensing that stress levels in our family are becoming contagious, we hold a "Laffy Taffy ceremony." I keep a bag of these candies handy, and we open them and read the jokes on the wrappers to each other. These are some of the cringiest "dad jokes" and riddles you could ever read, but they really work to get us giggling! You could just as easily use a joke book or take turns telling jokes you've memorized.

Top-Down Strategies

Daily Mindfulness Journaling

Top-down strategies mean dealing with a situation, or your emotions, head-on. Sometimes, that means thinking through a situation, even if you'd rather avoid thinking about it at all. Sometimes, that means taking an action. You may need to set a boundary, change a schedule, or have a complicated conversation. Once you see how many psychological resources you are using by avoiding a situation, you can see how it may be interfering with your parenting.

I'm also a big believer in keeping a daily mindfulness journal. It is less an exercise in writing and more of a daily recap. I think of it as straightening out the drawers of my brain and collecting data I can use in the future. The mindfulness part is that you're tapping into your observing self. Throughout the day, there's a part of you that's experiencing your day and another part of you that is narrating the story in your head, making sense of what happens. Often for PTPs, that narrator's voice is judgmental or mean (*Of course I forgot to defrost the chicken. I'm such a loser . . . as usual, I messed up*). It's our job to try to replace that mean voice with a narrator who is simply observing what's happening and then update that narrator so the story is told from a more positive perspective (*Amazing me, who forgot to defrost the chicken but has containers of microwaveable meatballs in the freezer for just such an emergency! Go, me!*). When we journal about our day, it becomes easier and easier to notice the judgmental voice and separate it from our sense of self. It becomes just another part, a voice inside of us, while the observing self becomes stronger. As a result, our automatic emotional reactions to anything that happens become a bit less unwieldy, a bit more manageable. The more we tune into that observer voice, the stronger it becomes, and ultimately, we're more self-regulated when we're more self-accepting.

In a journal, create three columns and commit to writing something down in each of them every day (see the chart below). Label the first column "What Went Right Today?" In this column, write down all the things that went well, even the smallest victories. Our brains are very good at noticing the bad and discounting the good unless we make a mindful decision to focus on them. Over time, you might notice how often your internal, self-critical voice pops up. For instance, when you write down "Everyone ate supper," you might hear a shaming voice that says, "Big deal." By noticing this shaming voice, you can see that this shaming voice isn't "you"; it's just one voice inside of you. This knowledge creates distance between the shaming voice and your sense of self, because you are more than your inner critic.

Label the second column "What Went Wrong Today?" As you fill this in, ask yourself one crucial question: What have I learned from that experience? For example, if you came home late from work tired and stressed and didn't handle the supper-homework-bedtime routine in a way that's consistent with your values, you may have learned that coming home late from work is a problem. You may have to set a boundary with your job or create a work-around for the days that you must work late (Maybe you skip a bath that night? Maybe you try the POD approach?). The goal is not to reinforce the shaming voice around the stuff that didn't go well; it's about facing it head-on and gleaning whatever data we can from those trouble spots. As you implement new strategies that address these issues, you may very well see that you lower your sense of shame, remind your inner child that there's a well-resourced grown-up in charge, and increase your sense of agency and empowerment.

The third column is labeled "Dump the Mental Load." These are the thoughts that inevitably come up surrounding the daily tasks that need to be accomplished. When we don't try to keep a zillion lists in our brain and instead off-load those tasks onto a piece of paper, they become a bit more manageable. It's also easier to delegate and outsource them. If "wash the soccer uniform—urgent" ends up on the list too often, it's time to either delegate that task or buy more uniforms so cleaning them isn't an emergency all the time. I find that when I dump my mental load, I'm so much calmer and much more able to relax into my bedtime routine, because my life feels more doable.

What Went Right Today?	What Went Wrong Today?	Dump the Mental Load

Core Parenting Competencies You Now Have

Can we sit for a moment and reflect on the journey you just went through as you read this book and completed the exercises? These core parenting competencies are what you need to parent in accordance with your values. At this point, you either have them or have a clear path toward developing them. In developing these competencies, you've also set yourself on the road to healing.

- An accurate understanding of your emotional states. Reading each emotion accurately, understanding that emotions are messengers and interpreting those messages correctly.
- Being comfortable with discomfort. Breaking our trauma responses like people-pleasing or dissociating is going to feel uncomfortable. But discomfort is not an emergency, even if our trauma app tells us that it's intolerable.
- The ability to regulate. Being able to lower adrenaline levels, or to raise them, in accurate response to the situation at hand.

- A strong and continuous sense of self. Knowing who we are, what our values are, and the ability to narrate the story of ourselves in a cohesive manner, remembering that which is the core of our values.

When to Seek More Help

If you have been struggling with the acceptance or integration stages of the AIM model or continue to feel that your trauma is too big, too overwhelming, or too painful, you may want to get professional help. Our trauma app often tells us to be self-sufficient, but there's no shame in asking for help from a mental health professional, licensed in their jurisdiction, who has significant trauma training. The more help you have from trained professionals, the more you can focus on enhancing your own parenting skills.

You may be reluctant to see a therapist. You may be worried about opening the door to difficult memories. Sometimes, our hyperindependence makes us feel like we have to manage on our own and that it would be weak or shameful to rely on someone else. I hope you can see that's the trauma app talking! Some of us come from cultures, or families, where therapy is seen as self-indulgent or wasteful. Some of us have had a bad experience with a non-trauma-informed therapist in the past, who made us feel worse instead of better. For some trauma survivors who attended therapy as kids, they may have seen the therapist as untrustworthy or more allied with the parents than the actual patient in front of them. This is particularly true if there was family dysfunction or coercive control.

In terms of opening up the door to upsetting memories, think of it as walking around with a toothache. The toothache hurts constantly at a level 4. It's not terrible (unless I forget and chew on that side or drink something really hot or cold), but it can be annoying and persistent. If I go to the dentist, the pain will rise to about a level 10 in the moment that they're drilling. But once the cavity is filled, I will feel much better, all the time. Therapy can be like that. When we open that door to upsetting memories, at first, our discomfort will rise to very high levels. But it's in service of addressing the source of the pain and clearing it up. And in the long run, we will feel much better.

In terms of hyperindependence, I see therapy as an opportunity for both teaching and learning. If I attend a party and one of my neighbors brings a delicious cake, I can try to guess all the ingredients and the exact cooking methodology. I might come close, but I might waste a lot of time trying to figure it out. Wouldn't it be smarter to just call the neighbor and ask for the recipe? You can figure out how to process your own trauma, or you can work with someone who is specially trained to do that. And just like it's not shameful to take swimming lessons or call a plumber, it's not shameful to get help from a therapist.

Trauma therapy options can be confusing. There are so many acronyms, schools of thought, and licensures. Here's a quick overview of what to look for.

Choose a Therapist

It is okay to interview a bunch of therapists to find a good fit. First, look for someone who is licensed by a board in the jurisdiction in which you live. In the United States, disciplines like clinical psychology, clinical social work, clinical counseling, and marriage and family therapists are regulated by licensing boards. Ask the therapist for the name of their board and then check with that board (most state boards for mental health professionals have searchable databases for licensed professionals). You want a licensed therapist because that means that the therapist is accountable to a professional board and must meet standards for practice, as well as engage in ongoing professional development to keep them informed of the latest treatment approaches. Look for a therapist who provides trauma-informed psychotherapy and can talk about their training in trauma-informed treatment. A license to practice as a mental health professional doesn't necessarily mean that a therapist has dedicated training and supervised experience treating trauma, so be sure to ask. Your therapist should also be participating in ongoing supervision or be part of an ongoing psychotherapy supervision group.

It's also important to pay attention to how you feel when you're with your therapist: if you trust that person and if you feel an alliance between you and the therapist. If something happens in therapy that makes you feel uncomfortable, it's okay to discuss that with your therapist. A good therapist should be open to feedback and will have a good explanation for why they're recommending certain strategies.

A therapist is there for you no matter what. You can't "trauma dump" on your therapist—that's what we signed up for. Your therapist is trained to handle any emotions that come up for them that are caused by hearing so many difficult stories and helping people handle so many overwhelming emotions. You don't have to protect them or avoid talking about anything that could "trigger" them.

It's worthwhile to periodically take the temperature of your therapy, to ask your therapist how they think therapy is going and what future directions for treatment are. A good therapist is always thinking about how therapy is going now and where the future is projected to be. It's totally okay to start therapy thinking it's going to be about one topic and end up focusing on something else. Your life evolves, and concerns that were important before may no longer be as important. Just make sure that both you and your therapist agree that you're working on valid, valuable goals.

Sometimes, a therapist wants to take us down a therapy path that doesn't make sense to us.

Imagine you have intense pain in your left arm. You go to the emergency room and they take one look at you and say, "Quick! We need interventional cardiology. This patient is having a heart attack." You say, "Wait, it's my arm that hurts," and the ER doc explains that the nerves supplying the heart and other parts of the body (like the arm) converge in the spinal cord, causing the brain to misinterpret the origin of the pain. You feel it in your arm, but it's your heart that's injured.

In the same way, you might go to therapy for difficulty setting boundaries with your toxic boss, and the therapist might start asking about your childhood history of being bullied and your difficult stepmom. You might say, "I wanted help with the boss, not the memories of third grade!" If your therapist can explain that the origin of the "pain" is third grade and that's why they want to work on those memories, you can follow that logic. If the doctor says, "Well, I don't know what arm pain has to do with your heart, but since I'm a cardiologist I really like to operate on hearts," you need to find another doctor. If the therapist says, "Well, I don't know what this therapy approach has to do with your toxic boss, but I just got certified in it, so let's use it," find another therapist.

Understand Your Therapist's Trauma-Informed Approach

There are many approaches for treating trauma. Each one has a distinct theory of *pathology*—what causes trauma—and a distinct theory of *treatment*—what to do about it. Some of the approaches that I have been trained in, or that I am aware of the efficacy of, include *trauma-focused cognitive behavioral therapy*, *psychodynamic psychotherapy*, *dialectical behavioral therapy*, *acceptance and commitment therapy*, *internal family systems therapy*, *eye movement desensitization and reprocessing*, *prolonged exposure therapy*, *polyvagal-informed psychotherapy*, *somatic psychotherapy*, and *cognitive processing therapy*.

There are accrediting boards for each of these approaches, and you can find out if your therapist has been certified by them. Accreditation in an approach is not the same thing as a license to practice: a license covers general competence as a clinician; accreditation covers specific training in a therapy approach. For trauma work, a therapist needs both.

Join My Community

This book might be your first introduction to the post-traumatic parenting community: welcome! Now you can join us on all our socials. Before I wrote this book, post-traumatic parenting was a social media community, and it still is.

I'm so impressed by my community because I have met some of the most courageous, dedicated, and committed parents through it. The people who participate in my social media community are grappling with their trauma and continuously trying to bring their best selves to parenting. I am humbled by the questions we all ask, the commitments we're willing to make, and the sense of ongoing, shared mission we all have. The people I meet are some of my own personal heroes. They're willing to do the work and to unflinchingly face their traumas and parent. They're willing to break the cycles that almost broke them. That's what I want for you.

There are a lot of ways to interact with me on social media because I value every single person's journey and we all learn from each other. On my Instagram Lives, people are constantly interacting with one another and finding new allies, friends, and supports. We have a subscription where people can ask very specific questions about their parenting, which I then respond to throughout the week, and all the subscription members can watch the responses, so we're all learning together and benefiting from each other's processes. We have a Facebook group where people can interact with one another. I do my best to respond to every message I receive from my social media community.

I offer a post-traumatic parenting newsletter, the post-traumatic parenting YouTube channel, and the post-traumatic parenting podcast. All these resources fill different needs for the community. On YouTube, I have dozens of twenty-minute videos on games, parenting strategies for specific issues, and more. These are searchable, so if you're looking for a specific topic, you can find it more easily. If you're looking for a technique to handle a challenging family holiday party, picture books and games to help a cautious child navigate the social world, or my take on a trauma-related story in the news, YouTube is where you can find those resources.

My goal is to change the world until post-traumatic parenting is no longer necessary, because children are being raised by healthy, integrated parents. I think we can do that, and now you've taken that first step. Using my AIM model, you can see how once you've achieved acceptance and integration, parenting in accordance with your values becomes your mission and meaning. You've transformed your trauma into the parenting superpower it now can be—because you know your "why," you've given your trauma meaning, and now you are on the mission to go from cycle breaking to cycle making.

You've got this. It's time to allow your children to meet your full, authentic, integrated self and for you to enjoy the experience of truly connecting with them. You've learned to restore, and share, your calm. Now find, and share, your joy, and in doing so, create a new foundation for your children and their joy.

Thank you for allowing me to be a part of that journey.

ACKNOWLEDGMENTS

The late, Dr. Esther Buccholz, my first dissertation chair, shared the gift of insight and intellect with me. She shared her memories and knowledge of object relations, child psychotherapy, and crucially, how to see the world through a child's eyes. Esther was the first person who helped me see the invisible effects of trauma on parenting, and helped me clarify my essential "me-search" question. You are missed.

Thank you to Dr. Sandee McClowry, my dissertation chair, professor, and mentor. You came into my life at such a crucial point, and reminded me that when a door is closed, a window opens. It's sad that Esther's death is what brought us together, and I believe our relationship was always meant to be. Thank you for introducing me to temperament research, believing in me, and teaching me so much about cross-cultural research design. Thank you for being a true mentsch, in every sense of the word. I hope you're proud of your intellectual grandbaby!

Thanks to the professors and faculty at NYU who were so helpful to a stranger in the strange land that is graduate school—Dr. Carola Suarez Orozco, Dr. Carol Gilligan, Dr. Gil Trachtman, Dr. Samuel Juni, Dr. David Pelcovitz, and Dr. Eileen O'Connor. Thank you for providing the rich research base, skills, and knowledge that allowed me to conceptualize this journey.

Thanks to the clinical supervisors who taught me how to be a therapist: Dr. Jean Bailey, Dr. Alejandra Morales, Dr. Tom Johnson, Dr. Kathy Forlenza, and Dr. Lucille Karr-Caffashan. Each of you embodies clinical expertise, broad knowledge, and true caring. You are all the best of what a psychologist can be, and my work is richer for having worked with you. Dr. Tom Johnson—I still have my scrawled WWTJD note (What Would Tom Johnson Do?) from internship, and I refer to it often. Thank you for stepping in at a crucial moment and helping me clarify the career path I truly wanted.

To my internship colleagues—Dr. Yoni Schwab, Dr. Kristin Candan, and Dr. Rose Zayco. Being friends with all of you extends my life span, and it also enriches my life. We are all so different in terms of theoretical orientation, life circumstances, and career paths, but at heart, we're all kindred spirits. Thank you for helping me hone my clinical skills, for supporting me throughout internship, and for the sincere friendship and understanding. Best internship class ever!

To Dr. Shimon Russel—thank you for your mentorship and support when I first began working in Lakewood so many years ago. Thank you for the example you set—that in the end, we heal by creating the world that we would have needed when we were going through our own stuff. You are a true exemplar of my AIM model—accepting and integrating your pain and finding its meaning and mission, thereby transforming it, and the world. Thank you for modeling honesty, courage, vulnerability, and authenticity. Thank you for the support and encouragement as I pushed through the writing process.

To Dr. Chaim Horwitz—thank you for the post-doctoral supervision, the mentorship, and the professional development. I'll never be a couple's therapist—but I've seen an excellent one up close, and that's saying something! What you taught me about working with families and systems will always be at the forefront of how I practice. Thank you for all your help, your collegiality, and your shining example of how to be a psychologist. I am lucky to have learned, and to continue to learn, from you.

I truly believe that my family deserves an independent reality outside of being "mine." That's why I'm going to respect their privacy, and not name them individually. To my husband—thank you for sharing this parenting and life adventure with me. Thanks for all the caring, laughter, and for always being there. I don't have enough words to convey my appreciation for twenty-five-plus years of that support, but know that you're the source of my earned security.

Sometimes we become a mother by birth; sometimes we become a mother through another relationship. To all of my children—you're the map, the mirror, and the mission. I am so proud of each and every one of you. I love you, I will always love you, and there's nothing you could ever do that would make me stop loving you. And to my children's spouses and my grandchildren—thank you for being you. Watching my adult children parent is the happy ending of this book. Guess what? I'm done with my homework! It's time to play.

To my in-laws—my parents in-law and siblings-in-law—thank you for being models of sturdy, reliable parenting. You are exemplars of what it means to be truly conscious of parenting as the most valuable career we'll ever engage in.

To Diana Carr and Lurline Hollinzed—thank you for being such kind, devoted caregivers for my mother. Caring for an elderly parent is never easy, but your supportive, confident, and gentle presence makes this task so much more bearable, even beautiful. You both truly model respectful, principled care, and I'm so grateful.

To my friends—to Idy, for being so wise, insightful, and self-aware. Thank you for the conversations, the emotional support, the sisterhood, and the laughter. You are valued so much more than you know, and I'm so glad to have you in my life. To Hindy—thank you for the walks, the friendship, and the emotional support. Thanks for being a model of true tact, kindness, and the ability to walk a mile in another's shoes. Also, thank you for telling me how to actually turn on the computer (you see, I did need a programmer after all!) And to my other friends—Anna, my BFF(er). Thank you for reminding me just how smart and capable women can be. Thanks for providing a model of achievement with grace. To Esty—thanks for being my first editor, my friend, and the person who reminded me who I am at a crucial moment. To Jeannie Rosenthal—thanks for being a model of true intellectual courage and supportive friendship always. I love how our relationship always picks up where it left off! And to my neighbors—I'm lucky to be living in a neighborhood with so many role models of ordinary heroism, good parenting, and kindness. Thank you.

To my therapist, Dr. A. You're not only a therapist's therapist—you're *this* therapist's therapist. Thank you for the wisdom, the insight, the challenges, and your ability to truly listen and help me reconnect to myself. Above all, thank you for the clarity, and the kindness.

To my associates—Mrs. Hadassah Schorr, Mrs. Mimi Kahn, and Dr. Amy Winters. Thank you for your patience as I worked on this book, thank you for your rich clinical questions, your essential hunger to grow and learn as therapists, and your ability to understand the clinical value of play, stories, and relationships. To my past and present associates and students: Thank you for the compliment of choosing to learn from and with me. And to Mrs. Hindy Goldberg, who runs my office (and my life) with such efficiency and grace. Thanks for being the buffer zone and for protecting my time, while still advocating for our patients and the schools. You are awesome!

To Emily May—I know I hired you to be a social media manager, but you're so much more than that. Thanks for being the number one brand ambassador, the person who translates my words to images, and for being a true example of what post-traumatic parenting is all about. When we met you instantly got me. Most of all, thank you for the friendship. Meeting a kindred spirit is one of the unanticipated benefits of this project.

To Tina Zimmer and Maria Cambria—thanks for being listening ears, friends, and supporters. You believed in me every step of this journey, and I'm grateful.

Thanks goes to my publishing team, starting with Wendy Keller, agent extraordinaire. Thank you for believing in me and understanding the value of this project. Thanks for your tireless efforts to champion post-traumatic parenting in all its forms, and for your example of true grit and fortitude.

To Pam Liflander—In every journey, a wise mentor must come to show the way. You were that person for me. What can I call you? Book midwife? Master wordsmith? In the end, I think you're the big sister I never had. Most of all, I'm proud to call you friend.

To Lisa Kloskin of Broadleaf—thank you for being the editor who believed in this project and supported me throughout. Thank you for your support and discernment through all the decisions, large and small. Thank you to Marissa Wold Uhrina for your patience and dedication to detail, and to Carlos Esparza for your visual representation of what post-traumatic parenting is all about.

Lastly, I would like to honor the members of the post-traumatic parenting community. Thank you all for your questions, insights, support, and most of all, your courage. The poet Alfred Tennyson says, "Tis better to have loved and lost than never to have loved at all." That may be true. But to love after loss, after pain—that's an act of courage. Protecting our hearts is often a trauma response. Opening ourselves up to love and vulnerability through parenting—that's an act of supreme courage. I see every single one of you. I salute every single one of you.

NOTES

CHAPTER 1: UNDERSTANDING TRAUMA

1. V. J. Felitti, R. F. Anda, D. Nordenberg, D. F. Williamson, A. M. Spitz, V. Edwards, M. P. Koss, and J. S. Marks, "Relationship of Childhood Abuse and Household Dysfunction to Many of the Leading Causes of Death in Adults. The Adverse Childhood Experiences (ACE) Study," *American Journal of Preventive Medicine*14, no. 4 (May 1998): 245–58. https://www.ajpmonline.org/article/S0749-3797(98)00017-8/fulltext.
2. Podcasts Notes, "Dr. Lisa Feldman Barrett: How to Understand Emotions," *Huberman Lab*, podcast, October 20, 2023, https://podcastnotes.org/huberman-lab/dr-lisa-feldman-barrett-how-to-understand-emotions-huberman-lab/.
3. Gavin de Becker, *The Gift of Fear* (Bloomsbury Publishing, 2000).

CHAPTER 2: YOUR INNER CHILD CAN'T RAISE A CHILD

1. Erik H. Erikson, *Identity and the Life Cycle* (W. W. Norton, 1994).
2. D. W. Winnicott, *Playing and Reality*, 2nd ed. (Routledge, 2019), 10.

CHAPTER 3: HOW TRAUMA SHOWS UP IN PARENTING: TRIGGERS AND RESPONSES

1. Lisa Feldman Barret, *How Emotions Are Made: The Secret Life of the Brain* (Houghton Mifflin Harcourt, 2017).
2. Ofer Perl, Or Duek, Kaustubh R. Kulkarni, Charles Gordon, John H. Krystal, Ifat Levy, Ilan Harpax-Rotem, and Daniela Schiller, "Neural Patterns Differentiate Traumatic from Sad Autobiographical Memories in PTSD," *Nature Neuroscience* 26 (2023): 2226–36, https://doi.org/10.1038/s41593-023-01483-5.

CHAPTER 4: THE ENTANGLED PARENT

1. Hazel Rose Markus, "You Can't Be a Self by Yourself," in *Pillars of Social Psychology: Stories and Retrospectives*, ed. Saul Kassin (Cambridge University Press, 2022), 236–46.

CHAPTER 5: THE PERFECTIONIST PARENT

1. Daniel J. Siegel and Tina Payne Bryson, *The Power of Showing Up: How Parental Presence Shapes Who Our Kids Become and How Their Brains Get Wired* (Ballantine Books, 2020), 16.
2. Carol S. Dweck, *Mindset* (Ballantine Books, 2008), 24.
3. M. Mikolajczak, M.-E. Raes, H. Avalosse, and I. Roskam, "Exhausted Parents: Sociodemographic, Child-Related, Parent-Related, Parenting and Family-Functioning Correlates of Parental Burnout," *Journal of Child and Family Studies* 27, no. 2 (2017): 602–14, https://doi.org/10.1007/s10826-017-0892-4.
4. M. M. Linehan, *Cognitive-Behavioral Treatment of Borderline Personality Disorder* (Guilford Press, 1993), 49.
5. Ester Schaler Buchholz, *The Call of Solitude: Alone Time in a World of Attachment* (Simon & Schuster, 1997).
6. Aliza Pressman, *The 5 Principles of Parenting: Your Essential Guide to Raising Good Humans* (Simon & Schuster, 2024).

CHAPTER 6: THE DISENGAGED PARENT

1. Patrick Teahan, "11 Oddly Specific Childhood Trauma Issues," premiered April 5, 2023, YouTube, 39 min., 2 sec., https://www.youtube.com/watch?v=lULd-wnWjT4.

CHAPTER 7: THE PARALYZED PARENT

1. S. W. Porges, *The Polyvagal Theory: Neurophysiological Foundations of Emotions, Attachment, Communication, and Self-Regulation* (W. W. Norton, 2011).
2. E. A. Piazza, L. Hasenfratz, U. Hasson, and C. Lew-Williams, "Infant and Adult Brains Are Coupled to the Dynamics of Natural Communication," *Psychological Science* 31, no. 1 (2020): 6–17, https://doi.org/10.1177/0956797619878698.
3. Russell Harris, "Acceptance and Commitment Therapy (ACT) Introductory Workshop Handout," 2007, 9, https://thehappinesstrap.com/upimages/2007%20Introductory%20ACT%20Workshop%20Handout%20-%20%20Russ%20Harris.pdf.
4. Becky Kennedy, *Good Inside: A Guide to Becoming the Parent You Want to Be* (Dial Press, 2022).
5. Adam Grant, host, *WorkLife*, podcast, season 4, episode 3, "The Science of Productive Conflict," TED Audio Collective, April 13, 2021, https://www.ted.com/podcasts/worklife/the-science-of-productive-conflict-transcript.
6. Daniel J. Siegel and Tina Payne Bryson, *The Whole-Brain Child: 12 Revolutionary Strategies to Nurture Your Child's Developing Mind* (Delacorte Press, 2011), 27.

7. *The Wizard of Oz*, directed by Victor Fleming (MGM, 1939).
8. J. Herman, *Trauma and Recovery* (Basic Books, 2015).
9. Porges, *The Pocket Guide to the Polyvagal Theory.*

CHAPTER 8: THE SURVIVOR PARENT

1. Tina Payne Bryson, *The Bottom Line for Baby: From Sleep Training to Screens, Thumb Sucking to Tummy Time—What the Science Says* (Ballantine Books, 2020).

CHAPTER 9: BECOMING THE PARENT YOU WANT TO BE

1. Siegel and Bryson, *The Power of Showing Up.*
2. I. Blix, A. B. Kanten, M. S. Birkeland, Ø. Solberg, A. Nissen, and T. Heir, "Thinking About What Might Have Happened: Counterfactual Thinking and Post-Traumatic Stress in Individuals Directly and Indirectly Exposed to the 2011 Oslo Bombing," *Applied Cognitive Psychology* 30, no. 6 (2016): 983–91, https://doi.org/10.1002/acp.3289.
3. M. D. Barnett and I. V. Maciel, "Counterfactual Thinking Among Victims of Sexual Assault: Relationships with Posttraumatic Stress and Posttraumatic Growth," *Journal of Interpersonal Violence* 36, nos. 17–18 (2021): 8652–67, https://doi.org/10.1177/0886260519852629.
4. I. Blix, K. A. Glad, A. Undset, T. Wentzel-Larsen, A. A. Ottesen, T. K. Jensen, and G. Dyb, "'My child Could Have Died': Counterfactual Thoughts and Psychological Distress in Parents of Trauma Survivors," *European Journal of Psychotraumatology* 15, no. 1 (2024). https://doi.org/10.1080/20008066.2024.2326736.
5. S. Huang, L. Faul, N. Parikh, K. S. LaBar, and F. De Brigard, "Counterfactual Thinking Induces Different Neural Patterns of Memory Modification in Anxious Individuals," *Scientific Reports* 14, 10630 (2024), https://doi.org/10.1038/s41598-024-61545-x.
6. Linehan, *Cognitive Behavioral Treatment of Borderline Personality Disorder.*
7. Judith Lewis Herman, *Trauma and Recovery* (Basic Books, 1992).
8. Friedrich Wilhelm Nietzsche, *Basic Writings of Nietzsche* (Modern Library, 1968).

CHAPTER 10: R2 PARENTING: BEING BOTH RESPONSIVE AND RESPONSIBLE

1. D. Baumrind, "Effects of Authoritative Parental Control on Child Behavior," *Child Development* 37, no. 4 (1966), 887–907.
2. A. Pressman, *The 5 Principles of Parenting* (Simon Element, 2024), 18.

3. Sandee Graham McClowry, *Your Child's Unique Temperament: Insights and Strategies for Responsive Parenting* (Research Press, 2003).
4. J. Cuartas, D. G. Weissman, M. A. Sheridan, L. Lengua, and K. A. McLaughlin, "Corporal Punishment and Elevated Neural Response to Threat in Children," *Child Development* 92, no. 3 (2021): 821–32, https://doi.org/10.1111/cdev.13565.
5. E. T. Gershoff, "Corporal Punishment by Parents and Associated Child Behaviors and Experiences: A Meta-Analytic and Theoretical Review," *Psychological Bulletin* 128, no. 4 (2002): 539–79, https://doi.org/10.1037//0033-2909.128.4.539.
6. Jonathan Haidt, *The Anxious Generation: How the Great Rewiring of Childhood Is Causing an Epidemic of Mental Illness* (Penguin, 2024).

CHAPTER 12: BRINGING OUR WHOLE SELVES TO PARENTING

1. DBT: Dialectical Behavior Therapy, "T10: TIPP," https://dialecticalbehaviortherapy.com/distress-tolerance/tipp/.